Rome and the Barbarians
Parts I–III
Kenneth W. Harl, Ph.D.

PUBLISHED BY:

THE TEACHING COMPANY
4151 Lafayette Center Drive, Suite 100
Chantilly, Virginia 20151-1232
1-800-TEACH-12
Fax—703-378-3819
www.teach12.com

Copyright © The Teaching Company, 2004

Printed in the United States of America

This book is in copyright. All rights reserved.

Without limiting the rights under copyright reserved above,
no part of this publication may be reproduced, stored in
or introduced into a retrieval system, or transmitted,
in any form, or by any means
(electronic, mechanical, photocopying, recording, or otherwise),
without the prior written permission of
The Teaching Company.

Kenneth W. Harl, Ph.D.

Professor of Classical and Byzantine History, Tulane University

Kenneth W. Harl, Professor of Classical and Byzantine History, joined the faculty of Tulane University after he completed his Ph.D. in history at Yale University in 1978. Professor Harl teaches courses on Greek, Roman, Byzantine, and Crusader history from the freshman to graduate levels. He has won numerous teaching awards at his home university, including the coveted Sheldon H. Hackney Award (twice voted by faculty and students), as well as the Robert Foster Cherry Award for Great Teachers from Baylor University. Professor Harl, a recognized scholar on coins and classical Anatolia, takes Tulane students on excursions to Turkey or as assistants on excavations of Hellenistic and Roman sites in Turkey. He is currently working on publishing coins from the excavations of Metropolis and Gordion.

Table of Contents
Rome and the Barbarians

Professor Biography i
Course Scope 1
Lecture One   Greek and Roman Views of Barbarians............ 2
Lecture Two   The Roman Republic 7
Lecture Three   Roman Society... 12
Lecture Four   The Roman Way of War.................................... 17
Lecture Five   Celtic Europe and the Mediterranean World ... 22
Lecture Six   The Conquest of Cisalpine Gaul 27
Lecture Seven   Romans and Carthaginians in Spain 33
Lecture Eight   The Roman Conquest of Spain 39
Lecture Nine   The Genesis of Roman Spain............................ 44
Lecture Ten   Jugurtha and the Nomadic Threat..................... 49
Lecture Eleven   Marius and the Northern Barbarians................. 54
Lecture Twelve   Rome's Rivals in the East 59
Lecture Thirteen   The Price of Empire—
                           The Roman Revolution 65
Lecture Fourteen   Julius Caesar and the Conquest of Gaul........... 70
Lecture Fifteen   Early Germanic Europe..................................... 76
Lecture Sixteen   The Nomads of Eastern Europe 81
Lecture Seventeen   Arsacid Parthia.. 87
Lecture Eighteen   The Augustan Principate and Imperialism........ 93
Lecture Nineteen   The Roman Imperial Army 98
Lecture Twenty   The Varian Disaster 102
Lecture Twenty-One   The Roman Conquest of Britain 107
Lecture Twenty-Two   Civil War and Rebellion 113
Lecture Twenty-Three   Flavian Frontiers and the Dacians................... 118
Lecture Twenty-Four   Trajan, the Dacians, and the Parthians........... 123
Lecture Twenty-Five   Romanization of the Provinces 128

Table of Contents
Rome and the Barbarians

Lecture Twenty-Six	Commerce Beyond the Imperial Frontiers	133
Lecture Twenty-Seven	Frontier Settlement and Assimilation	138
Lecture Twenty-Eight	From Germanic Tribes to Confederations	143
Lecture Twenty-Nine	Goths and the Crisis of the Third Century	148
Lecture Thirty	Eastern Rivals—Sassanid Persia	153
Lecture Thirty-One	Rome and the Barbarians in the Fourth Century	157
Lecture Thirty-Two	From Foes to Federates	162
Lecture Thirty-Three	Imperial Crisis and Decline	167
Lecture Thirty-Four	Attila and the Huns	172
Lecture Thirty-Five	Justinian and the Barbarians	177
Lecture Thirty-Six	Birth of the Barbarian Medieval West	182
Maps		186
Timeline		198
Glossary		231
Biographical Notes		246
Bibliography		269

Rome and the Barbarians

Scope:

The history of the Romans and the barbarians on their frontiers has, in large part, been written as one of warfare and conquest. Driven by memories of a Gallic menace, Rome's legions advanced the frontiers of Classical civilizations far north and east of the Mediterranean core by the first century A.D. Yet the Roman conquerors and native peoples intermarried, and exchanged ideas, mores, and objects. The ensuing provincial Roman cultures became the basis of Western European civilization.

The first third of this course deals with the Roman mastery of the Celtic peoples, first in northern Italy, and then in Gaul and Central Europe. Simultaneously, the Roman Republic conquered Spain. Roman exploitation of resources in the peninsula transformed Iberian society into the first successful provincial society. But wars against new barbarian foes in North Africa, Gaul, and Asia Minor proved a costly victory that undermined the Roman Republic.

The second third of the course deals with the barbarian peoples encountered by imperial Rome of the first and second centuries A.D. They comprised Germanic peoples of the forests, Iranian nomads of eastern Europe, and the Arsacid kings of Parthia. The emperor Augustus (27 B.C.–14 A.D.) consolidated the Western provinces, forged a professional army, and established frontiers along the Rhine, Danube, and Euphrates. He thus set the precepts of Roman frontier defense and diplomacy for the next two centuries.

The final third deals with commerce and cultural exchange between imperial Rome and the frontier peoples. The cultural exchange created a unique Roman frontier society as well as transformed the societies of the peoples beyond the imperial frontiers. Hence, the Germans, depicted as dreaded foes in Classical sources, are revealed by archaeology as settlers, merchants, and soldiers. The northern frontiers became a great mixing bowl of peoples and cultures. The ensuing martial society that emerged by 300 A.D. on both sides of the imperial frontier engendered both the defenders and foes of the late Roman world. The course concludes with the frontier wars and migrations of the third through sixth centuries that transformed the Classical into the Medieval world.

Lecture One
Greek and Roman Views of Barbarians

Scope: The clash with barbarians beyond the frontiers who threatened civilization was seen by the Romans as a major theme in their history. The Romans redefined Hellenic prejudices and idealized admiration of barbarians, whom Greeks regarded as "foreigners" who did not enjoy the rule of a law in a city-state (*polis*). In battling the Celtic-speaking Gauls who had settled in northern Italy, the Romans created the stereotype of the savage, indomitable warrior of northern Europe. For the Romans, however, conquered barbarians could become provincials tied by bonds of patronage and hospitality to members of Rome's great families. Provincials, in turn, could be assimilated, because Romans defined citizenship by political and legal rights rather than by descent. Hence, the foes of the republic were assimilated as provincials, and new barbarians, the Parthians in the east and the Germans in central and northern Europe, succeeded to the role of the Gauls. In short, the Greeks created the notion of barbarians, but Rome forged the means to master and assimilate them and, in so doing, created European civilization.

Outline

I. The aim of this course is to examine the interaction of the Romans and their so-called *barbarian* opponents.

  A. The word *barbarian* conjures up images of fur-clad, ax-wielding Nordic barbarians or the mounted Hun bowmen sweeping out of the Central Asian steppes.

  1. These images of barbarians are rooted in Greek and Roman sources and were transmitted to Christian peoples of medieval Europe.

  2. Hence, *barbarian* connoted uncouth, savage behavior and, after the conversion of Rome to Christianity, faith in demonic pagan gods.

  3. Since the Age of Discovery, such images of barbarians have been applied by Europeans to peoples they encountered in

Asia, Africa, and the Americas and have contributed to cultural and racial stereotyping.
   4. Such images of barbarians were behind European overseas imperialism since the 16th century.
   5. In the Enlightenment, Rousseau stressed an idealized image of the barbarian, unspoiled by corrupt civilization—another notion of barbarians also found in Classical sources. In this case, barbarians become the moral foils to the supposedly superior civilized peoples.
B. All these images are rooted in some fact, but the historical record is far more complex, and new evidence excavated by archaeologists, along with analysis and comparative studies by anthropologists, has corrected, supplemented, and confirmed the literary sources of antiquity about barbarians.
   1. In these lectures, we shall look at both Rome and the barbarians over the course of almost 1,000 years of Roman history.
   2. As we shall see, although the two groups clashed, they also intermarried and exchanged customs and material culture.
   3. Some historians, in fact, see Rome and the barbarians more as "bitter friends" than as enemies.
C. Keep in mind, too, that the identity of the barbarians constantly changed as Rome conquered new lands. Those defined as *barbarians* were always the next group that was not yet under Roman control. The "old" barbarians became provincials and, ultimately, were Romanized.

II. What are the main themes of this course?
A. In part, the course will address why the Romans were so successful in bringing barbarians to heel. The answer lies in Rome's peculiar institutions, which enabled the Romans to conquer, rule, and assimilate their barbarian foes.
   1. We shall look at political and military institutions, as well as the social bonds of Roman civilization.
   2. At the same time, we should note that the Romans' success in assimilating barbarian peoples often depended on existing conditions in a region before the Romans moved in. Celtic peoples, for example, had achieved a great deal of success in various aspects of their society, which the Romans built on.

3. The Romans' success in assimilating others was aided by their ability to adapt existing institutions and arrangements to their own ends, as well as their unique viewpoint in regard to these "outsiders."
- **B.** The second theme of this course will examine the barbarian societies at the time of Roman contact.
   1. This theme may be more difficult to trace, because the barbarians, with some exceptions, did not leave the same kind of written records as the Romans did.
   2. We shall see, however, how these barbarian cultures contributed to the establishment of Roman provinces.
- **C.** The last theme deals with the role of the barbarians in bringing down the Roman Empire.
   1. This theme ties in with the popular images of barbarians mentioned earlier.
   2. We shall explore the factors that gave these peoples, particularly the Germanic tribes and the Sassanid Persians, the military and political edge to bring about the fall of Rome.

III. The term *barbarian* was coined by the Greeks to designate "foreigners" who were unable to speak the Hellenic tongue.
- **A.** The Hellenes ("Greeks") were distinguished from barbarians, because they lived under the rule of law in a *polis* ("city-state"; pl. *poleis*).
   1. This definition included a political dimension. Hellenes defined themselves in terms of their common altars, common ancestors, and common language, as well as their common political structure.
   2. Because barbarians did not live by the rule of law, they could be divided into only two categories: slaves or tyrants.
- **B.** In the Greek definition, the term *barbarian* is accurately translated as "foreigner"; it does not carry the cultural and moral implications found in the later Roman age.
   1. By the Greek definition, barbarians included all non-Greek races, peoples as diverse as the Thracians, Scythians, Phoenicians, Egyptians, and Persians, some of whom were even admired.

    2. The Phoenicians were viewed ambivalently as rivals and teachers; the Egyptians were admired as members of the oldest civilization.
    3. The Persians were seen as the noble masters of the Near East; Herodotus (ca. 490–425 B.C.) admired the Persians for their moral virtues and devotion to their king.
    4. Xenophon (427–354 B.C.) praised the Persian prince Cyrus the Younger (408–401 B.C.) as a model gentleman and a chivalrous prince worthy of emulation by all Greeks.

C. The Hellenic notion of barbarian changed in the course of Greek history.
    1. The conquest of Alexander the Great brought the Persian Empire under the domination of Macedonian kings, which extended the concept of what it meant to be Greek.
    2. Even before Alexander's day, Athenian intellectuals, the *panhellenists*, had already added the political dimension to the definition of *Hellenic*.
    3. Indeed, the Athenian orator Isocrates (437–336 B.C.) asserted that barbarians could become Greeks if they lived in a *polis*.

D. In the 4th and 3rd centuries B.C., when the Greeks first experienced contact with the Romans in Italy, the Romans fell under the Greek definition of barbarians as foreigners who did not live under the rule of law.

E. The Romans inherited the term *barbarian* and the Greek definitions of it, but they also added their own connotations to it.
    1. The Roman use of the term was more along the lines of what we think of as a barbarian today.
    2. An erroneous Roman etymology claimed that the word *barbarian* came from the Latin *barba*, meaning "beard." The term came to designate "uncivilized outsiders."
    3. Even for the Romans, however, the condition of barbarians was a result of their laws and culture, not their race. Once subdued, barbarians could become civilized.

F. These two views of barbarians, the Greek and the Roman, can be traced to the critical periods of formation of these two civilizations.
    1. The Greeks evolved their definition, centered on the *polis* and the rule of law, in a period of relative security. In some ways,

this definition restricted the Greeks' ability to bring outsiders into their communities.
2. In contrast, when the Roman Republic was declared, Rome was in the middle of the invasion routes of central Italy. The Romans quickly learned that unless they forged alliances with the people around them, they would be conquered.
3. The Romans, thus, devised the political and military institutions to conquer and assimilate their neighbors that allowed them to master Italy, first, and then, the Mediterranean world.

Readings:

Harrison, Thomas, ed. *Greeks and Barbarians*.

Sherwin-White, A. N. *The Roman Citizenship*, 2nd ed.

Questions to Consider:

1. What were Roman notions and prejudices about barbarians? How did the Romans define barbarians, and why were barbarians able to be assimilated into the Roman order?
2. Why were Romans regarded as barbarians by Greeks? How did Greeks come to terms with Romans as members of a wider Hellenistic world? How did the Romans contribute to this process?
3. How have stereotypical images of barbarians influenced prejudices and attitudes in the Classical world? What was their impact on the medieval and modern worlds? What accounts for the persistence of such images? Why have notions of a noble savage likewise persisted in literature and popular perceptions in Western civilization?

Lecture Two
The Roman Republic

Scope: Rome's political and legal institutions proved decisive in ruling and assimilating defeated barbarian foes, even if the Romans never articulated any policy of Romanization. Between 509 and 264 B.C., Rome united Italy into a confederation. Rome demanded military service from the "togated peoples," but she did not interfere in local affairs. Furthermore, loyal allies could be promoted to favored Latin status or even be granted Roman citizenship; in other words, citizenship was based on political and legal rights rather than descent. In 264 B.C., Rome in her constitution resembled a Greek city-state, possessing annually elected magistrates, assemblies, and the Senate. Rome, however, was an aristocratic republic dominated by 30 great families (*gentes*) that monopolized high office and the Senate. Yet the political elite (*nobiles*) and the majority of citizens shared a devotion to the republic and achieved a rule of law praised by the Greek historian Polybius as the model of a "mixed constitution." The Roman political elite adapted the political offices of their republic to govern provinces of a great overseas empire after the First Punic War.

Outline

I. This lecture covers the constitutional and political institutions of Rome in the period called the *Middle Republic*, the years 264 B.C. to 190 B.C.

    A. Our main source for this period is a Greek author, Polybius.

    B. This period saw the Romans expand the limits of Mediterranean civilization beyond peninsular Italy into the barbarian lands.

    C. This lecture focuses on how the political institutions operated in the republic and looks at why these institutions were so important in overcoming and assimilating barbarian foes.

    D. In understanding Roman legal and political institutions, we must keep in mind that the Romans never carried political reform to its logical conclusion and never abolished any political or social practice that was obsolete.

II. What was Roman citizenship like?

    A. As mentioned in the first lecture, the Romans defined their citizenship as a group of political and legal rights. Citizenship was not based on descent, nor was it necessarily based on culture.

    B. The Romans were mainly concerned with bringing people into the Roman body politic, because they needed military power. These military needs saw expression in the term *ex formula togatorum*, which was a legal classification of the peoples of Italy requiring "military service of the togated peoples."

    C. In 264 B.C., Rome went to war with Carthage, her first major war outside of Italy and the event that transformed Rome into a Mediterranean power.

        1. At the time, Rome was in possession of about 65 percent of peninsular Italy.

        2. The population there was divided into four major legal categories: Roman citizens, citizens without the franchise (*cives sine suffragio*), Latins, and Italian allies (*socius*, pl. *socii*).

        3. Roman citizens had full rights, including the right to vote in assemblies, hold offices of state, and serve in the Senate.

        4. The citizens without the franchise had been incorporated into the Roman body politic but generally lived in more distant regions, such as the cities of Campania. They enjoyed the protection of Roman law and were eventually incorporated as full citizens.

        5. The Latins were members of the 30 Latin communities or colonies (*colonia*), self-governing military settlements. They enjoyed a "half-citizen" status, although they could return to Rome and resume full citizenship as long as their military obligations were met. The Latin colonies each had a separate treaty with Rome but not among themselves.

        6. The last category, comprised of the *socii*, included various members of Italian or Greek communities, tribes, or cities. These allies owed military service to Rome but retained their own institutions.

D. Thus, in 264 B.C., when the Romans embarked on their first overseas war, the majority of those serving in their armies were not Roman citizens.

III. From the founding of the republic in 509 B.C., Roman citizens were classified into two orders: patricians and plebians.

A. The patricians represented an elite class (*nobiles*), whose ancestors had held high offices of state and the priesthood. They alone had the right to hold high office, including the consulship. The plebians did not have the right to hold these offices, but they were not all poor.

B. Between 367 and 287 B.C., the plebian order (*ordo*) had mobilized to force concessions that opened offices to all citizens, ended debt slavery, distributed land taken from defeated foes, and recognized the plebian assembly (*concilium plebis*).

C. A new magisterial class of nobles (*nobiles*)—patricians or plebians—was created in Rome. By 264 B.C., then, most of the Roman aristocracy was not the original patrician elite.

D. Further, the plebians had gained a number of important rights. They had the protection of special groups of officials known as *tribunes*, which could appeal arbitrary decisions of magistrates on behalf of plebians.

E. By 264, the Roman constitution functioned, in the words of the Victorian constitutional historian Walter Bageot, "because of the reasonableness of men."

IV. Three components of the Roman constitution operated in this arrangement of patricians and plebians.

A. Romans voted in assemblies based on property, age, or residence, rather than as individuals.

B. For our purposes, the two key assemblies were the Centuriate Assembly and the Tribal Assembly.
   1. The Centuriate Assembly was based on units in the Roman army and was heavily weighted toward age and property. Its members were the landowners, and it elected high officials of state.

      2. The Tribal Assembly was based on residence; citizens were registered in one of 35 tribes, or large districts. This assembly voted on legislation.
- **C.** Neither of these assemblies had independent initiative; their roles, ultimately, were passive. The Tribal Assembly was the closest the Romans ever came to democracy.
- **D.** In addition to these assemblies were various levels of elected magistrates, including *consuls* and *praetors*, who were restricted in significant ways.
    1. All public officials were paired with colleagues, the offices were elected annually, and in the event of a dispute, the negative vote won. These measures were taken to prevent any one official from gaining too much power.
    2. Other limitations also applied to these offices, including age and class restrictions. In particular, only the members of the *nobiles* were thought to be suited for political or military command, by virtue of their birth, training, and tradition.
    3. This arrangement had a number of benefits for the members of the 30 great clans (*gens*, pl. *gentes*) of the patrician-plebian noble class. All members of this class had the opportunity to hold office, to acquire booty, and to gain *auctoritas* ("influence").
    4. This arrangement also presented some peculiar problems, particularly in the military. For example, in several situations, two consuls commanded the same army together. One solution to any conflicts was for the two to lead on alternate days. This "safeguard" led to a number of military disasters, notably the defeat at the Battle of Cannae in 216 B.C.
    5. Such weaknesses in the Roman political and military structure became evident as the Romans expanded overseas, but the Romans were always able to adapt their institutions to suit changing conditions. For example, they created a new class of *pro-consuls*, *pro-praetors*, and so on to conduct overseas wars.
- **E.** The key institution that came to run the republic was the Senate, which was made up of former magistrates.
    1. The Senate was the advisory body of the republic, acting through its *auctoritas*. Magistrates were reluctant to initiate

radical legislation in the assemblies, because they ultimately wanted to sit in the Senate themselves.
2. The Senate dominated the Roman state during the period of expansion overseas, because it was the only permanent standing institution in Rome, and it had the collective experience of all the former magistrates.

F. These three public institutions endured for almost 250 years and won Rome her empire.
1. It is often thought that a great deal of the success of the Romans rested on this hierarchical organization.
2. The Romans' success can also be traced to the political consensus that existed in the Middle Republic and the bonds of society that tied the classes together, which we shall discuss in the next lecture.

Readings:

Mitchell, Richard E. *Patricians and Plebians: The Origin of the Roman State*.

Nicolet, Claude. *The World of the Citizen in Republican Rome*. Translated by P. S. Fall.

Questions to Consider:

1. How did legal and political institutions of the Roman Republic contribute to the success of Roman expansion? How did Roman attitudes to citizenship influence how they would view barbarians?
2. What were the unique features of Roman citizenship? What were the prime political institutions of the Roman Republic in 264 B.C.?

Lecture Three
Roman Society

Scope: In 264 B.C., political loyalty to the republic (*res publica*) was rooted in the values of early Roman society that connected lesser citizens as clients to patrons of the great families. Bonds between patrons and clients were reciprocal and hereditary, determining voting, military service, and litigation. The political success of the republic rested on the stability of a hierarchical social order. Since 367 B.C., patricians, who had originally constituted the only order (*ordo*) allowed high office, shared political power and patronage with plebians of prominent families to form an expanded aristocracy by 264 B.C. This political elite, or *nobiles*, dictated the course of Roman expansion and the destiny of Roman civilization for the next three centuries. These nobles applied their notions of patron and client in dealing with defeated foes, which assisted in assimilating barbarians into the ranks of provincial clients and ensuring the success of a republic governing a vast empire.

Outline

I. The bonds of society cemented the Roman citizen orders and the Italian allied peoples into the larger Roman Republic. Particularly important were the bonds of patrons (*patronus*, pl. *patroni*) and clients (*cliens*, pl. *clientes*).

    A. The bonds of patron and client were inherited and reciprocal. The patrons at the top of the hierarchy had certain obligations to those at the bottom.

    B. Rituals and traditions sanctified the patron-client relationship, including the morning *salutatio* ("salutation").

    C. The ties of patronage had both political and military implications. Clients were expected to vote in the direction of their patrons and to turn out for the draft when called.

    D. In return, patrons gave a great deal of protection and advantage to their clients, including legal protection.

    E. These obligations were powerfully felt and were sanctified by *mos maiorum* ("the custom of the ancestors"). The Romans were

innately conservative and looked to past precedent to justify present-day actions. This conservatism explains their reluctance to abolish outmoded political institutions.
- **F.** Patrons could accept not only individuals and families but also other types of groups, such as the *collegia*, which were organizations similar to guilds.
- **G.** The depths of these patronage ties are revealed by public and private inscriptions erected by dutiful and grateful clients to their patrons.

II. As mentioned earlier, these social bonds explain much of the political conservatism in Roman assemblies.
- **A.** Again, the Roman assemblies did not have the same initiative as, for example, the Athenian assemblies.
- **B.** Further, the electorate was conservative because the voters were tied to patrons, who were members of the political elite.
    1. In rare cases, someone from outside the order of *nobiles* might be elected to the Senate. Such an officer was called *novus homo* ("new man").
    2. From 367 B.C. to 46 B.C., Rome had 640 consulships, but only 21 of these offices were held by new men, and this number represents only 11 individuals.
- **C.** The social bonds of Rome all but ensured that the voters would not elect anyone who did not have the traditions of the *nobiles* behind him to hold high office.
- **D.** These ties also explain the relationship among the Roman senatorial elite themselves. The study of patronage connections among aristocrats is termed *prosopography* (the "study of faces") by modern scholars.
- **E.** When these bonds of client and patron, as well as *amicitia* ("friendship" ties), began to dissolve at the end of the 2nd century B.C. as a result of social and economic change, the republic itself began to break down.

III. The powerful social bonds of Roman society were also seen in the institution of slavery, which must be understood as an extension of the family.

A. We must make a distinction between state slaves and slaves who were attached to individuals. Most slaves had come to that condition as captives in war; race was not a factor.

B. In the households of the great families, slaves were often liberated. On manumission, a freedman (*libertus*, pl. *liberti*) became, in effect, a "super-client" of his former master. Slavery served as an avenue to assimilate large numbers of foreign captives into the Roman body politic.

    1. Between 200 B.C. and 50 B.C., at least 1 million captives were sold on the slave markets of Italy.

    2. In 225 B.C., perhaps 500,000 out of 4.5 million residents in Italy were slaves, or about 10 percent of the population.

    3. By 50 B.C., slaves numbered at least 2 million out of 6.5 million residents, or about 30 percent of the population. Of the whole population, many had servile origins, because their ancestors had been captured and enslaved in Spain, Gaul, or the Greek world.

    4. We should also note that when they were given their freedom, former slaves acquired Roman citizenship and the right to vote.

C. The arrangements of slavery in the Roman Republic presented some dangers. In the later republic, the great wars of conquest overseas, in Spain, Gaul, North Africa, and elsewhere, flooded the Italian market with slaves and brought about changes to the social organization.

    1. A powerful propertied order emerged between the political elite and the plebians. In 129 B.C., this group was recognized as the *ordo equester* ("equestrian order").

    2. This group should not be confused with the middle class; they are best described as "the gentlemen outside the Senate."

    3. The equestrians amassed fortunes, clients, and slaves in government contracting, tax farming, banking, and law.

D. The Late Republic saw other dramatic changes in economic and social arrangements.

    1. By 150 B.C., the profits of conquest were so great that the political elite could begin to separate themselves physically, socially, and culturally from their fellow Roman citizens.

      2. Cato the Elder had warned against this situation, urging senators to retain their connections with their Roman clients. This warning was ignored in the generation after Cato.

IV. How did these social ties relate to the barbarians?
- **A.** The Romans were extremely interested in understanding the foreign peoples that they conquered and administered.
- **B.** The bonds of client and patron were easily extended to the defeated, both those who were enslaved and those who remained in their homelands.
- **C.** The Romans first began to extend this system into the region of Cisalpine Gaul, that is, northern Italy, where Celtic tribes had settled.
  - **1.** The Celtic warrior elites quickly found that, upon surrendering, they could become the representatives of their tribes to the Roman patrons. In turn, the patrons offered legal protection to these new provincials.
  - **2.** As early as 171 B.C., conquered Spanish tribes learned to appeal to individual senators to represent judicial complaints before the Roman Senate.
- **D.** This patron-client system, which tied Italian society together, assisted in the assimilation of conquered peoples and enabled Romans to extend their control over the Mediterranean world and push the frontiers of that world deep into central and northern Europe.
- **E.** Of course, this system also gave rise to some peculiar situations. For example, some of the great rebel leaders, such as Arminius, a German prince, had served as representatives of their tribes and gained Roman citizenship.
  - **1.** The brother of Arminius, Flavus, pointed out that the prince had betrayed his patron, the emperor Tiberius, while Flavus had remained loyal to Rome.
  - **2.** Indeed, most of the members of Arminius's family remained pro-Roman.
- **F.** Romans were willing to enfranchise the elite classes of provincials and, eventually, the provincials themselves. This attitude is captured vividly in a speech by Emperor Claudius in 48 A.D.,

reported by the historian Tacitus, when the emperor championed the admission of Gallic nobles into the Senate.

G. Some historians have argued that all of Roman foreign policy can be understood in terms of the relationship of patron and client. Although the Romans were capable of more subtle diplomacy than this theory implies, it does contain a great deal of truth.

Readings:

Brunt, P. A. *Social Conflicts in the Roman Republic.*

MacMullen, Ramsay. *Roman Social Relations, 50 B.C. to A.D. 284.*

Questions to Consider:

1. How did the bonds of patron and client account for the success of the Roman Republic? Why were such ties so powerful in early Italian society?
2. How did the stability of the Roman social order contribute to political institutions? How were elections and the administration of law premised on this social order? How was the social order reflected in the politics among the ruling classes?
3. How did the Roman social order affect attitudes to barbarians and provincials? By what means could these outsiders be assimilated into the Roman order?

Lecture Four
The Roman Way of War

Scope: Romans excelled in war, and the citizen legions of the republic gained a reputation for discipline, courage, and skill still envied by professional armies. Roman consuls levied citizens and Italian allies from a draft that mobilized trained soldiers on a scale not again attained until the 18th century. Legionaries were drilled by centurions to fight in open-order tactics using the sword, the famed *gladius*. Hence, Roman armies, even in defeat, inflicted high casualties on opponents. In the 4th through 3rd centuries B.C., the Romans perfected tactics to defeat fierce barbarian opponents, first in northern Italy, then in Spain, the Balkans, and northwestern Europe. The Romans mastered siege warfare and logistics, and they linked Italy by a network of military highways and colonies. These bastions broke the power of rebels or invaders and served as bases for the conquest of the Gauls of northern Italy. Above all, Roman commanders and soldiers were determined to conquer to win glory and booty. This tenacity won the republic a Mediterranean empire. As many barbarian opponents learned, the Romans were, in the opinion of Polybius, to be feared most when they were most pressed.

Outline

I. The Romans perfected the weapons and tactics of their citizen legions in the course of waging campaigns against the tough hill peoples of Italy, such as the Samnites, and the dreaded Celtic tribes of northern Italy (Cisalpine Gaul). Most of our information about the Roman army covers the period from 150 B.C. to 200 A.D.

  A. The Roman army was commanded by magistrates, who were elected with *imperium* (the "right to command citizens"). These magistrates had the right, even in the imperial age, to levy a draft (*dilectus*) on all citizens.

  B. In 264 B.C., Romans of property (*assidui*), that is, those who could equip themselves as heavy infantry troops, were compelled to respond to the draft.

        1. Those who did not have the full arms could also be summoned as members of the light infantry or missile soldiers.
        2. The members of the senatorial and political elite served as officers, as generals, and in the cavalry.
        3. Citizenship depended on military service. Men were expected to provide their own weapons, and a man's position in the army reflected his property and his worth to the state.
    C. Further, all citizens were expected to train themselves for military service. Even propertied men were accustomed to hard manual labor and would have served ably. These factors, along with the social bonds of the patron-client relationship, contributed to the effectiveness of the Roman draft.

II. Between 264 and 200 B.C., the Roman army was in a state of evolution in its weapons and tactics.
    A. Two descriptions of the Roman army come to us from literary sources, one penned by Livy, looking at the army in about the 3rd century B.C., and the other by Polybius, writing in about 150 B.C.
    B. From these sources, we know that by about 150 B.C., the Roman armies were shifting their tactics to shock action relying on a sword.
        1. The tactical units were also undergoing change. In 264 B.C., soldiers fought in smaller units, known as *maniples*. These units arranged themselves in three ranks, the *principes*, *hastati*, and *triarii*.
        2. The front two ranks probably had a version of the *pilum* (pl. *pila*), a spear thrown to disable or kill an opponent.
        3. A classic Roman attack in the 2nd and 1st centuries B.C. used an open-order formation, not a column. It would open with a volley of *pila*, followed by close shock action with the sword (*gladius*).
    C. Using these tactics, Roman legionaries combined the mobility and ease of maneuver of cavalry with the staying power of infantry, and they inflicted heavy casualties. Romans fought in close and were trained to go for the kill, demoralizing their opponents.
    D. The Roman body armor was perfectly designed for this type of fighting. A soldier was protected by a large, semi-cylindrical shield (*scutum*), which enabled him to fight individually with full protection.

- **E.** The power and effectiveness of the Roman army depended on the individual skill of each soldier and his ability to operate in teams with his fellow *centuries*. Each Roman soldier was interchangeable with any other soldier, and the reserves were just as skilled as the men who were first called to the colors.
- **F.** The Romans' effectiveness gives rise to such terms as *Pyrrhic victory*. Twice the Romans were defeated by the mercenary King Pyrrhus in 280 and 279 B.C., but they also inflicted heavy casualties on Pyrrhus's army.
- **G.** In terms of fighting ability, the Roman army was superb, and the Romans continually incorporated innovations into their equipment and tactics. Further, in their skill and sense of devotion to their units, Rome's "citizen soldiers" were as professional as any army could be.

III. The Romans had other advantages over their opponents, including their vaunted engineering skills and their devotion to glory.

- **A.** Whenever they were moving in enemy territory, the Romans laid out perfectly regular camps according to a grid system. These sites would then become permanent camps in the territory, and the grid would ultimately become a system of streets that can still be seen in some of the cities of Western Europe.
- **B.** The most impressive example of the Romans' engineering ability comes from Julius Caesar's siege of Alesia in 52 B.C., which included two concentric lines of fortifications, 12 and 14 miles in diameter.
- **C.** Above all, Romans valued bravery and glory. The commanders were expected to exhibit *virtus* ("bravery") and aspired to gain a *triumph*, which meant that they had killed 5,000 barbarian foes.
- **D.** Commanders were expected to lead from the front, that is, to serve as examples to their men.
  1. Nothing is more vivid in this regard than the orations of Julius Caesar exhorting his men to battle or Caesar's own cool reserve in the Battle of the Sambre in 57 B.C.
  2. *Centurions*, the non-commissioned officers, and the *tribunes*, the junior officers, were also expected to inspire courage and initiative.

- **E.** The Romans had to master the logistics involved in feeding, equipping, and transporting their armies.
    1. In 225 B.C., Rome could mobilize well over 1 million Romans, Latins, and Italian allies. At the height of the Second Punic War (218–201 B.C.), more than 280,000 men were under arms.
    2. Between 264 B.C. and 31 B.C., one-half to two-thirds of all Romans and Italian allies served in legions.
    3. After 200 B.C., 150,000 men served overseas annually, but major wars in the east, in Spain, and against northern barbarians required expeditionary forces, often supported by fleets.
    4. It is a testament to the Romans' logistical abilities that they could sustain these large armies overseas. On average, 17 percent of the adult male population was under arms; early-modern armies, such as that of Louis XIV, could mobilize only about 5 percent of the population.
- **F.** We might also compare Roman military power to that of its opponents.
    1. A consular army could number 20,000–40,000 men, one-third to one-half of whom were Romans. Such manpower was the average for ancient armies.
    2. The Romans, however, had the ability to mobilize more men as needed. King Philip V of Macedon (r. 223–179 B.C.), for example, could call on an absolute maximum of 150,000 men; the Romans had 1 million.
    3. In the first three years of the Punic Wars, the Roman army lost 100,000 men, 10 percent of its manpower. In response, Rome raised more legions.
    4. In time, this strategy would take a terrible toll on the citizen population and contribute to the breakdown of the republic.
- **G.** Livy captures the spirit of pride and patriotism of the Roman soldier in his account of a speech given by the centurion Spurius Ligustinus in 171 B.C.

Readings:

Goldsworthy, A. K. *The Roman Army at War 100 B.C.–A.D. 200.*

Keppie, L. J. F. *The Making of the Roman Army from Republic to Empire.*

Questions to Consider:

1. What were the consistent advantages enjoyed by the Romans in the way they waged war during the republic? How important were weapons and tactics, generalship, and logistics and engineering to Roman success?

2. How important were morale, social bonds, and patriotism in motivating officers and men? How important were booty and land? What accounted for the success of Roman mobilization of citizens and allies?

Lecture Five
Celtic Europe and the Mediterranean World

Scope: In the 6th century B.C., Celtic-speaking peoples dwelling in northern and eastern Gaul and the lands of the Upper Danube attained a sophisticated level of culture, known as *La Tène*. With improved iron technology came prosperity and the growth of fortified towns, trade, and monetized markets. From their heartland, Celts migrated to settle in Britain, northern and central Spain, northern Italy, and the Balkans. In 390 B.C., a Gallic host sacked Rome. In 281–277 B.C., Celtic tribes, dubbed *Galatians*, ravaged Macedon and northern Greece, then crossed into Asia Minor. To the peoples of the Mediterranean world, who had long traded with Celts, these invaders epitomized the barbarian. Classical literature and visual arts depicted Gauls as pale-faced, savage warriors, who were worthy opponents to defeat or mercenaries to hire. Yet the achievements of Celtic civilization laid the foundations for the success of Roman rule in northern Europe; the history of Romans and Celts was far more than a record of wars, because by commerce, settlement, and military service, the two peoples ultimately created new provincial Roman societies in northern Europe.

Outline

I. This lecture introduces the Celts of western and central Europe, who in many ways, represented the epitome of barbarians to both Greeks and Romans.

    A. The preferred term for these peoples is *Celts* or, in Greek, *Keltoi*.
        1. The term has acquired a linguistic meaning, denoting a large group of related languages, spoken from Spain to France, central Europe, the British Isles, and northern Italy.
        2. The language was even brought by a group of Celtic invaders into central Turkey; the Celtic people who settled there were known as *Galatians*.

    B. The Romans called the Celts *Gauls*, although *Gaul* has come to mean the extended region of France that encompassed parts of the

Rhineland and the Low Countries. Hence, for clarity, we refer to these peoples as Celts.

C. In modern parlance, Celts denotes Irish, Scots, Welsh, and Bretons, but the core of Celtic civilization was really in southern Germany and eastern France; it later spread to these "fringe" regions.

II. Who were the Celts? They are known to us from both Greek and Roman literary sources as early as the 7th and 6th centuries B.C.

A. We have reports of Greek merchants having contact with the Celts in the Greek colony of Massilia (modern-day Marseilles). The sources recognize the Celts as a group of related barbarian peoples.

B. We also have significant archaeological evidence about the Celts from southern Germany and France. This evidence reveals a much more complicated material culture than the literary sources relate.

C. Archaeologists recognize two phases in the material culture. The first is known as the *Hallstatt* period (c. 800–450 B.C.), which takes its name from a major salt-mining region in Austria. The second phase is called *La Tène* (c. 450–50 B.C.).

   1. The Hallstatt period saw a dramatic shift in the material culture of central Europe and eastern France: Iron technology was adopted, more land was put under cultivation, and certain settlements were fortified.

   2. These settlements were clearly not based on subsistence but included regional trade. In time, that trade began to extend to the Mediterranean shores.

   3. Between 600–450 B.C., trade with the Greek and Etruscan cities of Marseilles, Tuscany, and Milan, along with other regions, was important in stimulating development of these fortified Celtic towns. By 450 B.C., these settlements were called *oppida* (Latin, sing. *oppidum*).

   4. Archaeological finds around these *oppida* also include impressive burial mounds, which reveal the products imported from the Mediterranean world. These products include ceramics, wine, jewelry, textiles, and carved ivories.

   5. In return, the Celts made advancements in their own products for export, which included salt, iron technology, timber, hides, woolens, and slaves.

- **D.** This trade resulted in the transition from the Hallstatt period into La Tène culture and a shift in the gravity of Celtic economic and political power from southern Germany to eastern France, the Rhineland, and the Alpine regions.
- **E.** By 300 B.C., the Celts had developed a sophisticated culture.
    1. Their economic systems and political structures served as the basis for Roman provincial success several centuries later.
    2. At the time, the Celts had adapted Greek and Etruscan alphabets into a writing system. In addition, the priestly caste, the *Druids*, had already evolved, later to be described by Julius Caesar.
    3. The Celts were successful traders and merchants and were skilled in constructing wheeled vehicles. Most of the loan words in Latin for *cart*, *harness*, and so on come from Celtic.
- **F.** Emphasis on the Celts' material and cultural achievements should not downplay their abilities as warriors. They were formidable opponents, which gave them an advantage when they migrated throughout Europe.
    1. In Spain, for example, the Celts were known to the Romans as Celtiberians. They were distinct from the Spaniards in their methods of fighting.
    2. Both Celtic infantry and cavalry were regarded as exceptional. The Celts are reported to have gone into battle half-dressed, painted blue, and wielding large slashing swords.

III. We turn to the two points of contact that the Celts, or Gauls, had with the Romans and Greeks, which influenced developments in Rome and the wider Greek world.
- **A.** The Gauls crossed the Alps at the end of the 5th century B.C. and began to settle in northern Italy, especially in the upper reaches of the Po valley.
- **B.** A group of these Gauls, the Senones, drifted down the Po and positioned themselves where they could easily swoop into the Etruscan heartland and Rome.
    1. In 390 B.C., one such war party came down the Tiber, attacked Etruscan cities, and met with a Roman army on a tributary of the Po, the river Allia, on July 18.
    2. At the time, the Roman army was only about 15,000 strong and was overwhelmed by the initial charge of the Gauls.

3. The Gauls, under the leader called Brennus, proceeded to Rome and sacked the city, although they did not take the citadel.
   4. The Romans never forgot this humiliation; July 18 was observed, for centuries, as a "black day." Afterwards, the Romans fortified the city with the Servian walls.
   5. In the course of the 4th and 3rd centuries, the Romans perfected their tactics of the legions to cope with Gallic charges. They shifted to the use of different types of javelins and missiles, culminating in the *pilum*, to counter the Gauls.
C. Ultimately, Rome benefited from these Gallic raids, because they weakened the older, wealthier Etruscan cities and Umbria, which enabled Rome to bring these regions under control in the 4th and 3rd centuries B.C.
D. The Celtic migrations also followed traditional trade routes farther east, to the Balkans and, ultimately, to Greece and Asia Minor.
   1. These tribes were not interested in settling in the mountain zones of the Balkans; they were looking for areas where they could farm and herd animals. They followed the Save and Drave Rivers to the routes leading south into the northern regions of the Aegean world.
   2. In 281 B.C., a group of Gallic tribes appeared on the borders of Macedon (Macedonia). King Ptolemy Ceraumus and his army was annihilated by the Gauls. The Gauls then raided Macedon and crossed into northern Greece.
   3. These Gauls got as far as central Greece and even came close to raiding Delphi. The Greeks were terrified of these barbarians.
   4. The Gauls withdrew into the Balkans, then received an invitation from Prusias, king of Bithynia in northwest Turkey, to serve as mercenaries in Asia Minor. Perhaps as many as 10,000 Galatian warriors, with their families, responded to this invitation and terrorized Asia Minor for the next generation.
   5. Eventually, these Galatians were brought under control by the Seleucid kings. In particular, King Antiochus I defeated the Galatians at the Battle of Elephants in 269 B.C. The tribes were pushed onto the Anatolian plateau and settled there.

6. The Galatians then adopted the Hellenistic lifestyle and, eventually, hired themselves out as mercenaries to the Greek armies. This development helped make Gordion, their capital in Anatolia, an important commercial center.
7. The Galatians' role in the region did not stop the Greeks from portraying them as noble, ferocious warriors. Hellenic sculpture groups and relief panels, particularly the *Galliomachy*, show the triumph of civilization over the Gauls but encapsulate the Greek and Roman view of these Celtic peoples as barbarian warriors.

Readings:

Dyson, Stephen. *Creation of the Roman Frontier*.

Schutze. Herbert. *The Prehistory of Germanic Europe*.

Questions to Consider:

1. How did technological change, along with improvements in agriculture and trade, contribute to the emergence of a Celtic civilization based on towns by the La Tène period? Where did Celt tribes seek new homelands?
2. What was the early Roman reaction to the Gallic invasions of Italy? How did the defeat in 390 B.C. shape later Roman attitudes and institutions? How did Greeks view the Galatian migrations of the 3rd century B.C.? How stereotyped and misleading were Roman and Greek opinions about the Celts?

Lecture Six
The Conquest of Cisalpine Gaul

Scope: In 264 B.C., Romans defined Italy's northern boundary as the rivers Arno and Rubicon, because beyond them lay Cisalpine Gaul ("Gaul on the nearer side of the Alps"). Following ancient trade routes, Celtic tribes of La Tène crossed the Alps and settled in the rich valleys of the Po's northern tributaries between the 5th and 3rd centuries B.C. The Celtic newcomers occupied Etruscanized cities, such as Comum (Como) and Mediolanum (Milan). Other Celts crossed the lower Po and penetrated to the upper reaches of the Tiber. In 390 B.C., Celtic raiders, dubbed a *tumultus* in Latin, defeated the Roman army on the Allia and sacked Rome. For the next century, Rome battled to avenge the humiliation, ending in the expulsion of Celtic tribes of the lower Po. From 223 B.C., consular armies crossed the Po and imposed Roman authority over the Gallic tribes. But the Celts, who found an ally in Hannibal, rose in rebellion during the Second Punic War (218–201 B.C.). For two decades thereafter, Rome methodically pacified Cisalpine Gaul. Between 170 and 90 B.C., Romans and Italians thickly settled the lands south of the Po. To the north, Celtic tribes were integrated into Roman society by ties of patronage, commerce, and military service. Cisalpine Gaul was transformed into Transpadane Italy; the urban communities received the Latin status in 89 B.C., and the entire province was merged with greater Italy in 42 B.C.

Outline

I. This lecture continues our exploration of Celtic Europe to explain the role of the Gauls in northern Italy and the influence they had on the development of early Rome.

    A. In 264 B.C., the Romans were pulled in two directions: north into central and western Europe or east into the Mediterranean world.

    B. The Romans had close dealings with the Gauls for 200 years before they brought these peoples under control and turned the region north of the Arno and Rubicon Rivers—Cisalpine Gaul—into northern Italy.

- **C.** We shall look at the diversity of people in Cisalpine Gaul, examine how the Romans moved into this area and conquered the Gauls, and explore the process of Romanization in the region.
    1. Eventually, the residents of this area received the full Roman franchise, and northern Italy was merged into the rest of Italy in 42 B.C.
    2. This Romanization was not a conscious policy but more of a byproduct of the Roman conquest, in which the barbarians acquired the material culture and language of Rome.
    3. At the same time, the Romans also learned a good deal from these Celtic peoples.

II. In 264 B.C., diverse peoples dwelled north of the line of the rivers Arno and Rubicon, which the Romans did not consider a part of Italy.

- **A.** Celtic tribes dominated the fertile lands of modern Lombardy in the upper Po valley area. Mediolanum (Milan) was a major Celtic settlement, and the Celts had also founded a number of *oppida* in the region.
- **B.** Such tribes as the Insubres, Cenomani, Senones, and Boii had settled in the area. These Celts had also settled south of the Po in an area that later became the Roman district Aemilia.
- **C.** These Celtic settlements had two distinct zones, one in the northern reaches of the Po and one in the southern reaches of the Po and the piedmont area of the Apennines.
- **D.** Other settlements included an area to the far west, home of the Ligurians.
    1. These people spoke a language related to the Iberian dialects of Spain.
    2. The Ligurians were part of an ancient Mediterranean population, going back to the Bronze Age, that stretched from Italy through southern France and into Spain.
    3. These people were pastoralists, practicing a simple form of agriculture and herding.
    4. The Ligurians were also regarded as superb light infantry and posed a constant threat as raiders to Etruscan cities and Celtic tribes.
- **E.** In northeastern Italy were the Venetians, an Italic people who opposed the Celts and saw Rome as an ally.

- **F.** Therefore, when Italy was reorganized in the time of the emperor Augustus at the end of the 1st century B.C., these people represented four distinct zones in Italy, which were numbered VIII, IX, X, and XI.
- **G.** The Celts played an important role in these regions.
    1. They had brought in their metallurgy and their town organization from central Europe.
    2. They also established important trade routes going into central Europe and Gaul. They were active in trading with Genua (Genoa) and with the Venetians.
    3. The Romans saw the Celts as a dynamic force in this region and their most serious opponents; they termed the area *Cisalpine Gaul*, although it included large numbers of non-Gallic peoples. *Transalpine Gaul* was, essentially, "Gaul on the other side of the Alps," what is today France, the Low Countries, and the Rhineland.

III. By 264 B.C., the Romans had devoted about 150 years to unifying Italy and had gained experience in dealing with Celtic tactics.
- **A.** The Romans never forgot the sack of their city in 390 B.C. by a Celtic tribe, and indeed, the Senate declared a state of emergency (*tumultus*) whenever the Celts were on the move.
- **B.** The whole first half of the 3rd century B.C. was an effort by the Romans to bring the Celtic invasion routes under control.
    1. The Romans finally smashed Gallic resistance, particularly that of the Senones and the Boii, in a series of significant battles in the 280s B.C.
    2. These battles allowed Rome to secure Etruria and Umbria, block the invasion routes, and begin to think of taking the offensive into the heartland of Cisalpine Gaul.
    3. These victories also gave the Romans the sense of security to take on Carthage in 264 B.C. in the First Punic War.
- **C.** The First Punic War transformed Rome into a Mediterranean power and allowed the Romans to exploit, indirectly, the wider western Mediterranean.
    1. The Romans always imposed harsh terms on their defeated foes. Carthage, for example, was slapped with an enormous indemnity that had to be paid in silver.

> 2. To pay this indemnity, Carthage had to conquer a colonial empire in Spain that, ironically, revived Carthaginian power and allowed Hannibal to reopen the struggle with Rome in 218 B.C.
> 3. Hannibal recruited a large number of Celtiberians in Spain, marched them over the Pyrenees and the Alps, and attacked Italy from the north, nearly bringing Rome to her knees in the Second Punic War.
> 4. This war, in part, was sustained by the large numbers of Cisalpine Gauls who were willing to join Hannibal's army as mercenaries. These Gauls attacked the Romans, forcing Rome to detach legions into Cisalpine Gaul.
> 5. This war came at a critical point in Roman relations with the Celts, because the Romans had spent the past two decades moving into the region, had already established two important colonies in the Po valley, had brought the Venetians into alliance, and had imposed treaties on the Celtic tribes around Milan.
> 6. The Romans had to keep two to four legions in Cisalpine Gaul during the whole of the Second Punic War. Even after Hannibal's army evacuated Italy in 201 B.C., the Romans repeatedly sent consular armies into northern Italy.
> 7. The Gauls sacked one of the Latin colonies, Placentia, around 200 B.C. In addition, the Romans suffered some embarrassing defeats at the hands of the Gauls, and the casualties were high on both sides.
> 8. It was not until 190 B.C. that the final Gallic resistance was broken, although the Ligurians continued to give the Romans difficulty for the next generation.

IV. The Romans' policies in northern Italy differed after these regions were secured.

- A. Certain areas saw intensive Roman colonization. Large numbers of Italians, Latins, and Romans moved into the regions immediately south of the Po, that area called Aemilia.
  1. In 173 B.C., the Roman consul Marcus Aemilius Lepidus distributed individual land grants (*viritim*) to Italian and Roman settlers of Aemilia. Other settlements (*fora*) were also established.

2. Many Latin colonies were established or refounded at this time; the modern cities of Bologna and Parma trace their origins to these Roman municipal foundations.
   3. The region south of the Po was, essentially, incorporated into greater Italy.
B. North of the Po, where the Celtic tribes and Venetians dwelt, the pattern was different.
   1. Initially, merchants moved into this area but very few settlers. The Via Annia, originally a military highway, linked Aquileia (the area of Venice) with Genua (Genoa) and became an important trade route.
   2. Within a generation, the Celtic warrior elites in this region learned to operate under the patronage system with Rome. They also quickly acquired the Mediterranean culture and tastes, and their goods became essential to Rome.
   3. The northern zones of Italy were indispensable in feeding Rome, which grew enormously during the 2nd and 1st centuries B.C.
   4. This economic development had major social implications. Many of the descendents of Celtic warriors undertook Roman military service and gained citizenship. They acquired the Latin language and linked themselves by marriage and hospitality to the Latin colonies.
   5. By 100 B.C., this area, which had formerly been part of Celtic Europe, was quickly being integrated into the wider Roman world, but many of the older Celtic traditions were maintained.
C. In two or three generations from the conquest, a northern Italian provincial culture had emerged.
   1. In 106–105 B.C., barbarian Germanic peoples migrated into southern Gaul and attempted to cross into Italy. The peoples of Cisalpine Gaul felt no identity with these new barbarians and demanded protection from Rome.
   2. In 90 B.C., Italian allies staged a major revolt against the Romans in southern and central Italy, clamoring for Roman citizenship. Ultimately, the Romans gave into these demands and enfranchised the Italian allies as Roman citizens.
   3. At the same time, consul Cn. Pompeius Strabo proposed to make all the Latin colonies officially Roman and all the

people residing there Latins. The Romans, thus, potentially extended the franchise to the Cisalpine Gauls.

4. Further, Julius Caesar was successful, in part, because he made himself the patron of this area. He recruited many of the legions that would conquer Gaul from northern Italy, people who were, in their ancestry, Celtic.

5. In the 50s–60s B.C., Julius Caesar championed the cause of Roman citizenship for these peoples, and when he became dictator of Rome, he delivered. In 42 B.C., after Caesar's assassination, the people obtained citizenship, and Cisalpine Gaul was abolished as a province and merged into Italy.

Readings:

Chilver, G. E. F. *Cisalpine Gaul*.

Livy. *Rome and Italy*. Translated by B. Radice.

Questions to Consider:

1. How diverse were the peoples and culture of northern Italy in 300 B.C.? What was the impact of the Celtic tribes in shaping the civilization of northern Italy? What material achievements of La Tène civilization were exported to Italy?

2. How extensive was Roman settlement? In what ways did Romans and indigenous populations interact to create a new provincial society? How important were the building of roads and Latin colonies, promotion of trade, and military service in accelerating social change?

Lecture Seven
Romans and Carthaginians in Spain

Scope: In 300 B.C., the Spanish peninsula was home to diverse cultures. Greek colonies along the northeastern shores stretched from the Pyrenees to the lower Ebro River. Iberian towns along the Levantine littoral and in the Baetis (Guadalquivir) valley were linked by commerce with Carthage. On the great central plateau of Spain, the Meseta, dwelled martial Celtiberian tribes. In 237–219 B.C., generals of the Barcid family—Hamilcar, Hasdrubal, and Hannibal—built a colonial empire in Spain to pay off the indemnity owed Rome as the price of Carthage's defeat in the First Punic War. Spanish silver and Celtiberian mercenaries restored Carthage's military might, and she challenged Rome again in the Second Punic War (218–201 B.C.).

From bases in Spain, Hannibal invaded Italy. Roman forces arrived under the brothers Publius and Lucius Cornelius Scipio to check Spanish reinforcements from reaching Hannibal in Italy. Each brother, betrayed by Celtiberian allies, was defeated and slain in 211 B.C. The Senate commissioned Scipio Africanus, son and namesake of the elder Publius, to restore the situation. Scipio Africanus not only broke Carthaginian power in Spain, but he built a network of alliances among Spanish tribes and towns that committed the republic to the conquest of the peninsula. Although the Romans entered the peninsula out of military necessity, they chose to remain out of a desire for glory and riches.

Outline

I. This lecture deals with the Roman conquest of the Iberian peninsula, which would include the modern countries of Portugal and Spain today.

    A. The Romans understood the Spanish peninsula geographically; that is, the region did not encompass a uniform culture. In fact, the Romans arriving in Spain in the 3rd century B.C. would have seen the kind of diversity that they had encountered in northern Italy.

- **B.** In some ways, the Spanish peninsula overtaxed the Roman Republic, although the wars fought there were important to the social and economic transformation of Rome. These wars also contributed directly to the breakdown of the political consensus in Rome that led to the collapse of the republic.
- **II.** We begin with a picture of the Iberian peninsula just before the Romans arrived.
  - **A.** The name *Iberia* was used because it was the name given to the earliest people dwelling on the peninsula.
  - **B.** Iberian languages seem to be part of a wider language group that included those spoken in parts of Italy and southern Gaul, but the commonalities of language did not mean that Iberians thought of themselves as belonging to a single nation.
  - **C.** The culture and patterns of settlement had also divided the Iberians into distinct groups.
    1. In 300 B.C., the Iberians occupied a good portion of the southern and eastern peninsula, as well as the far northwest, where the Basques are today.
    2. Much of the central portion of the peninsula, modern regions of Portugal, and southwest Spain were occupied by Celtiberians and native people with whom they intermingled.
  - **D.** The contact of the Spanish peninsula with the Mediterranean world had a long history.
    1. As early as 1000 B.C., Phoenicians were already active in trading with southern Spain. These merchants traded for metals and foodstuffs with Tartessus, which emerged as a leading state in Spain around 600 B.C.
    2. A couple of hundred years later, the Phoenicians were followed by Greeks, who never managed to break into the Spanish markets. The Greeks established some colonies in the northeast corner of Spain, but the majority of cities on the eastern shore and in the far south were settled by the Phoenicians.
    3. The Phoenicians were primarily merchants, not agriculturalists. They transported goods along trade routes that followed the North African shore. The key city on the western Mediterranean shore was Carthage ("New City").

E. In the 5th and 4th centuries B.C., Carthage emerged as a great commercial republic. At the time of the First Punic War, in 264 B.C., she was a bustling Hellenistic city.
  1. The Carthaginians were content with controlling the points of trade; they did not feel the need to subject the tribes of Spain or North Africa.
  2. Carthage had built a commercial empire that influenced indigenous Spanish groups. What changed the situation was the defeat of the Carthaginians in the First Punic War.
  3. Carthage was slapped with two indemnities totaling 17 million *denarii*, the basic Roman silver coin. The *denarius* would have represented the equivalent of a week's wage to a Roman legionary. The only way for Carthage to pay that debt was to develop an empire in Spain.

F. Forging that empire became the work of the wealthy Barcid family.
  1. The majority of the Carthaginian soldiers were mercenaries recruited from Africa, Spain, and elsewhere. They were drilled into a professional army by Carthaginian generals.
  2. General Hamilcar Barca landed in southern Spain in 237 B.C. and established what would become the capital of the Carthaginian empire at New Carthage.
  3. Hamilcar was succeeded by his son-in-law Hasdrubal and his son Hannibal. These three men built, effectively, an empire in Spain without committing the Carthaginian government to any central administration; instead, they relied on ties of patronage.
  4. In Carthage, unlike Rome, the military and the government were kept separate. The generals were not elected and were subject to the scrutiny of the Senate. Generals could, however, hold command for a number of years, as the Barcid generals did.
  5. The Barcid generals married Iberian women and cemented personal ties with Celtiberian elites. The Barcid family developed a network of alliances that tied the tribes of the interior to the Carthaginian administration at New Carthage.
  6. In this way, the Carthaginians were able to field a mercenary army of infantry and cavalry and exploit the mineral wealth of

Spain. Their involvement in the mining trade ultimately enabled the Carthaginians to pay off their indemnities.
   7. Ironically, Rome's treatment at the end of the First Punic War pushed Carthage into the business of empire building and enabled her to take on Rome again in the Second Punic War.

III. The Second Punic War had profound consequences for the barbarian peoples of Spain.
   A. At the start of the war, when Hannibal invaded Italy, one of the consuls assigned to defeat him was Publius Cornelius Scipio. He was the father of Scipio Africanus, who eventually defeated Hannibal.
   B. When Italy was invaded, Scipio recalled his fellow consul, who was headed toward Carthage, to return and oppose Hannibal in Italy, while Scipio sent his own army to Spain.
   C. That Roman army landed in Spain under the leadership of Scipio's brother, Gnaeus, who defeated the Spanish fleet at the Battle of the Ebro. He set up a base at Tarraco and began to wage war to reduce the power of Carthage in Spain.
   D. Publius Scipio realized that the only way Hannibal could be reinforced in Italy was with the support of the colonial empire in Spain. The Romans' entrance in Spain, then, was dictated by the strategy of the Second Punic War, not with any thought to Romanization of Spain.
   E. In Spain, the Romans quickly found that their city-state institutions were taxed. Spain was so distant from Rome that the annually elected magistrates simply did not have time to accomplish anything in a year in office.
      1. When the consulship of Publius Cornelius was up at Rome, he was sent to Spain to join his brother, and the two held a proconsular *imperium*. By propagation, their right to command armies was extended each year, and they served as military governors.
      2. Further, the Romans found towns on the shores of Spain with which they could make treaties, but beyond these towns was a variety of different peoples, especially Celtiberian tribes, who had gained a military ethos from serving in the Carthaginian armies.

3. Publius and Gnaeus found that the only way they could win the war would be to cement relations with the towns, to provide supplies, and to contact the Celtiberian leaders, who would provide large numbers of soldiers.
   4. The two brothers essentially ran the war in Spain as a private enterprise, and when they were killed in separate actions in 211 B.C., Publius Cornelius Scipio the younger (Africanus) was sent in to reopen the offensive.

F. At the time, Scipio Africanus was in his early 20s and was holding the power of a proconsul. He proved to be a charismatic and brilliant general.
   1. In 209 B.C., he took New Carthage with a combined naval and land assault and won over the Celtiberians.
   2. Although the Spaniards referred to Scipio as "king," he never posed a threat to the Roman constitution.
   3. Scipio did achieve primacy in Roman politics. He returned to Rome in 206 B.C. and was elected consul at the age of 29 or 30.

G. The Romans learned that taking on Spain would be far more difficult for their institutions than they ever imagined. The diversity of the region would also make control extremely difficult.
   1. The Celtiberian tribes were tough warriors, and the hinterlands, beyond the Mediterranean zone on the southern coast, were studded with well-fortified Celtiberian and Iberian towns. The countryside of Spain would pose logistical problems of campaigning that made northern Italy look like a cakewalk.
   2. The victory in Spain, which had begun as an effort to break Carthaginian power to protect Italy, saddled Rome with its first major overseas barbarian province. Rome also saw that it had to stay in Spain because of the region's mineral wealth.
   3. The lessons of assimilating barbarian foes that the Romans had learned in Cisalpine Gaul could not be applied on the Iberian peninsula. Rome would have to come to terms with the fact that it was no longer a republican city-state but a Mediterranean power with a host of new demands and responsibilities.

Readings:

Curchin, L. A. *Roman Spain: Conquest and Assimilation.*
Goldsworthy, A. *The Punic Wars.*

Questions to Consider:

1. How did Punic colonists, followed by imperial Carthage, transform the civilizations in Spain? How did the Barcid family forge a Carthaginian order in Spain?

2. Why was the rule of Spain so daunting to the Roman Republic? What were the dangers to the constitution? In what ways did Rome have to forge new policies and institutions in the control of Spain?

Lecture Eight
The Roman Conquest of Spain

Scope: In the war against Carthage, Spanish towns and Celtiberian tribes had sworn allegiance to P. Cornelius Scipio Africanus, rather than to the Senate and people of Rome. With Scipio's departure in 206 B.C., Rome faced a daunting task in governing her Spanish allies. Celtiberian warriors of the Meseta, denied employment in Carthage's mercenary armies, raided the two new Roman provinces, Hispania Citerior and Ulterior (Nearer and Farther Spain). For 25 years, Roman commanders waged costly wars against this determined foe. Rome took political, fiscal, and military measures to meet this crisis, notably the extension of annual commands by prorogation to enable proconsuls to direct frontier wars and govern provinces. In 180–178 B.C., the proconsul Tiberius Sempronius Gracchus established market towns and veteran colonies and secured peace for two decades. In 153 B.C., the restless Celtiberians again challenged Rome. They were joined by the Numantines of the middle Ebro and the Lusitanians, smarting from oppressive foreign rule. Twenty more years of fighting ensued, until the triumph of Scipio Aemilianus in 133 B.C. In securing the Iberian peninsula, Rome paid the high price of political agitation over the draft—the first step in the fateful Roman Revolution.

Outline

I. This lecture looks at the Roman conquest of Spain, from 197 to 133 B.C., a period in which the Romans were forced to face up to the commitments they took on by defeating the Carthaginians in Spain.

   A. We must keep in mind that the Roman expansion in the 3rd–1st centuries B.C. was still Mediterranean based; in other words, Roman armies were sent to Spain by sea, and the Romans depended on the coastal cities of the Iberian peninsula to supply and equip these armies.

   B. Between 206 and 196 B.C., the Romans imposed control over their Spanish possessions in the interior very loosely. They sent out magistrates, but they wanted to dodge the responsibility of administering the area.

C. Although the Romans in the Late Republic often fought wars simultaneously, they were more focused on the pacification of Cisalpine Gaul at this time than they were with control of the Iberian peninsula. With the assimilation of northern Italy in the 190s B.C., the Romans shifted their attention to Spain.

II. In 197 B.C., the Roman Senate divided Spain into two provinces, Hispania Citerior and Hispania Ulterior, that is, Nearer and Farther Spain. Farther Spain comprised the southern coast around New Carthage, and Nearer Spain was the Ebro valley.

   A. From 179 B.C. on, the Romans found themselves saddled with tough wars against the Celtiberian tribes. These well-armed and well-disciplined warriors progressed from raiding in outlying areas to attacking the towns along the coast. The Romans had to take action to protect these areas and the routes linking the coast to the mines.

      1. In 195 B.C., Marcus Porcius Cato (the Censor) arrived as a consul to Hispania Citerior and waged campaigns there for two years. Cato gives us a fairly detailed account of the fighting at that time.
      2. From the start, Cato faced the problem of supplying his army, which probably numbered 50,000 men. He also encountered tough fighting in the middle and upper Ebro valley, especially against the cities of Segontia and Numantia.
      3. Cato's governorship represents the opening of a long and desultory war from 197 to 179 B.C., in which both Iberian provinces called for repeated Roman attention.

   B. From the Celtiberian point of view, their actions were perfectly logical. They were suffering from overpopulation, which could be relieved only through migration, mercenary service, or the slave trade.

   C. The Romans did not attempt to delineate borders, because they knew such boundaries would be meaningless. The only way to cope with the situation was to establish alliances with the native populations and to regulate the frontier zones.

   D. From 197 to 179 B.C., wars were waged primarily to break the power of individual tribes, which Cato accomplished in northern

Spain, around the area of Emporium. Restoration of order in one region, however, did not mean that the Romans had control elsewhere.

E. By the 180s B.C., two-thirds of the Roman soldiers going into Spain were Italian allies or allies of Latin status. Probably all of the cavalry was Latin, and most of the infantry was Italian allies. In essence, this was an imperial army.

III. This first phase of fighting was brought to a close by the *praetor*, Tiberius Sempronius Gracchus.

A. Gracchus campaigned for two hard years, broke several tribes, negotiated terms with Numantia, extended some control over the high plateau, and signed a series of settlements in which he gave land to tribes in the provinces.

B. Gracchus understood that the only way to stabilize the situation in Spain was to adapt what was learned in northern Italy, that is, to establish towns, cement alliances, promote trade, and move excess populations to vacant lands.

C. As a result, for the next 20 years, the Spanish provinces were quiet. Gracchus's efforts set in place a set of economic and social relations that tied a number of these tribes to the towns and, ultimately, linked them to the wider Mediterranean community.

IV. Some Celtiberian tribes in the west, particularly the Lusitanians, were not brought into this alliance structure. Further, tensions arose with the settlement of Roman veterans in Spanish communities, and the population pressures mounted. A rough frontier society emerged.

A. As the Romans began to increase their garrisons to deal with these problems, several wars erupted simultaneously.

1. Essentially, these wars, fought in the 150s–130s B.C., were actions against different tribes who had never really stopped fighting the Romans.

2. The Romans found that this set of wars was far different than the ones they had fought initially in Spain. The Romans now faced guerilla operations that exploited their weaknesses.

3. The Lusitanian wars were led by Punicus and Kaiseros, who had imposed some discipline on their warriors.

4. These tribes were organizing in larger groups and carried out some embarrassing ambushes of the Romans. For example,

Lucius Mummius, *praetor* of Farther Spain, was lured into an ambush in 153 B.C. in which 9,000 men fell.

B. Every major figure of any political or military importance in Rome in the second half of the 2nd century B.C. saw significant service in Spain at this time.
   1. Quintus Fabius Maximus Aemilianus and Publius Cornelius Scipio Aemilianus went into Spain with armies of volunteers. This fact suggests the increasing hardship of fighting these wars.
   2. The Romans also engaged in sleazy tactics to break Spanish resistance. In 150 B.C., for instance, Ser. Sulpicius Galba convinced a tribe of Lusitanians to surrender on the promise of land, then immediately slaughtered them.
   3. The Romans found themselves unable to use the methods they had used in Cisalpine Gaul of luring opponents into a pitched battle. This situation characterized the wars running from 154 to 133 B.C.

C. The fighting of the Third Celtiberian War (143–133 B.C.) in the middle Ebro valley illustrates the problems the Romans faced.
   1. Numantia was an important Celtiberian stronghold in the northeast, one of the major threats against Nearer Spain. From 153 to 133 B.C., the city was put under siege several times, but the Romans still could not reduce it.
   2. In 141 B.C., Q. Pompeius, a new consul, brought his army to Numantia and was tactically defeated but concluded a treaty with the Numantines that enabled him to claim a triumph in Rome. The Senate, however, wanted a victory.
   3. In 137 B.C., Gaius Hostilius Mancinus blundered into an ambush near Numantia and surrendered on the promise of a generous treaty.
   4. Finally, the city was broken with the arrival of Scipio Aemilianus and his volunteer army in 133 B.C. The fighting in the Ebro valley and the west eventually wore down the Spanish opponents and broke the power of the Celtiberian tribes, although some fighting continued.

D. Some regions of Spain remained outside Roman control for the next century. Not until 25–19 B.C. were the far northwestern tribes pacified by the general M. Vispanius Agrippa. In short, the fighting in Spain was costly and brutal.

1. In the course of fighting these wars against the Celtiberian tribes in the interior, the Romans learned some important lessons.
2. First, there were not clear frontier lines, and they could not be effectively established.
3. Second, it was imperative to win over the local elites, not to treat them dishonorably in a bid to win a triumph.
4. Finally, the Romans found that to succeed in Spain, they had to win over Spanish allies and build towns and highways to establish a provincial society.

Readings:

Harris, William V. *War and Imperialism in Republican Rome, 327–70 B.C.*

Richardson, J. S. *Hispaniae: Spain and the Development of Roman Imperialism, 218–82 B.C.*

Questions to Consider:

1. Why did the Romans enter the Spanish peninsula, and what motives convinced Rome to remain in Spain after the Second Punic War? How well did the Romans comprehend the peoples and cultures in Spain in 200 B.C.? What were Spanish perceptions of Rome?
2. Why did the Romans face so many problems in securing the Spanish provinces in the generation after the departure of Scipio Africanus in 206 B.C.? Why did the peace and settlements of Tiberius Sempronius Gracchus in 180–178 B.C. prove so successful?

Lecture Nine
The Genesis of Roman Spain

Scope: During the 2nd century B.C., Spaniards endured the most destructive features of Roman rule: brutal frontier wars, tribute, and exploitation of mines. But the wars of conquest contributed to the development of an urbanized provincial society tied to the Mediterranean world. On discharge, many Roman veterans settled in such colonies as Carteia, Italica, or Cordoba in the Baetis valley. Roman fiscal demands compelled Spanish provincials to expand vastly regional trade, commercial farming, and mining—activities that promoted the growth of market towns. By 125 B.C., the pace of Romanization accelerated not only in towns but also among the Celtiberians, who acquired by trade a taste for the luxury goods of the Mediterranean world. The Roman army in Spain, too, stimulated prosperity by its demand for consumables. More Spaniards sought service as auxiliaries in Rome's frontier armies and were assimilated by military service. By the accession of the emperor Augustus (27 B.C.–14 A.D.), Roman-style municipalities that used Latin in speech were homes to a vibrant Hispano-Roman culture. Only in the rugged northwestern regions had the Vascones and Cantabrians escaped Roman rule. But archaeology reveals that they, too, were deeply influenced by the Roman impact two generations before Augustus conquered these last independent barbarians.

Outline

I. This lecture discusses the genesis of Roman Spain, which includes the social and economic changes brought on by the Roman conquest.

    A. After 133 B.C., most of the peninsula was more or less under control, although sporadic fighting took place in the far northwest until 19 B.C.

    B. This lecture looks at what happened once the major fighting ended. Why was Spain such a success story for Romanization?

II. The case of Spain reveals several important patterns in the process of Romanization and the transformation of barbarian cultures that are instructive for looking at other areas of the Roman Empire later on.

   A. In 205 B.C., the Romans inherited an urban-based set of communities stretching along the Mediterranean and southern shores of Spain. These towns were of Punic, Greek, and Iberian origins but would have had lifestyles that were compatible with Mediterranean civilization.

   B. Romans who stayed in Spain tended to settle in areas that approximated their homelands in central and north-central Italy; therefore, settlement was heavier in the Baetis valley in southern Spain, now known as Grenada.

   1. In 171 B.C., Carteia was founded as a Latin colony for veterans, many of whom had married and produced offspring with local women.

   2. Other cities, such as Seville, Cordoba, and Italica, were homes to veterans because they approximated conditions in Italy.

   3. There was also a certain amount of settlement around New Carthage and to the west, where the mines were located.

   4. The result of this settlement was that the southern area, essentially modern Granada; the area of the lower Ebro valley, where modern Barcelona is; and the area around Cartagena became Romanized by the opening of the 1st century B.C.

III. Romanization of the Iberian peninsula can be documented in several ways.

   A. For example, literary and archaeological sources reveal the growth of Roman institutions and a thriving economy in exports from Spain. Spanish olive oil, for instance, was exported to Italy. Further, the cities began to mint bronze coins based on Roman standards.

   1. By 48 B.C., the city of Gades (modern Cadiz) boasted that it had 500 citizens of Roman equestrian status, that is, men who had sufficient property to be in the class just below the political elite in Italy.

   2. L. Cornelius Balbus, a financial agent of Julius Caesar, was the first provincial to receive Roman citizenship and to be selected into the Roman Senate. He held the consulship in 40 B.C., the first non-Italian ever to do so.

3. The Spaniards became adept at manipulating the patron-client system. In fact, the first efforts to prosecute corrupt governors in the provinces came from the Spanish towns.

B. Another important force in the Romanization of Spain was mining.
1. Initially, the Romans indirectly exploited the mines by imposing tribute and indemnities on Spanish towns and Celtiberian tribes.
2. In the 150s B.C., the Romans financially reorganized the Spanish provinces and shifted from a system of tribute to taxation (*tributum*).
3. At the same time, the mines came under state regulation. Polybius reports in 150 B.C. that the mines near New Carthage employed 40,000 workers daily and produced an annual output of silver of 8⅓ tons. By the 170s B.C., the Roman Republic was probably receiving about 10 million denarii in revenue from the mines.
4. In the early imperial age, gold was found in northwest Spain, spawning a gold rush.
5. The mining operations also brought in large numbers of residents, who transformed traditional societies in the area.
6. Spain had other minerals besides gold and silver, including copper, iron, and lead. Areas around mines in the remote locations where these minerals were found became thoroughly Romanized.

C. Service in the Roman army helped in the assimilation of Spanish warrior elites, although in this area, the defeated foes also had a significant impact on their conquerors.
1. When the Roman army first moved into Spain in the 2nd century B.C., its forces were largely from Italy; the Romans did not hire the Celtiberian tribes as mercenaries.
2. In the course of fighting, especially during the second surge of wars in the 150s–130s B.C., the Romans found that they had to make use of their Spanish allies, who were prized as members of the cavalry and light infantry. From the end of the 2nd century B.C. on, the Romans began using these forces outside of Spain.
3. This practice became institutionalized in the imperial age as the auxiliary army. This army encompassed provincial

soldiers, fighting according to their specialties in Rome's wars of expansion overseas.
4. We have documentation noting that the consul Gnaeus Pompeius Strabo enfranchised 30 Spanish cavalrymen in 90 B.C., after their service in the Social War. Many provincial soldiers also took Roman names when they were discharged and received citizenship.
5. Military service, then, became a way to acculturate local populations, provided social advancement, and furthered the patron-client system under which the Romans operated.

IV. Romanization, however, was a two-way street.
   A. By about 40 B.C., many of the cities in the southern and eastern districts of Spain were adopting the Latin language and were applying for municipal charters. This process would continue for 150 years and climax in the Flavian age (69–96 A.D.).
   B. From the Roman viewpoint, the experience in Spain had put a great deal of strain on Rome and transformed the republic in a number of ways.
   C. First, Rome had to make administrative adjustments to control Spain effectively.
      1. Prorogation was used, that is, the practice of extending the terms of annual magistrates, who eventually developed into governors.
      2. In addition, the meaning of the term *provincia* ("province") was extended from "theater of operation" to a definable area with an administration and regular taxation.
   D. Second, the Romans began to transform their citizen army into a professional army.
      1. During the years of heavy fighting, in 197–178 B.C. and 154–133 B.C., as many as 100,000 Romans, Latins, and Italians saw service in the army and fleet in Spain. These men often served for at least six years, and during that time, they became professional soldiers.
      2. Changes in weapons and tactics came about, as did the development of the *cohort*, the larger military unit of 600.
      3. Veterans were expected to take on, train, and socialize 10,000 recruits yearly.

- **E.** Finally, the mortality rates in Spain were nothing short of frightening, especially in the second set of wars, which resulted in political agitation in Rome.
    1. It was not uncommon for the forces involved in the siege of Numantia, for example, to experience a casualty rate of 40 percent.
    2. In Rome, disputes arose over the draft. Bills were also introduced to redistribute public land in Italy to restore the status and property of veterans. This political agitation was the immediate cause of the Roman Revolution.
- **F.** The historic result of the Roman conquest of Spain was to create provinces in the southern and eastern regions that were, by the 1st century A.D., regarded as Italy overseas.

Readings:

Sutherland, C. H. V. *The Romans in Spain, 217 B.C.–A.D. 117.*

Wilson, A. J. N. *Emigration from Italy in the Republican Age of Rome.*

Questions to Consider:

1. What military and fiscal policies pursued by Rome led to the transformation of the towns and tribal societies of Spain? Why were towns and markets so important in this process? How did the native elites contribute to this process? How did they exploit the network of patrons and clients to advance the interests of themselves and their own communities?
2. What was the role played by discharged Roman veterans, contractors, and merchants in creating a Hispano-Roman society? Why did they have such a profound impact?

Lecture Ten
Jugurtha and the Nomadic Threat

Scope: Upon destroying her hatred rival Carthage in 146 B.C., Rome annexed the Punic cities as the province of Africa (modern Tunisia). Rome then faced new barbarian opponents in the Berber-speaking nomads of North Africa. Rome blundered into an ugly frontier war with Jugurtha, king of the Numidians, the nomads of eastern Algeria. The Jugurthine War (112–105 B.C.) discredited the Senate and catapulted Gaius Marius to the consulship, a new man posing as a popular reformer. Marius, who recruited a volunteer army, waged a war of pacification against Jugurtha, but victory brought no annexations. Rome judiciously learned to court Numidian princes to maintain the borders, while Roman veterans and Italian merchants settled in the province of Africa. A later Numidian king erred in opposing Julius Caesar during the Roman civil war, and Numidia was annexed in 46 B.C. Rome's African borders were advanced, but the principles remained constant. The Roman army, ultimately based at Lambaesis in the 1st century A.D., mounted aggressive patrols to direct and regulate, rather than to halt, the seasonal movements of Berber nomads, who entered into a beneficial symbiosis with the agriculturists and Romanized towns. The North African provinces thus enjoyed an unparalleled prosperity down to the 5th century A.D.

Outline

I. This lecture turns to the relationship between Romans and barbarians in North Africa, beginning with the Roman understanding of *Africa*.

   A. The Romans applied the word *Africa* to a very restricted area of the continent, what would today be Tunisia and the western coastal fringe of Libya. Many of the Punic settlers, that is, the Carthaginians, were located in this area, as were the Libyans.

   B. Historians, however, use the term *North Africa* to embrace a much larger area, the coastal lands that include modern-day Libya, Tunisia, Algeria, and Morocco.

    C. By entering this region, the Romans inherited a long border of desert zones. Egypt, however, was regarded as a separate land of an ancient civilization.

II. The Romans invaded North Africa because they had to defeat Carthage, which they did in 201 B.C., reducing this rival to a client state.

    A. Some historians—and the Romans themselves—argue that they originally came to North Africa in self-defense. In 149–146 B.C., Rome embarked on the Third Punic War with the intention of humbling Carthage. Indeed, the Romans besieged and sacked the city, and it remained unoccupied for more than 100 years.

    B. One of the results of the Third Punic War was that the Romans gained control of the fertile area they called *Africa*, most of which was probably annexed as Roman public land. Colonists moved into this area, continuing the brisk trade that already existed between the Punic towns and the wider Mediterranean world.

    C. In North Africa, the Romans also inherited a problem that they had never encountered before: In defeating Carthage, they faced a potentially dangerous barbarian opponent in the form of desert nomads, the ancestors of the modern Berbers today.

        1. These nomads had perfected the means of traveling across the Sahara and living off oasis farming. Note that the Sahara was not as dry then as it is today.

        2. These people never threatened Roman security, but they did present some unique difficulties to the Romans.

        3. The earliest literary accounts dismiss these nomads as simple barbarians, known for their treachery. Given that the nomads did not live in towns, the Romans saw them as culturally inferior.

        4. Most nomads, however, were able to exploit the landscape in sophisticated ways. The inhabitants of the mountainous regions of the west survived through a combination of agriculture and herding. Along the desert rim of the Sahara, the people engaged in oasis farming and transhumance, that is, the practice of moving seasonally with the herds.

        5. With the Punic towns of the coast and the arid highlands of the Aurès region, North Africa was divided into four distinct zones. This diversity was somewhat puzzling to the Romans.

III. For the first 50 years after the Third Punic War, the Romans annexed the province of Africa but did nothing with it.
   A. Most of the Roman officials there were tax farmers, men of the equestrian order who held contracts to collect taxes.
   B. Security in North Africa essentially fell into the hands of the nomads.
      1. The Romans had found an ally in Masinissa (204–148 B.C.), a chief of a tribe of Numidians and a former Punic mercenary leader, who had struck up a friendship with Scipio Africanus.
      2. The Numidians were renowned as light cavalry and were superb in reconnaissance and skirmishing techniques; in fact, 10,000 Numidians had fought on the Roman side at Zama when Hannibal was defeated.
      3. Masinissa adroitly exploited his friendship with the Scipionic family and his alliance with Rome, using his influence to weld several tribes together into an effective Kingdom of Numidia.
      4. Masinissa also provided soldiers, grain, and elephants for Roman expeditionary forces in Spain and the Hellenistic East.
      5. Masinissa died at an advanced age in 148 B.C. and was succeeded by his son Micipsa (148–118 B.C.). When Micipsa died, succession problems arose immediately.
   C. An illegitimate grandson of Masinissa, Jugurtha, ultimately killed both of his rivals to the throne, his cousins Hiempsal and Adherbal. Jugurtha was a charismatic leader and had patronage ties to Rome.
      1. In the process of warring against his cousins, Jugurtha's Numidian forces killed a group of Italian allies at Citra in 112 B.C.
      2. Jugurtha expected to make his apologies to the Roman Senate and so to rule as the new Masinissa, but he had stumbled onto political unrest in Rome.
      3. The *populares* were reformers at Rome who were agitating for redistribution of public lands and a revision of the draft. The *optimates* ("best men") were conservatives interested in maintaining the status quo.
      4. The *populares* used Jugurtha's debacle to criticize the Senate's policy in North Africa and to demand war. The *populares* represented a powerful coalition of the urban dispossessed, rural voters, and the equestrian order.

5. The Senate sent in commanders to deal with Jugurtha but they bungled the operation. Jugurtha was even called to Rome under safe conduct to present his case to the Senate, but he failed to comprehend the depth of popular outrage against him.
6. Jugurtha returned to Numidia with nothing settled and the war continued. Eventually, the Senate sent in the impeccably honest C. Caecilius Metellus, who waged an effective war of pacification in North Africa but was unpopular in Rome.
7. Caecilius Metellus was undermined by one of his own subordinate commanders, C. Marius, who took over as consul in 106 B.C. Marius began to reform the Roman army, chiefly by dropping the property qualification for service and using land as a reward.
8. Eventually, Marius drove Jugurtha out of Numidia. L. Cornelius Sulla, Marius's quaestor, arranged for the surrender of Jugurtha by King Bocchus of Mauretania.

IV. With Jugurtha's surrender, the Romans reinstated the system that existed before the Jugurthine War. They installed another descendent of Masinissa in Numidia and maintained the existing provincial structure.

A. Only during the dictatorship of Julius Caesar did the Romans rebuild Carthage, establish a provincial administration in Africa, and come to terms with the desert nomads.

B. The Romans discovered that the only way to patrol the 2,500-mile-long frontier in Africa was to form a system of alliances with the nomadic chiefs.
1. The nomads could not really be conquered, but their princes could be given citizenship in return for patrolling the frontier. This system worked remarkably well.
2. The coastal areas and the immediate hinterland of Carthage were subject to Roman colonization and exploitation.
3. The intermediate region of Aurès was brought under intensive agricultural development. This region prospered the most because it was involved in feeding the coastal cities, Carthage, and Rome.

C. As in Spain, the towns in Africa became Romanized by the end of the 1st century A.D. The intermediate region experienced a mixed

Punic, Roman, and Libyan culture. The fringe areas had some ties with Rome but, in many ways, were still pursuing traditional ways of life. These divisions were also seen in the languages spoken in the different zones.

D. The Roman success in North Africa was in coming to terms with the society there, rather than defeating it.

Readings:

Broughton, T. S. R. *The Romanization of Africa Proconsularis*.

Cherry, David. *Frontier and Society in Roman North Africa*.

Questions to Consider:

1. How did climate, terrain, and economic conditions dictate developments in Africa from the 2nd century B.C. to the 2nd century A.D.? What attracted Romans to settle in Africa? How did they interact with the native populations?

2. What factors led to the growth of cities in Roman Africa? Why did the pace of social and cultural change accelerate in the late 1st century A.D.? How were the agriculturalists, pastoralists, and desert nomads drawn into Rome's economic orbit? How were they and their societies transformed?

Lecture Eleven
Marius and the Northern Barbarians

Scope: While Rome battled Jugurtha in North Africa, the Teutones and Cimbri quit their homes in Jutland and migrated into the Celtic lands of the upper Danube and eastern Gaul. They were the first Germanic-speaking peoples to enter the Mediterranean world. They disrupted the network of Roman alliances among the tribes of central Gaul and ravaged the Roman province in southern Gaul (modern Provence), which had been organized to secure the routes between Italy and Spain. In 105 B.C., these German barbarians annihilated two Roman armies in the Rhône valley—the greatest single defeat inflicted by barbarians since 390 B.C. Gaius Marius, elected five times as consul, destroyed the invaders in 102–101 B.C. Marius, hailed as the savior of Rome, set dangerous precedents for future ambitious generals. But it was significant that the Celtic tribes in northern Italy did not make common cause with these invaders. Instead, they, along with their kinsmen in Transalpine Gaul ("Gaul beyond the Alps"), clamored for Rome's protection from the Germans. Rome was, thus, drawn over the Alps to secure invasion routes into Italy and into northern Europe far beyond the limits of Mediterranean civilization. The stunning conquest by Julius Caesar was the logical conclusion to Marius's success. But this conquest was delayed a generation by a Roman civil war and was the cause of a second civil war that ended the republic.

Outline

I. This lecture introduces a new group of barbarians, the Teutones and the Cimbri. These were Germanic-speaking peoples whose home was what is now called Jutland, that is, the Danish peninsula.

  A. Along with these barbarians, we continue to follow the career of the Roman general G. Marius, who defeated Jugurtha and advanced the Roman frontiers in North Africa.

  B. How Marius and these barbarians ended up fighting a series of battles that shaped Roman foreign policy and Roman attitudes toward northern barbarians is a story that brings us back to the Celtic homeland.

C. As may be recalled, the Celtic peoples dominated most of central Europe, stretching from the British Isles deep into the Danube basin. Also remember that by 125 B.C., the Celts of Cisalpine Gaul were becoming integrated into Italy.

D. Our question, then, is how were the Romans drawn over the Alps into Gaul in the 2nd century B.C.?

II. To answer that question, we must begin by exploring the development of the region that the Romans called *Transalpine Gaul*, particularly the southern areas along the Mediterranean shore (Provence and Languedoc).

A. Most of the population dwelling in this area in 125 B.C. was descended from Iberian peoples; they were not part of Celtic La Tène civilization.

1. There were a number of Celtic tribes in the region, but they were relative newcomers. They had migrated in the preceding 100–200 years, bringing their skills in metallurgy and their construction of fortified towns (*oppida*).

2. Certain zones of southern France were inviting to Mediterranean peoples, including the lower reaches of the Rhône valley. In 600 B.C., the Greeks had founded Massilia (Marseilles) and established a string of colonies running from the Ebro in northern Spain to the modern city of Nice.

3. Along that coastal zone was the region of the valley of Carcassone, which offered fertile fields for grains, vineyards, and olive groves. The Greeks mingled successfully with the native populations in these areas.

B. The Celts who migrated to this region came down the Rhône from the heartland of La Tène civilization.

1. One of the most important tribes was a group known as the Salluvi, who settled near the lower Rhône. In the region stretching from Lyons to Geneva today were the Allobroges. The upper Sâone River was occupied by the Aedui. The region of central France was the homeland of the Averni.

2. Celtic tribes moved into areas that were suitable for their way of life; these migrations were not organized invasions. For example, Celts engaged in farming and stock raising in settlements around the town of Tolosa (Toulouse), which was primarily Iberian.

C. The Romans understood that Transalpine Gaul was quite distinct from the rest of Gaul, where the Celts were unquestionably in the majority.
  1. This area became known in Latin as the *provincia*, from which we derive the modern name Provence.
  2. The rest of Gaul, which was later divided into three parts by Julius Caesar, was called Gallia Comata (the "long-haired Gaul").

D. The Celts in southern Gaul quickly saw the potential of the existing civilizations they found. An important Celtic site in the Rhône valley was Entremont, which includes typical Celtic "decorations," such as heads nailed to the walls, along with Greek ceramics and imitations.

E. When the Romans moved into southern Gaul, they found a sophisticated culture. Institutions and trade routes were in place, on which the Romans could build an administration and urban civilization.

F. On the other hand, most of Gaul could still be classified as La Tène civilization, and there was always the possibility that other Gallic tribes could create pressures by moving into the region. Ultimately, this threat forced the Romans to become involved in southern Gaul.

III. The Romans had come to depend heavily on the Greek city of Massilia for their dealings with these northern barbarians.

  A. When the Romans received news that Massilia was under attack by the Salluvi, they retaliated.
    1. In 124–123 B.C., Tourtomotulus, leader of the Salluvi, had amassed the wealth and forces to put Massilia under siege.
    2. The Romans sent in armies, who drove the Salluvi away and pursued them up the Rhône. Eventually, these Celts were defeated by Cn. Domitius Ahenobarbus in 123 B.C.
    3. Domitius Ahenobarbus also set in place the alliance networks to protect the area and, in 121 B.C., organized a province. He extended the franchise and cemented patron-client ties with the Celtic chiefs.

B. This system held in place for a generation but broke down because of an unexpected wave of migrations out of northern Europe.
   1. As far as we know, the Cimbri and Teutones were the first Germanic-speaking peoples to enter the Mediterranean world. Why they moved from the peninsula of Denmark is not known.
   2. There is evidence that sometime in the 2nd or early 1st century B.C., the Celtic settlements in southern Germany were disrupted and abandoned, and La Tène civilization there went into decline.
   3. There is no archaeological evidence to trace the migrations of these Celtic tribes, nor do we have any literary records from the tribes themselves.
   4. Nonetheless, there was a migration that brought a frightening new people into southern Gaul.

C. By 113 B.C., the Cimbri and Teutones entered Noricum (Austria), an area rich in iron and gold deposits, and inflicted an embarrassing defeat on the consul, Cn. Papirius Carbo.
   1. The Senate downplayed the defeat, largely because of the crisis that was brewing in North Africa and popular outrage at home.
   2. Meanwhile, the Germanic tribes moved across the Alpine areas and into southern Gaul. These tribes were looking for food and a new homeland; along the way, they picked up other tribes.
   3. By moving into southern Gaul, these tribes disrupted long-established trade patterns and broke up Celtic political alliances. The Aedui, Allobroges, and Averni all had large networks of client tribes, which might be tempted to hire the Germanic warriors to cast off the control of their masters.

D. The Roman Senate finally responded, sending in forces in 105 B.C. to deal with the Germans.
   1. At Arausio, in the Rhône valley, the Cimbri and Teutones met and destroyed two separate Roman armies, one under the consul Cn. Mallius Maximus and one under the proconsul Q. Servilius Caepio.
   2. A much later report of the aftermath of this victory describes the destruction of booty in what may have been a dedication to the German god of war, later known as Odin.

- **E.** The result was a political crisis in Rome.
    1. Marius, who had just completed his victory against Jugurtha, was elected consul to meet the menace; he crushed the invaders in 102–101 B.C.
    2. Some of the Germans got as far as northern Italy before their defeat, a fact that was later used by Julius Caesar as justification for invading Gaul.
    3. A radical political consensus in Rome, led by Appuleius and Glaucia, backed Marius for reelection to the consulship, which he held five times.
    4. Marius again proved his ability as a general, and a number of military reforms are associated with him. He recruited his soldiers from volunteers, drilled them to a professional level, and rewarded them with land on discharge.
    5. Henceforth, each Roman legion had its own eagle (*aquila*), which provided the religious power for the unit. Further, the soldiers now fought with the expectation of acquiring booty, donatives (bonuses), and grants of land.
    6. The result of the victories over the German barbarians was to professionalize the army. When Marius returned to Rome and found rioting in the streets, he used this army to restore order on behalf of the legitimate government. Later leaders, notably Sulla and Julius Caesar, would see the potential for turning the professional army against the government.

Readings:

Goldsworthy, A. *The Roman Army at War 100 B.C.–A.D. 200.*

Plutarch. *Fall of the Roman Republic*. Translated by Rex Warner.

Questions to Consider:

1. Why did the Teutones and Cimbri prove to be such dangerous enemies to the Celts and Romans in 113–100 B.C.? What were the consequences of these invasions for Gaul and Rome?
2. How did the northern crisis catapult Gaius Marius to unprecedented political primacy? How was his example a potential threat to the republic?

Lecture Twelve
Rome's Rivals in the East

Scope: In the generation after the Second Punic War, Roman legions crossed the Adriatic Sea and swiftly crushed the great Hellenistic monarchies of Macedon and the Seleucid Empire. By 167 B.C., Rome exercised hegemony over the wealthy civilized lands of the eastern Mediterranean, but the Senate was reluctant to organize provinces lest ambitious generals emerge who could challenge the republic. The cities of the Greek world were ruthlessly exploited by Roman investors and tax farmers, while the republic offered neither protection nor justice. In 89 B.C., Mithridates VI Eupator, leader of the remote kingdom of Pontus in northeastern Asia Minor swept the Romans out of Asia, with mercenaries hired from barbarian races around the Black Sea, including the Thracians in the Balkans, Scythian nomads of southern Russia, and the warlike races of Armenia and central Anatolia. Rome responded with her traditional resolve, dispatching the commanders (*imperatores*) of the Late Republic—Lucius Cornelius Sulla, Lucius Licinius Lucullus, and Gnaeus Pompeius Magnus. The Mithridatic Wars (89–63 B.C.) compelled Rome to reorganize her Eastern provinces and to advance her frontiers to the lower Danube and Euphrates. Rome next faced far more deadly barbarian rivals in the East, foremost the Parthians, steppe nomads famed as horse archers, who had succeeded to the Seleucid Empire in the Near East.

Outline

I. We now shift our focus away from the West to the eastern half of the Mediterranean.

    A. It might be wondered what barbarian peoples were living in this area, because the Aegean world was the home of Greek civilization and Egypt was one of the oldest civilizations in the Near East. Although the Nile valley and the Mediterranean zones from Greece through Asia Minor and along the Levantine shore were civilized, the interiors of these regions were anything but.

    B. The Balkans were largely unexplored. The great plateau of Turkey and the high tableland of Armenia to the east (Transcaucasia) were also forbidding barbarian lands. Farther to the east were other groups: the Arabs, desert nomads, and the Parthians.

C. Initially, Rome battled the civilized states, but in reducing the Hellenistic powers, Rome inherited the problem of coping with frontiers and new barbarian peoples.

II. We begin by looking at exactly what the Romans acquired when they took over the hegemony of the Greek world.

A. The defeat of the Greek civilized powers was accomplished quickly by the Romans. The kingdom of Macedon, for example, was reduced in 197 B.C. and again in 168 B.C.

B. The other leading rival in the region was the Seleucid Empire, that is, Macedonian kings who ruled over the Asian possessions of Alexander the Great. That empire was smashed in a decisive battle in 190 B.C. at Magnesia.

C. The Romans inherited a complicated political situation in the East, and as it had in North Africa and Spain, the Roman Senate did its best to dodge any responsibility for running these areas.

1. The Senate hoped that the lesser Greek powers that were left in place, such as Pergamum or Athens, along with the reduced Seleucid Empire, would rule the area as dutiful clients.

2. At the same time, these civilized areas bordered frontiers that would require the attention of Rome, because these regions were extremely profitable. Indeed, the preponderance of wealth and population was in the eastern half of the Mediterranean.

3. The Romans never faced a serious opponent in the Balkans in the Late Republic. The Thracians, who lived in the region of Bulgaria, had been very much Hellenized and were brought into the republic under a client arrangement.

4. East of the Aegean in Asia Minor, the Romans came into possession of Greek cities and installed governors. This region was also open to tax farmers, merchants, and bankers.

5. On the whole, the Roman presence in the Greek world was rather unimpressive. The main barbarian opponents, the peoples in central Anatolia and Armenia and the steppe nomads of southern Russia, were probably not impressed with Roman power.

III. This situation resulted in the emergence of a barbarian, Mithridates VI Eupator (c. 120–63 B.C.), King of Pontus in northeast Asia Minor, who styled himself as the new Alexander the Great.

   A. Mithridates ruled a rugged area of what is now Turkey; for warriors, he could draw on a number of martial races, including the people of Pontus, the Galatians, and Iranian-speaking steppe nomads. He also had contacts with the Georgians, the Armenians, and the barbarians of the Balkans in central Europe.

   B. Mithridates, along with other client kings in Asia Minor, was supposed to patrol the Roman frontiers in Anatolia under a system similar to what the Romans had used in North Africa.

   C. Mistakes in handling these regions, however, resulted in a military crisis that nearly toppled the Roman Republic in the eastern half of the Mediterranean.

   1. First, no regular military forces were stationed east of the Aegean, although the Romans had sent in governors and tax farmers and had built some important highways.

   2. The Romans exploited the Greek cities ruthlessly. The worst corruption that one could imagine occurred in the Roman province of Asia. Tax collecting, in particular, was contracted out to equestrians, who were also charged with hearing charges of corruption in this business in the courts.

   D. King Mithridates had been warned by Marius in 99 B.C. to make either himself stronger than the Romans or to obey the will of Rome in silence.

   1. Not only did Mithridates style himself after Alexander the Great, but he also possessed a good deal of Alexander's organizational skill and knowledge of warfare.

   2. Mithridates was, to some extent, bullied into a war with the Romans in 90 B.C. But he was also looking for an issue to test his power against Rome.

IV. In 90 B.C., the Italian allies of southern and central Italy rose in rebellion against their Roman masters.

   A. These allies, many of them veterans, had been clamoring for citizenship. When the Roman politician who had tried to broker an honest agreement to meet their demands was assassinated, 150,000 Italian allies rose and threatened to destroy Italy.

- **B.** In 89 B.C., Mithridates declared war. While the Romans were fighting for their lives in Italy, the armies of the king of Pontus swept Asia Minor. In the course of three months, Mithridates smashed three Roman armies and the army of one client king, overran the Roman province of Asia, and sent his forces into Greece.
- **C.** The news that the Eastern Empire had been overtaken brought about the near collapse of money markets in Rome.
- **D.** The Romans did not realize the depths of Greek hatred, brought on by Roman misrule over the last generation and a half. Mithridates did not have to give the Greeks much encouragement to slaughter the Romans in their midst, and 60,000 Romans and Italians were said to have been killed in the province of Asia.
- **E.** In the aftermath, Mithridates proved himself to be not so much Alexander the Great as a barbarian king. He began to tax the Greeks, and he quartered his barbarian soldiers in Greek cities.
- **F.** In 88 B.C., the Romans concluded the Social War with the Italian allies quickly in order to take on Mithridates.

V. The political scene in Italy was complicated.
- **A.** The Italian allies were enfranchised by a series of bills in 89 B.C. The Romans also extended the potential of the franchise to the people of Cisalpine Gaul.
- **B.** All these new voters had to be included in the Roman constitution, registered in tribes, counted in a census, and so on. In fact, new citizens would now make up 60 percent of the citizen body.
- **C.** Whoever registered these allies would become the patron of a great number of potential voters. Again, this caused political upheaval in Rome.
- **D.** Marius came out of retirement to back the *popularis* faction, which wanted to distribute the new citizens evenly among the tribes and property districts so that they would have full representation in the assemblies. The conservatives wanted to manipulate the unit voting system to neutralize the power of the new citizens.
- **E.** Marius also believed that he should be chosen to take on Mithridates, even though he had been inactive as a commander for 12 years. The consul who was supposed to receive this command

was L. Cornelius Sulla, who had become the darling of the Roman conservatives.

1. At one point, Sulla agreed to give Marius the command, but he then convinced his former legions to march on Rome, claiming that Marius had taken command illegally.
2. Sulla's forces reached Rome, defeated the *populares* in a bloodbath, and initiated the first Roman civil war. Sulla then marched east and handily defeated the armies of Mithridates.
3. Mithridates negotiated a treaty and retreated to his kingdom in 85 B.C. Sulla decided to consolidate his position in the East, tax the Eastern provinces, raise more forces, and return to Italy. In the meantime, Marius and the *populares* had reoccupied Rome in 87 B.C. and declared Sulla a rogue consul.
4. Sulla returned, swiftly crushed his opponents, carried out brutal reprisals, and imposed a dictatorship on Rome.

F. The experience in the First Mithridatic War proved that a general who had been victorious against barbarians could take power in Rome and legitimize himself.

G. Mithridates challenged Rome again in 74 B.C. when the Romans were involved in repeated civil war actions.
1. In response, the Senate sent out, first, L. Licinius Lucullus, followed by Pompey the Great.
2. The Romans had extended the commands of consuls in the past but never on the order that they did with Lucullus and, especially, Pompey.
3. In the East, Pompey had 120,000 men under his command, 120 warships, and 24 *legates* (lieutenants), along with overriding power to make treaties and supercede the orders of any governor. He was, in effect, a king.
4. Pompey defeated a number of different barbarians, reordered the Eastern provinces, installed a provincial administration, and set up a system of client kingdoms. He made all these arrangements as a "super-magistrate," a man who held powers above the Roman constitution.
5. Like Marius, Pompey was reluctant to seize power in Rome, but he had written the blueprint for doing so for Julius Caesar.

Readings:

Magie, David. *Roman Rule in Asia Minor to the End of the Third Century A.D.* 2 vols.

Seager, Robin. *Pompey: A Political Biography*.

Sherwin-White, A. N. *Roman Foreign Policy in the East, 168 B.C. to A.D. 1*.

Questions to Consider:

1. Why was the Roman Senate so reluctant to assume responsibility for administering the Greek world? How did the acquisitions of provinces in 146 and 133 B.C. alter this policy? Did the Senate's policy make the outbreak of the Mithridatic Wars inevitable?

2. What factors resulted in Mithridates VI emerging as Rome's barbarian foe in the East? Did Mithridates deserve the title as the greatest king since Alexander the Great?

Lecture Thirteen
The Price of Empire—The Roman Revolution

Scope: Rome's acquisition of empire eroded the republican constitution, Italian society, and the citizen legions. The influx of money and numerous slaves promoted commercial estates farming over subsistence farming. As the number of citizens with the property qualification for military service declined after 150 B.C., Roman armies suffered embarrassing defeats from barbarian opponents. Simultaneously, the political elite removed themselves from fellow citizens, creating an opulent Hellenized life of the villa staffed by slaves. Roman politics grew ever more violent as poorer citizens clamored for distribution of public land and relief from military service. Moderate reforms, proposed by the *populares* tribunes Tiberius and Gaius Sempronius Gracchus in 133 and 123–121 B.C., ended in failure and violence. Gaius Marius solved the immediate military crisis by making property a reward rather than a requirement, but in 90 B.C., the Italian allies rose in rebellion when denied citizenship and their share of public lands.

The ensuing Social War resulted in the enfranchisement of all Italy, but it sparked another civil war that ended in the dictatorship of Lucius Cornelius Sulla. With Sulla's retirement from politics, power in the republic shifted from the Senate, magistrates, and assemblies to popular commanders (*imperatores*) who had the reputation to raise legions; win glory, money, and clients in frontier wars; and dictate Roman politics. The last generation of the republic witnessed the struggle among these great dynasts to secure legitimacy as monarchs in the guise of Roman magistrates.

Outline

I. What were the results for Rome of her overseas conquests?

    A. We started this lecture series with a sketch of Roman institutions in 264 B.C. We then looked at the wars that drew Rome into contact with barbarian peoples in northern Italy, Spain, North Africa, and southern Gaul. We have moved, in time, from 264 to 60 B.C.

- **B.** In this lecture and the next one, we shall explore the transition of Rome from an imperial republic, through the career of Julius Caesar, to an imperial monarchy, later known as a *Principate*.
- **C.** In the second third of these lectures, we shall study the new barbarian peoples, including Germans, Iranian-speaking nomads, and others, with whom the Romans came into contact under the Principate.

II. We begin by adding up some of the costs the Romans paid—politically, socially, and constitutionally—in acquiring their empire.
- **A.** This exploration requires us to address three issues, the first of which is the Roman Revolution, a series of crises that brought about violent civil war and undermined the political consensus that had allowed Rome to function successfully for so many centuries.
- **B.** Next, we shall look at efforts by the Romans to address some of the changes that were taking place in the state. The turning point was a land bill introduced in 133 B.C. by Tiberius Sempronius Gracchus, which initiated efforts to reform Roman society from within according to constitutional procedures. These efforts were thwarted, and the project ended in violence and civil war.
- **C.** That failure of the Roman Republic to reform itself brought on the breakdown of the constitution, which is our third issue. We will also look at how Rome managed to retain its empire and come through these civil wars with a stable political and social organization.

III. What were the costs of Roman imperialism?
- **A.** As mentioned earlier, the bloodletting in the Roman wars of conquest was beyond imagination.
    1. In 190–180 B.C. and 155–150 B.C. in Spain, 46,000 Romans, Latins, and Italian allies are reported to have been killed in action.
    2. The physical burden of acquiring the empire fell on citizens and allies who were of modest property status (*assidui*), were drafted into the legions, and had to do the bulk of the fighting.
    3. At least 150,000 men were serving in the military in the outlying regions of the empire in any given year.
    4. A state cannot sustain this effort without suffering certain consequences, the most obvious of which were the mutinies

that erupted in Spain in the 180s B.C., the low morale of the 150s–140s, and the setbacks in the Jugurthine War and in revolts in Macedonia and Asia.

5. Rome attempted to address the state of her military by, for example, lowering the property qualification for service 90 percent in the inflationary period 200–160 B.C.

B. The economic costs of Roman imperialism can be measured in several ways.

1. Ironically, the legions in Rome's wars were capturing their replacements in the labor market in the form of numerous slaves. From 200–50 B.C., at least 1.5 million people were removed from their homelands and sold on the Italian slave markets.

2. The Roman upper classes had an incentive to use slaves, because they reaped the vast majority of the profits from this labor so that they went into the business of commercial farming, which rapidly destroyed subsistence agriculture. The peasants, dispossessed by this development, then moved into the cities, particularly Rome.

C. The flood of newcomers into Rome had serious political and social consequences. The ties of patron and client were violated as peasants were pushed off the land. Further, the upper classes used their wealth to separate themselves from the majority of their clients.

1. The sense of concord among the classes broke down as the tribal assemblies became more vocal and violent.

2. In 133 B.C., some senators aimed to carry out reform. Tiberius Sempronius Gracchus, a junior figure representing a powerful clique of senior senators, proposed to distribute public land to the dispossessed so that they would be eligible for the draft.

3. The land bill was conservative, but it won the support of the *populares*. Whoever sponsored this bill would have gained numerous clients and future voters. Gracchus compromised the reform by the methods he used to secure passage of the bill.

4. This land bill sent a signal that carrying out reform would benefit the reformers to such an extent that the political

structure and voting patterns of the republic would be endangered.
5. Ten years later, Gracchus's brother made a similar attempt to introduce reforms. In 124–122 B.C., he held two successive tribunates; he reactivated the land bill and made other efforts at reform but he was deserted by most Roman voters on the issue of granting citizenship to the Italian and Latin allies.
6. The younger Gracchus was killed in a riot in 121 B.C., so that reformers took their revenge on the optimates through the Jugurthine War.
7. The last serious effort at reform came in 91 B.C. from Marcus Livius Drusus, who proposed a bill to give citizenship to the Italian and Latin allies. Most Romans were against this bill, which would have more than doubled the size of the citizen body.
8. Drusus was murdered, and by the spring of 90 B.C., the Italians rose in rebellion in the first of a series of Roman civil wars. This Social War was particularly brutal, and the only way that the Romans could win was to enfranchise the Italian allies.

D. The *populares* saw that all efforts at constitutional reform had been shot down and believed that they would have to resort to violence. Hence, they had to ally with a popular commander, who could support reform with the threat of military force.

E. In 88 B.C., Marius supported the allied enfranchisement bills championed by the tribune Publius Sulpicius Rufus in return for the Mithridatic command. But this power play drove the consul Lucius Cornelius Sulla to resort to violence by marching his legions on Rome. Sulla's brutal reprisals precipitated a second civil war, and by 82 B.C., he and the optimates had crushed the *populares*.

IV. In 90–88 B.C., the threat on the Eastern frontier aggravated the Roman civil war and jeopardized the Republic's overseas empire.

A. Any Roman commander, henceforth, could emulate Sulla. By defeating a barbarian foe in the provinces, he could forge a seasoned army, acquire provincial clients and vast amounts of wealth, and return to Rome to reorder the state according to his own wishes.

- **B.** In 83–82 B.C., Sulla and his veteran army seized power. Sulla, as a dictator, rewrote the constitution along conservative lines, then retired in 77 B.C.
- **C.** The ensuing competition among the great commanders (*imperatores*) erupted into a second round of civil wars after 49 B.C. as the great leaders fought for primacy in the Roman state.
    1. Julius Caesar, by his conquest of Gaul, drove Pompey into alliance with the optimates.
    2. Caesar's assassination in 44 B.C. set off another series of civil wars, leaving Marc Antony and Octavian as potential heirs.
    3. In 31 B.C., Octavian (renamed Augustus) brought these wars to an end as Caesar's heir.
- **D.** Ironically, the government that evolved in Rome in the aftermath of these wars was almost a constitutional monarchy. No one who aspired to a position of primacy in the Roman state could afford to pass himself off as a king. The only way to run the far-flung Roman Empire was through the traditional political classes in Rome and by preserving the guise of the republic.

Readings:

Gruen, Erich. *Last Generation of the Roman Republic*.

Seager, Robin, ed. *The Crisis of the Roman Republic*.

Questions to Consider:

1. How did the profits of empire result in economic change in Italy? Why were the profits so unevenly divided among the conquerors? What factors were driving the development of commercial crops, manufacturing, mining, and banking at the expense of peasant subsistence agriculture?
2. Why did the tribunes Tiberius and Gaius Sempronius Gracchus fail to achieve reform in 133 and 123–122 B.C.? Did these reforms promise success? How did the deaths of these tribunes mark a turning point in Roman politics? Why was the failure and assassination of M. Livius Drusus the signal for civil war?

Lecture Fourteen
Julius Caesar and the Conquest of Gaul

Scope: In 58 B.C., Gaius Julius Caesar, self-styled political heir to the *popularis* traditions of reform, assumed his governorships of Cisalpine Gaul, Transalpine Gaul, and Illyricum. In the next decade, he accomplished the extraordinary conquest of Gaul, that is, the Celtic heartland west of the Rhine River. In part, Caesar pressed the frontier policy of Marius to its conclusion; in part, he sought to elevate himself as *imperator* and first man at Rome. In 58 B.C., on invitation of Gallic allies, Caesar drove back two coalitions of migrating tribes, the Helvetians and Germans under Ariovistus. Each coalition posed a potential threat of invading Italy. In the next six years, Caesar imposed Rome's authority over Gaul. His campaigns were masterpieces of speed, and Caesar exploited tribal rivalries and courted Gallic princes. In 52 B.C. at the Alesia, Caesar broke the pan-Gallic insurgents under the charismatic Avernian chief Vercingetorix. In the world of late republican politics, Julius Caesar assured his political dominance by triumphing over the ancestral barbarian foe and forged veteran legions that won for him a civil war and a dictatorship. But he also laid the foundations of Western Europe, because the Gauls of the La Tène proved brilliant pupils of Rome and created a model provincial civilization for the next three centuries.

Outline

I. This lecture deals with an important period in the career of Julius Caesar, one of the most memorable of the Romans and one of the great commanders of history.

   A. We will concentrate on Caesar's conquest of Gaul, which would transform the axis of the Mediterranean world. With Caesar, the Romans conquered a vast area of central and northern Europe and, ever after, the Romans were committed to extending the range of Mediterranean civilization to farther frontiers.

   B. Julius Caesar also brought the Romans into contact with new barbarian peoples, including the Germans in central Europe and the natives of the isle of Britain.

- **C.** Caesar was hailed as the conqueror over the traditional Roman foe. The conquest of Gaul ended the primacy of Celtic civilization in western and central Europe, which had been dominant since the 5th century B.C.

II. Caesar's political career, first as consul, then twice as proconsul, set the stage for an imperial monarchy and the end of traditional republican government.

- **A.** In 59 B.C., Julius Caesar was elected as consul with the support of Pompey and Crassus, and the three forced through legislation on behalf of their clients. Together, these three men held so much power that they could dominate the Roman state, effectively suspending normal constitutional government.
- **B.** In 58 B.C., Julius Caesar was prorogued as proconsul for five years in the provinces of Cisalpine Gaul (northern Italy), Illyricum (the Balkans), and Transalpine Gaul (southern Gaul).
    1. The security of Gaul rested on a network of alliances that had been forged in 121 B.C. between the Romans and the leaders of important tribes in central France.
    2. One of these tribes, the Aedui, controlled the trade route of the Saône River and acted as guardians for the Roman province.
    3. Caesar aligned Rome with the Aedui and so put the Romans at odds with the Averni and their allies.
    4. When Caesar first went to Gaul, his attentions were directed east into the Balkans, but he received reports from the Aedui that there were movements, particularly of Germans, from central Europe into Gaul.
    5. These Germans, called Sueves, had been invited into Gaul by dissident Celtic tribes as allies and mercenaries. The Helvetii and Sequani, Celtic peoples from western Switzerland, were also migrating west at this time. This tribal movement threatened to pass through Genava (Geneva) in the Roman province.
- **C.** In 58 B.C., Caesar responded by moving in and taking on these groups of barbarian immigrants. The numbers of immigrants were probably exaggerated, but they gave Caesar the excuse to increase the size of his army. By the time he left his governorship in Gaul 10 years later, Caesar commanded 12 veteran legions. Caesar's

conquest of Gaul also gave him the resources to return to Rome and wield political influence.

D. Any other commander might have been overwhelmed by the dimensions of the Gallic conquest.
1. In 58 B.C., Caesar brought down the Helvetii at Bibracte and, later that same year, defeated the German forces, under the leadership of King Ariovistus, in Alsace.
2. Both of these battles showed Caesar at his best, and both are still remembered from the stirring speeches Caesar gave his men before they went into battle.
3. We have a good deal of information about this fighting from Caesar's *Commentaries*, which was based on reports that he sent back to Rome during the conquest.

E. From 58–56 B.C., Caesar used the necessity of fending off these tribal migrations as an excuse to intervene in the whole of Gaul, that is, everything west of the Rhine, including France, the German Rhineland, the Low Countries, and western Switzerland.
1. Caesar achieved his goals largely by dividing his army up into columns and by swift and audacious movements.
2. In 57 B.C., Caesar defeated the Belgic tribes in northeastern Gaul, where his troops were surprised while making camp. He rallied his men to win a brilliant victory over the Nervii on the Sambre.
3. Caesar also enrolled large numbers of Gauls into his cavalry, made personal friendships with members of Gallic communities, and even rewarded some Gallic leaders with citizenship.
4. By a combination of diplomacy, speed, and logistics, Caesar pacified Gaul within two and a half years.

F. Caesar had to keep his army mobile and divide his men into winter quarters quite frequently. For all the success of Celtic society at the time, it could not feed and house large numbers of Roman legions (75,000–80,000 men).
1. Significant demands were placed on the local populations for grain and supplies, which caused a great deal of resentment among the lesser tribes.
2. By 54 B.C., there was widespread discontent among Gallic tribes over Roman oppression.

      3. The Roman army's followers—entertainers, merchants, and investors—also sparked anti-Roman sentiment.
      4. Ultimately, the Gauls submitted, but they had not been defeated.

III. Caesar also carried off two operations that proved momentous for the later history of Rome and Rome's relations with barbarians.
  A. In 55 and 54 B.C., Caesar equipped a fleet, crossed the English Channel, and invaded Britain.
      1. The first expedition was, essentially, a reconnaissance in force. For the second attack, Caesar brought with him five legions and several Gallic nobles, whom he intended to set up as client kings in Britain.
      2. Caesar's forces penetrated into southeastern England, defeated the Catuvellauni, and received submissions. This invasion served as the "legal" basis for the Roman conquest of Britain in 43 A.D. by the emperor Claudius.
  B. Caesar also crossed into Germany twice, creating Germany as distinct from his province Gaul.
      1. Caesar crossed the Rhine by building pontoon bridges, which stunned the Germans.
      2. The Romans carried out swift punitive expeditions and reprisals, although the precise identity of their targets remains unclear.
      3. The pretense for the invasion was that the Germans were supporting Gallic rebels and harboring anti-Roman exiles, just as the Britons had been accused of harboring anti-Roman Druids.
  C. These expeditions distinguished the lands beyond the Rhine from those west of the Rhine, that is, the Celtic heartland, or Gaul.
      1. The Rhine was declared a barrier that designated the lands to the east as Germania.
      2. That demarcation cut across a cultural unity. Celtic civilization was centered in southern Germany and on both sides of the Rhine. Caesar arbitrarily drew a political boundary to signal his conquest of the Gallic foe.
      3. As we shall see, the distinction between lands on either side of the Rhine reoriented the axis of trade and connections in Gaul.

IV. Caesar's achievements as of 54 B.C. were stunning, and he was immensely popular in Rome.
  A. Indeed, Caesar's popularity drove Crassus to seek his own command against the Parthians, which proved disastrous, and drove Pompey to re-cement his ties with the political conservatives (*optimates*) at Rome.
  B. Caesar had put himself in a constitutional dilemma. As soon as he laid down his *imperium* (the right to command), he was subject to political prosecution for his many illegal acts as consul in 59 B.C.
  C. In 54 B.C., there was also evidence that Gaul was not quite as pacified as Caesar had led the Romans to believe.
    1. Widespread resentment arose from the onus of supporting Roman armies. Caesar's expeditions into Britain and Germany had caused him to neglect the political alliances he had cultivated among the Gallic elites
    2. In the fall of 54 B.C., the Eburones of northeast Gaul lured a Roman army of 6,000–9,000 men out of their camp and into an ambush. The army, led by Q. Tituris Sabinus and L. Aurunculeius Cotta, was destroyed.
    3. The Nervii also attacked the winter camp of Q. Tullius Cicero, but Caesar relieved Cicero and put down this and other revolts.
  D. These uprisings, however, were indicative of a much more general discontent that erupted in the spring of 53 B.C.
    1. The trouble started near the modern city of Orléans, where the local Celtic populations butchered the Roman merchants.
    2. The revolt then spread to the Averni, the leading tribe of central Gaul and long opponents of the Aedui, who were friends of Rome. The Averni found a leader in Vercingetorix, a charismatic prince.
    3. Vercingetorix managed to rally many of the Celtic tribes in a national revolt. Caesar responded quickly, but the revolt was so widespread that even the Aedui defected.
    4. Caesar suffered a minor setback when he failed to take Gegovia, but he rallied from this defeat and surprised the forces of Vercingetorix at the city of Alesia in central Gaul.
    5. Caesar trapped Vercingetorix in Alesia by constructing two concentric rings of fortifications, one 12 miles in diameter to

besiege the city and one 14 miles in diameter to ward off a relieving army.
   6. In the late summer of 52 B.C., Caesar brilliantly drove off the Gallic relief army in two days of battles, compelled the surrender of Vercingetorix, and forced the collapse of the national revolt.
V. The conquest of Gaul gave Caesar the confidence and the legions to risk civil war in Rome—and win.
   A. By the conquest of Gaul, Julius Caesar disrupted the Celtic world forever. He brought the vast lands of Gaul into the Mediterranean empire of Rome and reoriented the axis of Western civilization from Rome into western and central Europe.
   B. As a result, the Germanic tribes emerged as the new barbarians in central Europe, and the foundations of French civilization were established.
   C. In a decade, Julius Caesar achieved in Gaul what it had taken the Roman Republic two centuries to achieve in Spain and, in the process, marked the birth of the Roman Empire.

Readings:

Gelzer, Matthias. *Caesar, Politician and Statesman*. Translated by P. Needham.

Goldsworthy, Adrian. *Roman Army at War, 100 B.C.–A.D. 200*.

Questions to Consider:

1. What was the extent of Roman political and cultural influence in Gaul in 60 B.C.? How likely was a Roman conquest of Gaul in 60 B.C.? What forces drove the Germanic Sueves and the Helvetians to migrate into eastern Gaul?

2. What personal and political reasons motivated Julius Caesar to intervene in Gaul in 58 B.C.? Did Caesar's decision to conquer Gaul advance Roman security?

3. What were the consequences of the conquest and assimilation of Gaul into the Roman world? How did Julius Caesar, in effect, create Germany?

Lecture Fifteen
Early Germanic Europe

Scope: The Germanic peoples, distinct linguistically by 500 B.C., traced their cultural roots to the brilliant northern Bronze Age in Scandinavia and northwestern Germany. Archaeology has revealed German settlements and burials as distinct from those of their Celtic contemporaries, and Germans quickly came to appreciate superior Celtic goods. Caesar's conquest of Gaul disrupted the Celtic world and facilitated the migration of Germanic tribes into central Europe. Germans displaced, assimilated, or subjected Celtic-speakers of La Tène, which resulted in cultural exchange. But the fortified settlements (*oppidum*) of La Tène often gave way to a simpler Germanic way of life based on slash-and-burn farming, stock-raising, fishing, and hunting. Warrior elites, described by Tactius as the *comitatus*, were devoted to their lords and a god later known as Woden or Odin. This martial ethos and population pressure propelled Germanic migrations from the late 2nd century B.C. Twice, in 55 and 53 B.C., Julius Caesar crossed the Rhine to chastise Germans and, thus, drew a new political and cultural frontier (*limes*), marking off the Roman provincial world from the Germans. In 16 B.C., Augustus pursued the strategy of his adoptive father, opening a new war against the dreaded northern barbarians across the Rhine. Augustus expected triumphs hailing him as the newest savior of Rome, but instead, he encountered barbarians whom Rome never quite mastered.

Outline

I. This lecture introduces the Germans, who came to epitomize the most ferocious barbarians that the Romans had ever encountered.

    A. With this lecture, we also begin to bring in other new barbarians, including Iranian-speaking nomads of eastern Europe, the Parthians, the Arabs, and the Dacians of central Europe.

    B. In his writings, Caesar portrays the Germans as uncivilized but noble, while the Gauls are seen as immoral, too influenced by the good things in Mediterranean life.

II. The core of the Germanic peoples was the Baltic—the Danish peninsula, the Danish islands, southern Sweden, and the northern shores of Germany along the North Sea and the Baltic.

A. Archaeological evidence reveals a continuity in material culture of this civilization that goes back to the middle Bronze Age (1800–1700 B.C.).

B. By 500 B.C., the Germanic dialects had emerged as a distinct group of languages that were quite different from the Celtic languages then spoken in Gaul.

C. Archaeology also indicates that there was a great deal of trade between the Germanic peoples and the Celtic world and that many skills, especially skills in metalworking, were transmitted from the Celts to the Germans. A bronze solar chariot, found at Trundholm, Denmark (c. 1100 B.C.), epitomizes the German metalworking skills.

D. The Germanic peoples may have also learned about writing from the Celts, although scholars still debate this issue. North Italic alphabets were adapted as the Germanic *runes*, perhaps as early as 200 B.C.

E. In his writings, Caesar noted the Germans' tendency to migrate, which also marked these peoples as distinct from the Celts.

    1. The agriculture in northern Germany and Scandinavia was rather simple. Forests were cleared using slash-and-burn techniques, and the soil was exhausted rather quickly.

    2. The area called Germania, which included all of central Europe—sections of what is now Poland, the Czech Republic, Slovakia, and Scandinavia—was covered by dense, virgin forests. Northern Germany was filled with marshes and heaths, and in Scandinavia, the forests literally broke up the landscape.

    3. Settlements grew in the Danish islands and peninsula and the Swedish islands, because the arable land was accessible and connected by sea to trade routes. Tribes also occupied valleys along the river systems, including the Weser, Elbe, Oder, and Vistula Rivers.

    4. Large tracts of central Europe were, therefore, underpopulated or unpopulated. Caesar describes the Hercynian Forest (Black Forest), which extended from the lower Rhine across much of southern Germany and cut off the Celtic zone in the northern Danube valley.

F. For all of their contact with Romans, the Germans never acquired the habit of living in cities.
  1. In the Celtic world, the *oppidum* became the basis for Roman provincial civilization. Such towns were organized as *civitates*, that is, communities with constitutions, and could evolve into Roman-style municipalities.
  2. In contrast, the urban culture associated with the Roman Empire and Mediterranean-based civilization never penetrated into the Germanic lands. In fact, most of those regions did not have the agriculture to sustain towns until the later Middle Ages, with the introduction of the coulter plough, the three-field system, and manorial arrangements.
  3. These aspects of the land and settlement patterns also explain some of the peculiarities of Germanic warriors, who excelled at ambush but were not successful in open battles or siege warfare.
  4. Although these people are often called Germans, the Germanic tribes never acquired any sense of being a distinct nation. Even tribal ties were loose, and most people identified themselves by family and clan.

III. Both Caesar and the imperial historian P. Cornelius Tacitus, writing about 100 A.D., give us a fairly detailed account of the Germanic tribes.

  A. *The Germania* of Tacitus is relatively accurate in describing Germanic tribes living close to the Roman frontier but becomes increasingly fantastic as it moves into the northern reaches of Europe.

  B. Tacitus tells us about the various gods and cults of the Germanic peoples, including the fact that the Germans had no priestly caste.
  1. Caesar reports that the Germans have no images of the gods, although that is probably an overstatement. Some attributes of the early Nordic gods from the Bronze Age and Iron Age can be matched with gods of Norse literature from the later Middle Ages.
  2. Tacitus tells us that the Germans worshipped Mercury, Mars, and Jupiter, which were his names for the Old Norse Odin,

Tyr, and Thor. He also reports that tribes living on the Danish peninsula worshipped a mother goddess, Nerthus. Tacitus's description of this cult coincides with what is later reported about the cults of the Vanir, the gods of fertility, in Scandinavian sources.

3. Both Caesar and Tacitus report on the casting of runes, and Tacitus, in particular, details the types of sacrifice practiced. The Cimbri, after defeating a Roman army, and the Hermandurii, after defeating the Chatti in 58 A.D., are reported to have sacrificed all prisoners and booty.

4. Archaeological evidence and literary sources reveal a remarkable continuity in Germanic customs, material culture, and religious practices. Despite this continuity, we still have no sense of these people as a *natio* ("nation"), a fact that the Romans appreciated and, in some cases, delighted in.

C. Even if they were not skilled in open battles or siege warfare, the Germanic tribesmen were prized as warriors.
1. The Romans adopted a number of German military practices, including raising the war cry (*barbitus*) as they went into battle. The Romans also used the German wedge formation (*cuneus*) later in the empire as a way of attacking in forest zones.
2. Another practice that the Romans acquired from the Germans was the apparently ancient tradition of raising the king on a shield. In 360 A.D., the Roman emperor Julian was raised on the shield at Lutetia (Paris) by the Western army.

D. At the time of Caesar's and Tacitus's descriptions, the Germans appear to have had a rather limited set of political structures.
1. Most resolutions were passed in traditional tribal meetings, often compared to the *thing*, the assemblies reported in Germanic and Scandinavian sources of the later Middle Ages.
2. These meetings were attended by the warriors of Germanic communities to decide issues of law and war and to elect kings to lead them through a crisis in warfare.
3. The Germans did not seem to have a need to consolidate into larger political structures until Roman attacks forced these Germanic tribes into more comprehensive organization.
4. Tacitus describes a *comitatus*, that is, a body of warriors who attached themselves to a lord. These armed retinues formed

the nucleus of Germanic tribal armies and were compared to later Scandinavian reports of *beserkers*.

IV. Between 50 B.C. and 16 B.C., the cultural and linguistic landscape of central Europe was transformed into Germania of the Roman imperial age.

　A. Many of these areas had been part of the Celtic world, but by the time the emperor Augustus organized Gaul and moved across the Rhine to advance the Roman frontier, these lands were Germanic.

　B. In 16 B.C., when Augustus opened a new set of expeditions against the Germanic barbarians, he expected to win triumphs in the tradition of his adopted father, Julius Caesar. Ironically, he set the limits of Roman rule in Western Europe and placed Germania forever beyond the imperial frontiers.

Readings:

Millar, Fergus. *The Roman Empire and Its Neighbors.* 2nd ed.

Thompson, E. A. *The Early Germans.*

Questions to Consider:

1. How did the Germanic tribes evolve into a distinct ethnic people in 500–50 B.C.? What was the impact of the Celtic world? What was the role of trade? What accounted for the migration of Germanic tribes in 125–50 B.C.? What was the nature of such migrations and settlement?

2. Given the nature of early Germanic society, was expansion across the Rhine by Augustus a sound policy? What were Roman expectations in 16 B.C.?

Lecture Sixteen
The Nomads of Eastern Europe

Scope: Between the 2nd century B.C. and the 2nd century A.D., Iranian-speaking nomads, the Sarmatians, dominated the steppes of southern Russia. Mounted on Mongolian horses and armed with the composite bow, they proved formidable light cavalry. Excavations of graves in the Kuban reveal that the Sarmatians prospered on the brisk trade with Greek cities on the shores of the Black Sea and the caravans crossing the Eurasian steppes. By 50 A.D., scions of the Sarmatians had settled along the Danube frontier. The Iazyges in eastern Hungary and the Roxalani in eastern Rumania, by their contact with Germanic Sueves and the Dacians, gained the means to mount *cataphracti*, lancers in lamellar armor. Rome prized these newcomers as soldiers and colonists, and while Rome tolerated no raiders, she courted rather than conquered these steppe peoples as useful allies. Other Sarmatians, the Alans, migrated to the grasslands north of the Caucasus, threatening Roman Anatolia and Parthian Iran, but here, too, Rome appreciated the nomads as allies. In securing trade and alliances with the steppe nomads of eastern Europe, Rome gained security and prosperity in her northern provinces for nearly two centuries. This network of relationships was only disrupted by the arrival of the Goths in the 3rd century A.D.

Outline

I. This lecture introduces the Iranian-speaking steppe nomads of eastern Europe, whose range probably extended from the lower Danube, across the steppes of southern Russia, along the northern and eastern shores of the Caspian Sea, and into central Asia. These people were long known to the Greeks, who called them Scythians.

   A. Herodotus gives us our first report of steppe nomads from his account of a visit to a Greek town called Olbia on the northern shores of the Black Sea in about 450 B.C.

   B. We can trace these people archaeologically even farther back, to the 7th and 8th centuries B.C. We have found evidence of their saddles and the fact that they moved their herds over great distances with the seasons.

II. By Greek accounts, the Scythians were the most primeval of nomads.

A. They lived in felt tents, drank mare's milk, had no cities or institutions, and were constantly on the move. To the Greeks, the Scythians were barbarians both culturally and linguistically.

B. As warriors, the Scythians were thought of as absolutely ferocious. They were depicted as bowman and were known for using sophisticated light cavalry tactics.
   1. By the 6th century B.C., the quintessential depiction of an archer in Greek art was an Iranian nomadic bowman, wearing a distinct conical cap and trousers.
   2. The Romans later used that same generic image to designate all barbarians of the East.

C. Among the various customs that distinguished these nomads were their scalping of opponents and taking of heads. The Scythians were known for using the skulls of their enemies as drinking cups.

D. We also have accounts that both the Scythians and the Sarmatians, the Iranian people who would displace the Scythians in the 2nd century B.C. and encounter Rome, valued women as warriors. About a third of the excavated *kurgans* ("barrows") in southern Russian are of women with arms and riding equipment.

E. The earliest report of a Scythian war describes King Darius I of Persia, who in 512 B.C., marched from Asia Minor into Thrace, crossed the Danube, and tried to bring to battle nomadic Scythians.

F. The Scythians proved adept at subjecting various peoples. They exacted tribute in metals from the Carpathians; in grains from the agriculturalists of southern Russia; and in furs, timber, and honey from tribes dwelling in the forested zones of European Russia.
   1. The steppe nomads quickly learned that they could trade these goods for the prestige goods of the Mediterranean world. Indeed, Scythian wheat fed the Greek world from the 5th century B.C. on.
   2. The *kurgans* also reveal cultural exchange in the combination of Scythian animal-style decoration with Greek naturalistic traditions on such artifacts as jewelry, riding equipment, and quivers.

3. The Greek cities on the northern shores of the Black Sea, including Olbia and the cities in what is now called the Crimea, which the Greeks called the Tauric Chersonesus, were the linchpin in this trade. These Greek cities had long-term connections with the nomads of eastern Europe, and these connections passed to the Romans.

III. The Scythians were on the fringe of the Roman world through much of the republic. Only at the beginning of the imperial age did the Romans begin to encounter these nomadic horsemen of the steppes, who were quite different from the desert nomads they had encountered in North Africa or Syria.

　A. The Roman frontier in the east ran 750–800 miles, from modern Vienna to the mouth of the Danube. Along this frontier, the Romans found peculiar nomadic tribes, the Sarmatians, whom they came to both respect and dread.

　B. The Sarmatians originally dwelled east of the Don River, on the lower Volga, and north of the Caspian Sea. Sometime in the 2nd or 1st century B.C., they moved into the Scythian heartland from the lower Danube to the Don River.

　C. The Sarmatians did not represent a single, unified group, but they do embody a change in material culture. For example, the Sarmatians did not build the expensive tombs that the Scythians had constructed, so that we do not have as much information about the Sarmatians.

IV. The members of the eastern branch of the Sarmatians were called, by the Romans, Alans.

　A. The Alans settled on the eastern steppes, between the Black Sea and the Caspian, which put them in a favorable position for invading Transcaucasia, the region of Georgia, Armenia, Azerbaijan, and eastern Turkey. From there, they could threaten Mesopotamia and Iran.

　B. The Jewish historian Flavius Josephus reports fearful raids launched by these people in 35 and 72 A.D.

　C. The Alans were one of the causes behind the Roman reorganization of the northeastern frontier along the Euphrates in the 1st and 2nd centuries A.D.

- **D.** These Sarmatians fought differently than the Scythians had. By the 1st century A.D., they were equipping heavy cavalry, as well as horse archers.
    1. The Latin term for these heavily armed, mounted warriors was *cataphracti*. They wore overlapping leather armor, called *lamellar armor*, or chain mail and were armed with lances or two-handed swords for shock action.
    2. The Sarmatians also introduced a number of the military emblems that were used in the later Roman Empire, including inflated balloons of dragons and other heraldic devices.
    3. By the reign of the emperor Hadrian (117–138 A.D.), the Romans were mounting their own Sarmatians as *cataphracti*.
- **E.** One of the most remarkable accounts we have of the Alans is by Flavius Arrianus (Arrian), a Greek writer and Roman senator and governor of Cappadocia in Asia Minor.
    1. Arrian's work, *The Battle Line against the Alans* (c. 135 A.D.), tells how the Alans were armed and how they could be countered.
    2. This manual reveals a shift from the Roman tradition of depending on swords to the dense phalanx formation that characterized Greek warfare.

V. Other kin of the Alans moved into eastern Europe.
- **A.** One of the most important of these tribes was the Roxolani, who dwelled in eastern Romania, just north of the Danube.
- **B.** The Iazyges moved into the basin of the Theiss (the great river system flowing into the middle Danube), the eastern plains of Hungary, Slovakia, and western Rumania. The Iazyges were involved with transmitting Roman goods from the Danube markets into central Europe.
- **C.** The Sarmatians as a group, while feared and respected by the Romans were never targeted for conquest in the same way that the Germans were.
    1. There are reports of Sarmatian nomadic armies, combinations of horse archers and heavy cavalry, numbering between 5,000 and 10,000.

2. There are also reports of Sarmatians, especially Roxolani, surrendering themselves to the Romans and being taken into military service.

D. The Romans never felt that these groups of barbarians posed a serious threat to their overall security. Instead, Rome evolved policies to regulate the flow of trade and immigrants across the imperial frontiers.

E. One of the best descriptions of the problem of a lack of formal boundaries comes from the funerary monument of Tiberius Plautius Silvanus Aelianus, *legate* ("governor") of Moesia, erected at Tibur (modern Tivoli). Plautius Silvanus reports that he halted a migration of these nomadic peoples, settled some of them in vacant lands, and turned them into Roman provincials, thereby securing the peace.

F. Plautius Silvanus, in his own words, gives a sense that the Romans saw the Sarmatians as a secondary threat, which made them ill prepared for a new group of barbarians, the Turkic-speaking Huns, who swept out of the Russian steppes at the end of the 4th century B.C.

Readings:

Melyukova, A. I. "The Scythians and Sarmatians," in *The Cambridge History of Central Asia*, edited by D. Sinor, pp. 97–117.

Rice, T. Talbot. "The Scytho-Sarmatian Tribes of South-Eastern Europe," in *The Roman Empire and Its Neighbors*, edited by Fergus Millar, 2nd edition, pp. 281–294.

Questions to Consider:

1. What were the means of contact between the Iranian nomadic peoples of the steppes of eastern Europe and the urban Greek and Roman civilizations between the 7th century B.C. and the 2nd century A.D.? How did trade transform Scythian and, later, Sarmatian society? What accounts for the greater opulence of grave goods in Scythian *kurgans*, as opposed to later Sarmatian barrows?

2. What types of frontier policies were adopted by Rome? How formidable were the *cataphracti* and horse archers of the Sarmatians? Why did the Sarmatians fail to forge larger political confederations, as had the earlier Scythians?

Lecture Seventeen
Arsacid Parthia

Scope: By destroying Seleucid power at Magnesia in 190 B.C., ironically, the Romans created their most formidable barbarian rival in the East: the Parthians from the steppes of central Asia. The obscure Arsacid Parthian princes of northern Iran renounced Seleucid overlordship. In 140–129 B.C., the Parthians had overrun Iran and Mesopotomia, falling heirs to a great Near Eastern bureaucratic state. The Arsacid kings based their power on horse archers recruited from steppe nomads and *cataphracti*, lancers, furnished by the Parthian warrior caste. Hence, the Arsacids were, at best, tolerated by their Greek, Aramaic, and Persian subjects. Later Sassanid shahs blacked the reputation of Parthians as philhellenes and lax Zoroastrians. When Pompey reorganized the Roman East in 63 B.C., Rome confronted a unique foe on the upper Euphrates. The Parthians possessed the resources of a Hellenistic state and the military traditions of Asian steppes. At Carrhae in 53 B.C., Parthian cavalry annihilated the legions of M. Licinius Crassus, and twice, it checked expeditions of Marc Antony in Armenia. The emperor Augustus restored Roman honor by negotiating the return of captured standards and prisoners. Augustus preferred diplomacy to war and the services of a dutiful Armenian client king. In 54–66 A.D., the uneasy peace between Rome and Parthia erupted into a desultory war over the Armenian succession that revealed deficiencies in Roman logistics and policy. Emperors from Vespasian to Marcus Aurelius were forced to rethink Roman aims and commitments against the Parthians.

Outline

I. This lecture introduces the third group of new barbarians encountered by the Romans, the Parthians, who were ruled by the Arsacid kings.

    A. The Parthians, who had originated from the steppe lands just north of Iran, settled in modern Khurasan. By the time the Romans encountered them, the Parthians had fallen heir to a bureaucratic, Hellenistic kingdom, the former Seleucid Empire.

- **B.** This lecture explains how the Parthians became the dominant barbarian power in the Near East and, therefore, the great rival of Rome for almost 300 years.
- **C.** We shall also look at the nature of the Parthian kingdom, although most of our information about these people comes from Latin and Greek authors who regarded the Parthians as foes.
- **D.** Finally, we shall explore the war of Nero against the Parthians and the implications that war had for Roman relations with barbarian peoples in the East.

II. The Parthians were part of that large group of Iranian-speaking nomads that stretched from central Asia into eastern Europe.
- **A.** They appeared on the scene as clients of the Seleucid kings, who had succeeded to the Asian empire of Alexander the Great. The Parthians asserted their dominance in the Near East, because the Seleucids were decisively defeated by the Romans at Magnesia in 190 B.C.
- **B.** In 140 B.C., the Parthian King Mithridates I defeated and imprisoned the Seleucid King Demetrius II and so established Parthian power in the Near East. This Parthian king (not to be confused with his namesake, the King of Pontus) was named after the Persian god, Mithras.
- **C.** The successors of Mithridates I nearly lost their position to the Pontic King Mithridates Eupator and his son-in-law, Tigranes I of Armenia, who divided the Seleucid Empire between them. But Mithridates VI Eupator clashed with Rome down to 63 B.C., while Tigranes briefly controlled most of the Near East and assumed the title "King of Kings."
- **D.** Again, the Parthians were helped by Rome. The Roman commander, L. Licinius Lucullus, humbled the Pontic King Mithridates VI and broke the power of Armenia in 73–69 B.C. Pompey imposed a Roman hegemony over Armenia in 65–63 B.C.
- **E.** Ironically, in 190 B.C. and, again, two generations later with the defeat of the Mithridates VI of Pontus, the Romans enabled the Parthians to take over a position as heirs to the Eastern Empire of Alexander the Great.

III. The Parthians succeeded to a composite state.

- **A.** The Parthian kings ruled as a warrior elite, but they were not well remembered in the later Iranian tradition. Oddly, the Iranian population did not welcome the Parthians as liberators from Greek oppression.
- **B.** The Parthian kings styled themselves as *philhellenes*, cultivating the rich, Greek-style cities of Babylonia. The Parthians also tolerated all cults so that they were later viewed as dubious rulers because they were not strict Zoroastrians.
- **C.** The Parthians, however, proved themselves to be remarkably adaptable. They ruled Babylonia as the fiscal center of their empire. They tolerated existing institutions and set in place their own bureaucratic class. Babylonia was also the nexus of the caravan trade, as well as commerce on the Persian Gulf.
- **D.** The Parthian kings retained their connections with the nomadic tribes of central Asia, although they ruled as opulent Greek-style monarchs in the capitals of Babylonia. Hence the Arsacid kings recruited allies from the steppes.
- **E.** The Parthian kings never forged fiscal institutions and provincial administration comparable to those in the Roman Empire. The Parthian kings remained a warrior elite propped up by their nomadic allies, but they never welded their diverse subjects into an effective state.
- **F.** The Parthian period was prosperous, but as a state, the Parthian kingdom was not effective.

IV. Why, then, did the Parthians receive so much attention from the Romans?
- **A.** By 63 B.C., with the reorganization of the Roman East, Rome took over the guardianship of the Greek cities of the Near East and had provinces and client kingdoms in Transcaucasia and the Levant.
- **B.** The Romans initially took an arrogant view of the Parthians, but their attitude changed abruptly in 53 B.C., when they suffered a defeat at the hands of the Parthians.
    1. In 56 B.C., M. Licinius Crassus, one of the associates of Julius Caesar, received Syria as his province and campaigned in the East in 55–53 B.C., with the expectation of matching the exploits of Caesar in Gaul.

2. Crassus, who hoped to exploit a Parthian civil war, invaded Mesopotamia with 50,000 men.
3. On the arid plain of Carrhae (Harran in southeastern Turkey), the Romans first clashed with Parthian horsemen under Surena, the leading general of the Parthian king.
4. Surena probably had a smaller army than Crassus, but he had secured the water sources and his men had a seemingly inexhaustible supply of arrows.
5. The Roman army maintained discipline for as long as possible but eventually succumbed to the relentless missile barrages and scattered. Crassus and 20,000 Roman legionaries were killed, and 10,000 prisoners were taken.

C. This disaster resulted in no major change in the political frontier. The Parthian king, Orodes II, might have been relieved that a Roman army had not invaded Babylonia.

D. For Rome, however, this defeat was a humiliation that would have to be avenged. In 39 and 37–36 B.C., Marc Antony twice led expeditions in Armenia to bring the Parthians to battle.

E. When the emperor Augustus consolidated the Roman world after 31 B.C., he inherited this Eastern frontier, as well as the angry political sentiment in Rome that the eastern barbarians must be humbled.

V. The astute Augustus, who understood the difficulties of campaigning in the arid climates of the Near East, preferred diplomacy to war.

A. Augustus had no intention of waging difficult wars in the East, well beyond the logistical bases of the Roman army. He preferred to use diplomatic pressure to keep the Parthians in line.

B. In 20 B.C., by the threat of invasion, Augustus persuaded the then-ruling king of the Parthians, Phraates IV, to agree to a treaty. The terms of the treaty were celebrated in Roman literature and the visual arts as the equivalent of a military victory.

C. The Parthian king agreed to return the prisoners taken at Carrhae, as well as the standards that had been captured. Roman honor was restored.

D. The Parthian king also sent four of his sons to Rome as "privileged hostages" to be trained in the household of Augustus. These

hostages served as pretenders that Augustus could use in the future to incite a civil war.
- **E.** A significant Roman military presence was maintained in the East; at the time of Augustus, four Roman legions were stationed in the cities of northern Syria. These forces kept the Parthian and Armenian kings in line with Roman wishes.
- **F.** This arrangement by Augustus was quite successful; it lasted through the whole of the Julio-Claudian period, until the reign of Nero.
    1. The arrangement broke down under Nero, largely because of Parthian politics. The then-reigning king of the Parthians, Vologaeses I, designated his brother, Tiridates, as king of the Armenians to stave off any attempts on the Parthian throne by Tiridates.
    2. Armenia was the strategic gateway between the Roman East and the Parthian Empire, and her king was supposed to be crowned by Rome.
    3. The Armenian nobles, however, accepted this Parthian prince, whom they preferred to the kings sent from Rome.
    4. This situation resulted in the first formal war between Rome and the Parthians since the late republic.
    5. In 54 A.D., when Nero came to the throne, he sent Cn. Domitius Corbulo, a strict disciplinarian, into Asia Minor with two legions from Syria. Corbulo worked these legions for four years to elevate them to battle readiness.
    6. In 58 A.D., Corbulo marched into Armenia and captured the capitals of Artaxata and Tigranocerta in a brilliant campaign.
    7. Corbulo imposed a pro-roman Armenian king, Tigranes, who blundered into warring with the Parthians so that Tiridates returned as Armenian king in 62.
    8. By agreement in 64, Tiridates retained the Armenian throne, but he had to receive his crown from Nero at Rome in 66.
- **G.** This arrangement satisfied both empires, but it also revealed certain weaknesses in Roman organization in eastern Asia Minor. Above all, the Romans saw that their Eastern frontiers would require major fiscal and military commitments for the future.

Readings:

Isaac, Benjamin, *The Limits of Empire: The Roman Army in the East.*

Millar, Fergus. *The Roman Near East, 31 B.C.–A.D. 337.*

Questions to Consider:

1. What were Rome's interests in the East during the late republic? How did Romans view the Parthians before and after the disaster at Carrhae? Did the Parthians ever pose a serious threat to Roman security?

2. Why did Augustus devise such a successful policy towards the Parthians and Armenians? What was the strategic importance of Armenia and why was it so difficult to control?

Lecture Eighteen
The Augustan Principate and Imperialism

Scope: The emperor Augustus proved to be the greatest conqueror of barbarians, doubling the size of the Roman world. He pursued expansion to legitimize his extraordinary constitutional position as he transformed himself from the revolutionary military dictator into *princeps*, the leading senator of a restored republic. Augustus ended civil war and secured peace at the price of republican government. He transformed the senatorial aristocracy from a political into an administrative elite, and henceforth, members of Augustus's family monopolized the great commands and received the privilege of a triumph. Foremost, Augustus advanced the northern frontiers of the Roman world. His friend and general, Marcus Vispanius Agrippa, conquered northwestern Spain and broke the power of the tribes in the Balkans, securing the routes between Italy and Greece. In 16–12 B.C., Augustus's stepsons, Tiberius and Drusus, pacified the German tribes between the Rhine and Danube. Their ultimate target was Maroboduus who had transformed his Marcomanni into an effective Germanic kingdom in Bohemia. The Pannonians and Dalmatians of the Balkans rose in a great rebellion in 6–9 A.D., diverting imperial efforts away from Germany. In 9 A.D., unexpectedly, a charismatic leader, Arminius, destroyed three legions, thereby shattering Roman rule in Germany and Augustus's confidence. The Varian disaster forever changed Roman perceptions of Germanic barbarians and the course of Western history.

Outline

I. In this lecture, we again turn our focus back to the Roman world and look at some of the key developments of the early empire that will explain the relationship between Rome and the new barbarians we have been discussing.

II. We begin by looking at the nature of the "republic" under the first Roman emperor, Augustus.

A. Augustus would have described himself as the "leading citizen of the state" (*princeps*), rather than "emperor," which was later derived from the word for a military commander, *imperator*.

B. In his inscription, *The Deeds of the Divine Augustus*, the emperor tell us that on January 13, 27 B.C., he resigned his extraordinary powers to the Senate, whereupon the Senate immediately voted him new powers.

   1. Consulships were reserved for Augustus each year beginning in 27 B.C. into perpetuity. He was also given tribunician power (*tribunica potestas*), that is, the power of one of the ten tribunes who were the legislative officials of the republic.

   2. Augustus was also given proconsular *imperium*, the power to command armies, which he could exercise in his provinces of Gaul, Illyricum, and "the East."

   3. Augustus had the legitimate powers of a Roman magistrate to run the provinces and the armies in the provinces and to legislate in Rome, and he did not have the limitations of office. He had established a constitutional basis for his own military dictatorship.

C. This arrangement in 27 B.C. is usually marked as the birth of the Roman Empire. Augustus also received his name at this time.

D. The Senate and the people of Rome still officially governed many of the provinces of the Roman world. The offices of consul, praetor, magistrate, and so on had not been abolished under the empire. The provinces ruled by Augustus were run by legates, who were senators acting as his deputies.

E. All these arrangements had precedents in the republic, and all served to the benefit of the upper classes. The great 30 families that had run Rome since the early republic could still claim the traditional offices and honors. The difference was that while Augustus kept the old political forms in place, he subtly transformed them into administrative posts.

F. In 23 B.C., Augustus carried out a new settlement that set up the constitutional means of appointing his successor. Because he was not a monarch in law, Augustus knew that his death would result in renewed civil wars.

   1. In this settlement, Augustus ceased to hold the consulship, kept the proconsular *imperium* and the tribunician power, and claimed the right to associate these powers with a colleague, who would follow him as *princeps*.

   2. This arrangement embodied a constitutional weakness: If the emperor died without designating a successor, there was the possibility of civil war.

III. Under this arrangement, Augustus had to designate a successor, but he was plagued by several difficulties in this regard.

   A. First, he had only one child, his daughter, Julia, from his first marriage. He had two stepsons by his second marriage, the future emperor Tiberius and Drusus. To choose his successor, Augustus came up with five plans over the course of his career.

   B. The reason that Augustus had to revise his plans so frequently is that he outlived four of his designated heirs.

   C. The heir to the Roman Empire had to be, first of all, an adult male with Julian blood, that is, who could be traced through Augustus to Julius Caesar (who had adopted Augustus). Only those who were descended from Augustus's daughter, Julia, or from the children of Octavia, the sister of Augustus, could claim Julian blood.

   D. In addition, Augustus wanted to link the Julian family to the Claudian family, that is, the children of Augustus's second wife, Livia Drusilla. Ultimately, the Julio-Claudian heir that was produced by these complicated arrangements was the emperor Caligula.

   E. Under Augustus's first plan, Julia was to marry Augustus's nephew, but he died in 23 B.C., Julia was then married to the great general Agrippa, and they had five children. Two of their sons, Gaius and Lucius Caesar, were designated as the heirs of Augustus, but they predeceased him, as did Agrippa in 12 B.C.

   F. Under the third dynastic plan in 11 B.C., Julia married Tiberius, Augustus's oldest stepson, but the two never got along and never had any children. Despite these difficulties, Tiberius was ultimately left as the only remaining adult male heir.

   G. Tiberius, on Augustus's orders, adopted as his heir Germanicus, the eldest son of Drusus, Tiberius's brother. Augustus had always favored the charming Drusus over the morose Tiberius and so transferred this favor to Drusus's eldest son, Germanicus.

- **H.** When the final dynastic plans were made in 6 A.D., it was understood that Tiberius would follow Augustus and Germanicus would follow Tiberius, even though Tiberius had his own son from an earlier marriage. Not only was Germanicus of half Julian blood, but he was also married to one of Julia's daughters, Agrippina the Elder, and their children merged the Julian and Claudian lines.

IV. Why was this convergence of bloodlines so important? To answer that question, we must return to the patron-client arrangements.

- **A.** By the time of Augustus's death in 14 A.D., he was the patron of the Roman world and he wanted only a member of his household to inherit the loyalty that accompanied the ties of patron and client.
- **B.** The urban dispossessed were on a grain dole paid by Augustus. The Roman army swore its allegiance to Augustus and his family. Many of the provincial elites owed their loyalty directly to Augustus.
- **C.** The constitutional illusion that Rome was a restored republic was maintained for the benefit of the political classes, who were needed to staff the imperial bureaucracy and the upper echelons of the military.
- **D.** From 25 B.C. on, the only military commanders of any merit were members of the household of Augustus.
    1. For example, Agrippa, a close associate of Augustus, carried out the final pacification of Spain in 25–19 B.C. and was given military forces to crush resistance in the Balkans. Of course, Agrippa was also married to Augustus's daughter, and his loyalty was unquestioned.
    2. With the death of Agrippa in 12 B.C., command devolved on the two stepsons, Drusus and Tiberius, who were responsible for the great Roman expansion in northern Europe.
    3. Even subordinate commanders, such as P. Quinctilius Varus and L. Domitius Ahenobarbus, were linked to the imperial family. Varus, for example, was married to one of Augustus's grandnieces and owed his position to family connections.
    4. This situation caused some resentment among the upper classes in the 1st century A.D. because it meant that expansion in the provinces was controlled. Governors could no longer seek glory and booty in the provinces, because, henceforth, the *princeps* controlled expansion.

- **E.** Even the symbols of bravery that were so important to the Roman upper classes were increasingly monopolized by the imperial family. Triumphs were no longer awarded to anyone except members of the imperial household.
- **F.** In short, Augustus ensured that the achievements of the Roman Empire in defeating the barbarians were accorded to the emperor.

Readings:

Brunt, P. A., and J. M. Moore, trans. and ed. *Res Gestae Divi Augusti: The Achievements of the Divine Augustus*.

Syme, Ronald. *The Roman Revolution*.

Questions to Consider:

1. Why were the constitutional settlements in 27 and 23 B.C. so important for the stability of the Roman Empire? What did Augustus intend to achieve by these settlements? How was imperial power to be exercised and transmitted?
2. How was Augustus the embodiment of a traditional Roman politician and general? In what ways did he alter the rules of imperial expansion? Why were campaigns against the northern barbarians so important to Augustus and his future heirs?

Lecture Nineteen
The Roman Imperial Army

Scope: The emperor Augustus turned the Roman army into a professional service, comprising 28 legions, along with auxiliary units, whose total strength was 325,000 men. By 235 A.D., this army stood at perhaps 450,000 strong. Increases in pay and improved conditions of service attracted recruits. Legionaries, citizens who volunteered for 20 years, henceforth, fought with cool professionalism, rather than the tenacious patriotism of the republic. Auxiliaries, recruited from warlike provincials, were drilled by Roman officers to professional levels, learned Latin, and received citizenship upon discharge. Hence, the imperial army became a primary agent of Romanization. Furthermore, the army was stationed in base camps along the frontiers, where soldiers constructed highways, canals, depots, and fortresses that protected and promoted a provincial Roman society. Few armies in history have played so decisive a civilizing role, and few armies have ever enjoyed such success on the battlefield. But this army was an expensive professional force, perhaps representing three-quarters of the imperial budget. Emperors had to maintain the discipline and loyalty of their forces and guard against the rivalries that emerged among the three great frontier armies of the Rhine, Danube, and Euphrates.

Outline

I. The Roman imperial army was a different institution than it had been under the republic, and to a great extent, it reflected the larger history of the Roman Empire.

    A. Augustus transformed the legions of the late republic into a full-time, professional imperial army that defended the frontiers against barbarians and civilized the provinces.

        1. In the empire, soldiers signed on for 16–25 years, depending on their rank, and were paid an annual wage. In the republic, service in the army was not a career.

        2. In some ways, the Roman imperial army could be classified as an *ordo*.

B. The symbols, traditions, and military rituals of the republic were focused on the imperial family.
  1. The oaths (*sacramentum*) earlier sworn to military commanders and the republic were now sworn to Augustus and the Julian family.
  2. The legionary standards (*aquila*) were decorated with signs of the zodiac and protective symbols. These standards exemplified the history and traditions of the military units, which had a powerful effect in socializing recruits.

C. In 6 B.C., Augustus fixed the number of legions at 28, numbering about 150,000 fighting men. We know a good deal about the Roman imperial army at this time from archaeological evidence, literary sources, and several relief works, including Trajan's column, erected to celebrate the Dacian Wars.
  1. As a fighting force, the Roman soldiers of the Principate still depended on the sword (*gladius*) as their shock weapon and were trained to fight in close for the kill.
  2. The soldiers under the empire were organized into larger tactical units, called *cohorts*, each of which numbered about 480 men.
  3. The legions were still recruited from among Roman citizens. Funerary inscriptions from the 1st century A.D. indicate that 80 percent of legionaries in the West were recruited from Italy, Narbonensis, or Baetica. This situation would change in the 2nd and 3rd centuries, when increasingly, soldiers would be recruited on the frontier.
  4. In the East, Galatians and Cappadocians in Anatolia and Greco-Macedonian military colonists in Egypt and Syria were enrolled in the army, often on the grant of citizenship.

II. Another component of the army was the auxiliary units, which tended to increase in number over time.

  A. These units were commanded by Roman officers but recruited from allies. The cohort, for example, was the basic tactical unit of allied forces, originally numbering 500–600 men. The *ala* ("wing") was for cavalry, numbering again, about 500 men.

  B. Auxiliary units often provided the specialties that the legions didn't have, including light infantry, archers, cavalry forces, and slingers.

- **C.** Augustus professionalized these units, as well. Auxiliary soldiers signed on for 25 years and were paid a good wage, although not as much as the legionaries were paid.
- **D.** The auxiliary units were smaller, but they, too, had certain standards and traditions. Often, they were recruited as ethnic units; for example, 10 Batavian cohorts fought with the renowned legion XIV Gemina.
- **E.** The Romans specifically selected auxiliaries from among warlike peoples, such as Thracians, eastern Syrians from Palmyra, northeastern Gauls, Germans from the Rhineland, Berbers from North Africa, and Spaniards from northwest Spain.

III. In this way, for the first time in the Western tradition, Augustus forged a full-time, standing professional army, perhaps numbering 325,000.

- **A.** These forces were comparatively small to protect the thousands of miles of frontier, to deal with the great variety of barbarians beyond the frontier, and to defend the Roman Empire.
- **B.** This army would remain a professional force for the next 300 years, and its breakdown would be closely associated with the demise of the Roman Empire.
- **C.** The legionaries were not only highly trained soldiers but also superb engineers. Roman military manuals instructed soldiers to build entrenchments, roads, and fortifications.
    1. The Roman army built an elaborate system of all-weather roads for strategic mobility, as well as canals, bridges, and depots.
    2. In the time of the republic, the armies had perfected the marching camp, which was built in a grid pattern. This plan would be applied to the stone fortresses of the 2nd century A.D. and would survive as the downtown of many cities in Western Europe today.
    3. Their vast construction programs increased the Romans' strategic mobility and the advantage they had over their opponents. We see this advantage at work, in one instance, in the civil war of 69 A.D., when two columns of the Rhine legions, 45,000 and 35,000 strong, crossed the Alps in winter and arrived at the Po, ready for battle, respectively, within 10–12 weeks.

D. The Roman army would also be an important agent in Romanization. Wherever the army set up camp against the barbarians, they brought with them tools and material luxuries. *Canabae*, civilian communities, also emerged near legionary bases to supply soldiers with necessities and vices.

E. The Roman army both defended the frontiers and assisted in assimilating the provincials and barbarians, thus proving the truth of Livy's maxim that the Romans not only knew how to win victories but also how to use them as agents of Romanization.

Readings:

Parker, H. M. D. *The Roman Legions.*
Roth, Jonathan. *The Logistics of the Roman Army at War (264 B.C.–A.D. 235).*

Questions to Consider:

1. What were the crucial measures taken by Augustus to turn the Roman army into a fully professional force? How important were drill, discipline, and the conditions of service? What was the role played by Roman officers?

2. How did the imperial army assimilate auxiliaries and provincial populations? What types of exchange resulted between Roman soldiers and frontier peoples? How did frontier society evolve during the first two centuries of the Roman Empire?

Lecture Twenty
The Varian Disaster

Scope: In 9 A.D., Publius Quinctilius Varus, governor of Germany, was lured into an ambush by Arminius, chief of the Cherusci, in the Teutoburger Wald. Three legions were annihilated in a ghastly running retreat in the pathless forests. Varus and his officers committed suicide. This celebrated disaster (*clades Variana*) convinced Augustus to abandon Germany between the Rhine and the Elbe. The Romans were taken by surprise, because Arminius came from a loyal family with citizenship. Many Germans in auxiliary units were, just as the Gauls, being assimilated as Roman soldiers. But German society, far simpler than that of Celtic Gaul, could not sustain garrisons of legions or a Roman provincial administration. Legions from base camps on the Rhine had cowed the tribes into submission by demonstrations in 16–9 B.C. Therefore, in 9 A.D., Augustus accepted the Rhine as the frontier. The emperor Tiberius restrained his heir, Germanicus, from reviving the conquest in 14–16. Instead, eight legions, one-third of the imperial army, mounted guard on the Rhine, and the Germans became the most dreaded barbarians in Roman imagination. By his fateful decision, Augustus marked the northern limits of Mediterranean civilization and dictated the course of future Western history.

Outline

I. This lecture deals with the expansion of Roman power in central Europe, primarily Germany, but also the Balkans.

   A. Augustus inherited a number of unresolved frontiers from the republic, especially in North Africa and Spain, but he quickly put these in order. For example, massive forces were brought into Spain to crush the final resistance in the northwest by 19 B.C.

   B. The control of these regions allowed Augustus to concentrate his main efforts into Europe. The first zone that attracted his attention was the Balkan provinces, which would be difficult to pacify.

   C. Some areas of the Balkans, such as Pannonia (western Hungary), were inviting to the Romans, offering rolling hills and arable land.

Other regions, such as Dalmatia (encompassing parts of Serbia and Bosnia), had rough, mountainous terrain.

D. The keys to the operations conducted by Augustus and his heirs, Agrippa and Tiberius, were two important highways that ran from the Julian Alps to the two rivers today known as the Save and the Drave. The highways intersected at Singidunum (Belgrade), followed along the Danube briefly, then cut inland up the Margus River, and eventually led into Macedonia and Greece. This axis was a traditional invasion route.

1. Along these highways, the strategic lower Danube and the valley of the Margus were organized into the Roman province of Moesia.
2. Most of the effort of the Roman army in securing these highways was not in pacifying the tribes but in building roads. This task occupied the army for almost a generation after Augustus.
3. Once the Balkan provinces were pacified, the Romans could strategically march forces from Italy and Western provinces to Greece and points east. All military expeditions in the later Roman Empire followed these land routes.
4. Further, the Romans discovered gold mines in the region, especially in Bosnia, prompting a gold rush in the 1st century A.D.
5. The native peoples, the Dalmatians, Pannonians, and Moesians, were ideal fighting material for the Roman auxiliary armies. The Thracians, for example, were prized as cavalry and the Pannonians served as infantry throughout the empire.

E. A dangerous revolt erupted in 6 A.D. among the Dalmatian tribes in what are now Bosnia and Serbia, then spread to Pannonia.

1. The rebellion occurred just when Augustus was planning the conquest of Germany, so that he had to divert forces to bring these regions back under control.
2. The rebels in each region were led by a former Roman auxiliary, each named Bato. Typically, the leaders of such revolts in the imperial period were men who had served in the Roman military and, in some cases, enjoyed Roman citizenship.

3. From 6–9 A.D., 70,000 men were massed into the Balkans to bring the region under control.

II. It can be argued that success in the Balkans was purchased at the cost of Germany.
   A. Again, note that for the Romans, Germania encompassed the lands east of the Rhine and north of the Danube; today, this region includes southern Scandinavia, Germany, Poland, the Czech Republic, and Slovakia.
   B. Augustus decided to move into central Europe once Spain was brought under control and after his initial successes in the Balkans.
      1. Caesar had left little administration in Gaul, but Augustus arrived there in 16 B.C. to take the census and institute administrative reforms.
      2. Gaul was organized into three provinces: Aquitania in the far southwest; Lugdunesis in central Gaul; and Belgica in the northeast. The regions of the Rhineland were organized into two military districts, Upper and Lower Germany, where Augustus massed his legions.
   C. In 12 B.C., major advances were launched from bases along the Rhine, commanded by Tiberius and Drusus.
      1. The German tribes submitted, but the Romans found different social and economic patterns among these peoples than they had encountered in Gaul. The Germans had no cities or towns; they lived in scattered villages and concentrated on stock raising over agriculture.
      2. Despite their submission, the Germanic tribes were, by no means, conquered. Further, the agricultural and economic base was too weak to support the Roman army over the winter; hence, the legions chastised the tribes during the summer, but pulled back to winter on the Rhine. Nonetheless, by 9 B.C., Augustus could declare a victory in Germania.
   D. Of all the German tribes, the one that was seen as the most dangerous dwelled in what is now the Czech Republic: the Marcomanni.
      1. These people had been led to the region by their warrior-king, Maroboduus, who took the throne in about 20 B.C. This tribe was related to the Sueves, the tribe of Ariovistus.

    2. As Roman legions pushed east of the Rhine, Maroboduus had moved his people away from Roman power. They migrated into Bohemia, subjected a Celtic population, and built up an impressive kingdom from the existing towns and mining operations there.

    3. The Marcomanni reputedly fielded an army of 70,000 and so looked like serious opponents to Rome.

    4. Augustus had slated the kingdom of Maroboduus for conquest when the rebellions broke out in the Balkans. Once the rebellions were crushed, Augustus returned his attention to Maroboduus, but the destruction of the legions in the Teutoburger Wald ("German forest") thwarted his plans again.

III. The events in the Teutoburger Wald were among the most dramatic in Roman imperial history on the frontiers.

    A. Sometime in 9 A.D., P. Quinctilius Varus took over as governor of the German province between the Rhine and the Elbe. He had at his disposal five legions; three of these, Varus's main field force, were based in a camp on a northern tributary of the Rhine.

    B. A leader, Arminius, emerged among the Cherusci, one of the major tribes in the region. Arminius lured Varus into an ambush by claiming that there was the possibility of a rebellion among his people.

    C. Arminius had massed the tribes together and prepared the battlefield well. An earth wall has recently been found, which would have blocked a Roman retreat.

    D. Under repeated attacks and in the midst of thunderstorms, the Roman soldiers lost their cohesion. Many of the auxiliaries defected, and the 15,000 Roman legionaries were slaughtered in battle or killed as captives. Varus committed suicide.

    E. This defeat was a complete military catastrophe and changed Roman perceptions. Never again were the numbers XVII, XVIII, and XIX used for Roman legions. Augustus sent eight legions to the Rhine to protect the Gallic provinces from a Germanic attack that never came.

    F. For the future, Augustus called a halt; Roman armies would not retrieve that lost province. Henceforth, the Germans emerged as the most dreaded foes in the eyes of the Romans and their presence on the other side of the frontiers in northwest Europe would have long-term consequences for the Roman world.

Readings:

Wells, Colin M. *The German Policy of Augustus.*

Wells, Peter S. *The Battle That Stopped Rome: Emperor Augustus, Arminius, and the Slaughter of the Legions in the Teutoburg Forest.*

Questions to Consider:

1. Why did Augustus consider the conquest of the Balkans and central Europe vital to the security of Rome and of his own Julian dynasty? How did these barbarian opponents differ from the Gauls who had opposed Julius Caesar?

2. What accounted for the success of the Dalmatian tribes and Arminius in raising general revolts against Rome? What motivated these recently conquered barbarians to rebel? What were their strategies and aims?

Lecture Twenty-One
The Roman Conquest of Britain

Scope: In 55 and 54 B.C., Julius Caesar led two punitive expeditions into southeastern Britain to chastise the tribes for aiding their kinsmen, the Belgae of northeastern Gaul. The Britons in southeastern England participated in the wider Celtic civilization based on trade and towns. Britain was also home to celebrated schools of Druids, the Celtic priestly caste that opposed Roman rule. In the early 1st century A.D., Cunobelinus (Shakespeare's Cymbeline), king of the Catuvellauni, overran southeastern Britain. The emperor Claudius invaded Britain, officially to restore British exiled princes, but he sought to emulate Julius Caesar. The Roman province was initially based on the towns of La Tène, while the Iceni in East Anglia and the Brigantes in northern England entered into alliance. But Rome was drawn into desultory frontier wars in Wales, Cornwall, and northern Britain. In 60 A.D., the British provincials rebelling under Queen Boudicca were decisively defeated by the governor C. Suetonius Paullinus. Hence, the Flavian emperors ordered the conquest of the island in 71–85 A.D.. The Caledonians of the Scottish highlands escaped Roman rule because new barbarians on the Danube, the Dacians, threatened Rome. The emperor Hadrian thus accepted another limit to Roman power, ordering the construction of a great wall to mark off the province. South of the wall, Britons enjoyed the benefits of the imperial peace, but just as in Gaul, Roman success in Britain rested on the achievements of Celtic civilization.

Outline

I. This lecture looks at a new frontier in the northern reaches of the Roman world, the isle of Britain, and the Celtic civilization that was in place there when the Romans arrived in 43 A.D.

  A. In the last lecture, we discussed the emperor Augustus's attempt to claim the Julian heritage by his conquests in Germany. Augustus could also have looked to Britain, where Julius Caesar had led expeditions in 55 and 54 B.C.

- **B.** A number of the kings ruling over the tribes in southeastern England acknowledged the authority of Rome based on the second expedition by Caesar in 54 B.C.
- **C.** The most unlikely of Caesar's heirs, the emperor Claudius, directed the Roman invasion of Britain. Claudius believed that he had to prove himself by emulating the great deeds of Caesar, which he could do by conquering Britain.
- **D.** The Romans conquered what is today England and Wales, with an indirect control over the Scottish lowlands, but they had no interest in the Scottish highlands or Ireland.
    1. The regions conquered by the Romans had been influenced by Celtic La Tène civilization.
    2. About 75 B.C., Belgic tribes had emigrated into southeastern Britain, bringing with them the La Tène technology. In 43 A.D., the Romans found the land bristling with *oppida*.
    3. Beyond the core area of Belgic civilization, which included what would today be the Midlands, London and the Home Counties, and the southern shore, the technology had been transmitted west and north. The Brigantes tribes in the north, for example, are known to have adopted the burial customs of Belgic La Tène civilization.
    4. Cornwall was home to a Celtic tribe known as the Dumnonii, who had been involved in the tin trade with the Mediterranean world since the beginning of the Iron Age. The Dumnonii were also linked by trade to the Venetii of Brittany.
    5. Two tribes, the Silures and the Ordovices, dominated Wales, and proved to be tough opponents of Rome.
- **E.** When Claudius decided to invade Britain, he was motivated largely by political concerns. He was unpopular in Rome and not seen as a Julian emperor. His wars of expansion were conducted to gain honor and triumph in the empire.
- **F.** At the same time, Claudius was also motivated by political reasons.
    1. The links between Gaul and Britain were close. Julius Caesar's conquest of Gaul and the development of the provinces did not interrupt the trade and contact between the Celts in the British Isles and those now under Roman rule.

2. In the period 54 B.C. to 43 A.D., southeastern England saw an influx of Roman goods. A number of Belgic tribes in this region, including the Catuvellauni and Artebates, minted Roman-style coins, imported Roman wares and wine, and fused Roman traditions with their own native Celtic style in art.
3. Further, the Romans outlawed the Druids but were not opposed to the Celtic gods. In fact, many of the Celtic gods were readily assimilated to Roman counterparts.

II. In 43 A.D., when Claudius decided to invade Britain, he left nothing to chance.
   A. He mobilized four veteran legions, probably about 50,000 men, under experienced officers. This was the largest organized army ever to land in England.
   B. Claudius's principal target was the Catuvellauni, who had subjected tribes friendly to Rome, occupied Camulodunum (Colchester), and failed to pay the tribute.
   C. Claudius reasoned that if the Romans smashed this tribe, they could overrun the island, which is essentially what happened. The existing network of roads and hill forts in Britain sustained this large Roman force on the move.
   D. By 47 A.D., most of southeastern England had been incorporated into the empire, or the tribes had submitted and become clients and friends of Rome.
   E. In moving a massive military force into Britain, Claudius committed his successors to securing this province.
      1. The initial areas of Britain overrun were part of the Belgic civilization. But in the rugged regions of Wales and Cornwall, tribes offered stubborn resistance to Roman control.
      2. Throughout the 40s and 50s A.D., the Romans found themselves drawn into difficult guerilla wars in western Britain.
      3. These operations climaxed in 60 A.D. when the governor C. Suetonius Paullinus, an expert in guerilla warfare, captured and sacked the Druid sanctuary on the island of Mona (Anglesey) to break the resistance of the Welsh tribes.

- **F.** The dispersal of so many Roman forces across the province invited a major rebellion.
    1. The revolt was led by Queen Boudicca of the Iceni, who has been immortalized as a British heroine opposing Roman oppression.
    2. The king of the Iceni, Prasutagus, had ruled as a client of Claudius and Nero. When he died in 60 A.D., Nero sent in his procurator and freedmen to annex the Icenian kingdom.
    3. The queen and her daughters were abused by the Romans, and the Iceni resented the Roman tax collectors and census takers. Boudicca rallied her tribe against the oppressors just at the time that the Romans were engaged in Wales.
    4. This insurrection spread across most of southeastern Britain and was joined by the Trinovantes, the Catuvellauni, and lesser tribes. These tribes resented Roman taxation, the order to disarm themselves, and the loss of land to Romans at the military colony of Camulodunum.
    5. The insurgents swept over the southeastern portions of the island, burned Camulodunum to the ground, and butchered the colonists. The rebels also sacked Verulamium (St. Albans) and Londinium (London).
    6. Suetonius Paullinus quickly returned with two legions, evacuated London, and drew the Britons into a decisive battle on the Watling Road in the Midlands. The Romans cut the rebel forces to pieces; many of the Britons were trampled in the panic; and Queen Boudicca committed suicide.
    7. The Romans were faced with rebuilding the island frontiers, but at the time, they were also involved with consolidating control over the Belgic heartland. A civil war following the suicide of Nero in 69 A.D. plunged the empire into turmoil and interrupted the process of bringing Britain under control.
- **III.** The civil war of 69 forced the Flavian emperors to settle the issue of Britain.
    - **A.** Tough professional governors were sent in to undertake the conquest of Wales, northern Britain, and most of Scotland.
    - **B.** The third of these governors was Gnaeus Julius Agricola, father-in-law of Tacitus, who depicted Agricola as a model Roman governor in a biography. Tacitus attributes to his father-in-law the

conquest of the northern tribes and the construction of road systems running up the east and west coasts of England.

C. The push to conquer the whole of the island was cut short, however, by the third Flavian emperor, Domitian, who had concerns closer to home on the Danube. The garrison of four legions in Britain was permanently reduced to three, and the Roman advance was halted.

D. The Roman frontier in Britain approximated the boundary between England and Scotland today. The Romans constructed the famous wall marking the northern limit of the frontier during the reign of the emperor Hadrian.
  1. Hadrian's Wall was 15 feet high and 10 feet thick and ran for 77 miles. The wall acted as a political barrier and as a platform for aggressive patrols. These patrols operated along four major highways emanating from the forts along the wall deep into lowland Scotland.
  2. Behind the wall was a barrier to stop raiders returning to Roman territory with loot and cattle. The wall acted as a deterrent for low-level dangers. The legions were based in York and Chester, ready to move in the event of a major Celtic threat.
  3. Auxiliary soldiers numbering about 15,000 were well placed along the wall. The wall also had a series of gates, forts placed about every 5–7 miles, and signal towers. This system secured the northern limit of the island.
  4. Briefly, in 139–140 A.D., the wall was advanced north to a much shorter line, about 45 miles across.

E. The Hadrianic Wall was never breached; it secured the northern frontier of Britain into the early 5th century A.D. Behind the wall, a successful Romano-British civilization developed based on Belgic achievements.

F. The threat to the Romans would come later, in the early Middle Ages, not from the northern tribes, but from the east, across the North Sea, from the Anglo-Saxons, and so Hadrian's Wall lost its strategic importance and was abandoned.

Readings:

Birley, Anthony. *The People of Roman Britain.*

Hanson, W. S. *Agricola and the Conquest of the North.*

Questions to Consider:

1. What factors, other than the need for legitimacy, led Claudius to conquer Britain? What conditions assisted in a rapid and successful Roman conquest of Britain, in contrast to the conditions that obtained in Germany east of the Rhine?

2. What accounted for the outbreak of the British revolt under Boudicca in 60? How did this revolt resemble other native uprisings against Roman rule?

3. How did the Hadrianic and Antonine Walls epitomize the frontier policy of the high Roman Empire? Why were these systems so successful in securing the northern frontiers?

Lecture Twenty-Two
Civil War and Rebellion

Scope: In 68 A.D., the suicide of the emperor Nero plunged the Roman world into civil wars and rebellions that revealed imperial weaknesses to all. In the transfer of imperial power, the three great regional armies of the Rhine, Danube, and Euphrates henceforth were the ultimate arbiters. In 69 A.D., the legions of the Rhine championing Vitellius were pitted against legions of the Danube and the East declaring for Vespasian. The decisive battles in northern Italy between rival legions put Vespasian on the throne, but the northern frontiers, denuded of garrisons, were exposed to barbarian assault for the first time. Roxalani raided the lower Danube; the Brigantes and Welsh tribes defied Rome in Britain. In 69–70 A.D., Gaius Julius Civilis, an auxiliary officer, led his fellow Batavians, Germans dwelling on the Lower Rhine, in a rebellion that briefly united Gallic provincials and German barbarians against Rome. Quintus Petillius Cerialis, kinsman of the emperor Vespasian, crushed this rebellion, but the Flavian emperors had to reorganize the army and rethink their frontiers and relations with the barbarians.

Outline

I. This lecture discusses the civil wars and rebellions that tore apart the Roman Empire in 68–70 A.D. These events are important for two reasons.

A. First, they illustrate the institutional weaknesses we discussed earlier in the constitutional and military arrangements made by Augustus.

1. When the last representative of Augustus's family, Nero, committed suicide on June 9, 68 A.D., there was no adult male heir with the appropriate constitutional powers to succeed him.

2. Without a recognized emperor in Rome, the *acrana imperii* ("the secret of the empire") was revealed. The three regional armies that had been created to defend and advance the

frontiers became the arbiters of power. These armies included the legions of the Rhine, the Danube, and the Euphrates.
   3. The key to power was for a single leader to emerge who could command the loyalty of at least two of these armies, put himself on the throne, and gain legitimacy from the Senate.
- **B.** The civil war in 69 A.D. also revealed weaknesses in the Romans' relationship with the various provincials and frontier peoples.
   1. The legions of the Rhine and of the Danube essentially fought the same battle, almost at the same location, twice in one year. These battles were fought on the Via Postumia, running from Venice to Genoa, midway between Cremona and Bedriacum.
   2. The casualties in such battles must have been horrendous, giving the provincials and barbarians the opportunity to seek independence against weakened Roman forces.

II. From 62 A.D. on, Nero had alienated the imperial aristocracy and provincial elites. He also erred in not campaigning on the frontiers, especially in the Rhineland.

- **A.** Nero was opposed initially by the Roman elites in Spain; one of the governors there, Servius Sulpicius Galba, was declared emperor by the provincials and legions in Spain. By the time Galba reached Rome, Nero had committed suicide.
- **B.** Galba secured the necessary powers for ruling in Rome from the Senate; however, he was in his 80s and had no children.
- **C.** The man who had helped engineer the revolt in Spain was Otho, from a relatively new aristocratic family. When Galba failed to adopt Otho as his heir, Otho bribed the Praetorian Guard to mutiny and slay Galba, then proclaim Otho emperor on January 15, 69.
- **D.** This change of power in Rome went unnoticed by the regional armies.
   1. The armies of the Rhine had been subject to poor discipline under Nero, and on January 1 and 3, 69 A.D., they mutinied.
   2. The two men behind the revolt were legates, A. Caecina Alienus (IV Macedonica at Mainz) and Fabius Valens (I Germanica at Cologne).
   3. The legions saluted L. Vitellius, the governor of Lower Germany, or the northern province. The armies marched on Rome to put their man on the throne.

- **4.** By mid-April of 69 A.D., some 70,000 men from the Rhineland had poured into northern Italy. The first column of these armies engaged Otho's hastily improvised forces.
- **5.** Otho suffered defeat at Bedriacum and committed suicide in an effort to save the empire from civil war.

E. Meanwhile, T. Flavius Vespasianus (Vespasian) was in command in the war against the Jews in the East, who had revolted in 66 A.D.
- **1.** Vespasian had built up a coalition of equestrians, leading senators, and high officials of state and had secured loyalty among the armies in Syria and the Danube.
- **2.** On July 1, 69 A.D., the two Egyptian legions in Alexandria saluted Vespasian as emperor. Vespasian then sent an army from the East to contest the decision of April 69 A.D.
- **3.** As in the case of the mutiny on the Rhine, junior officers in the Danube legions seized the initiative. The legate L. Antonius Primus led the Danube legions into Italy.
- **4.** These forces were spoiling to settle scores from the defeat several months earlier. A second battle was fought at Bedriacum between the Rhine and the Danube legions over the course of two days.
- **5.** The Danube legions won and forced their way farther into Italy, but the fighting continued in the streets of Rome. By December 22, 69 A.D., the civil war had been decided in Vespasian's favor.

III. What were the repercussions of these civil wars on the frontier?

A. In some instances, there were minor disturbances, as in Britain. In addition, some rivalries arose among client rulers and cities in Gaul.

B. The real danger, however, was on the Rhine. The lack of discipline in the forces there and the tendency to keep German and Gallic auxiliary forces recruited in the Rhineland close to home almost undermined Roman authority in the northwestern provinces.
- **1.** The man who organized the rebellion in the Rhineland was Julius Civilis, a Batavian but a typical auxiliary commander who was at least partially assimilated to the Roman system.

2. In the summer of 69 A.D., while the other legions were battling out the succession in northern Italy, Civilis launched his revolt.
3. The reaction in the Rhineland was mixed. Most of the best Roman forces were in Italy, and the only forces remaining in the Rhineland were detachments left to defend the camps. The northern camp, Castra Vetera, was defended by only about 2,500 men. There was no organized response to the action of Civilis.
4. Civilis enjoyed initial success but had difficulty maintaining discipline and loyalty. The only way he could achieve unity was by appealing to Roman symbols. It is significant that this separatist military revolt in Gaul and Roman Germany could only express itself in Roman terms.
5. In the spring of 70 A.D., Vespasian's cousin Q. Petilius Cerialis, with a massive force, crossed the Alps, and swept down the Rhine. The majority of Celtic tribes and Romanized towns in the Rhineland welcomed these Roman forces, who smashed the insurgents.
6. Civilis eventually arranged terms for his tribe, which came back under Roman control, and Cerialis put the military garrisons back in place in the Rhineland in the summer of 70 A.D.

C. The Flavian emperors thus reformed the military system to ensure that the frontiers would never be compromised again.

D. Ultimately, the civil wars revealed weaknesses in the imperial system. Far more damage was caused in the Roman Empire by Roman armies in civil war than by any barbarian rebellion.

Readings:

Levick, Barbara. *Vespasian*.

Wellesley, K. *The Long Year: A.D. 69*.

Questions to Consider:

1. How did civil war reveal the institutional weaknesses of the Roman Principate? What were the qualifications for a successful emperor? How did the frontier armies determine the transfer of power among

dynasties? Why was control of Rome so vital for legitimacy to any emperor who won a civil war?

2. Why were civil wars so destructive to the professionalism of the Roman army? How did civil war lead to the collapse of morale and discipline in the Rhine army? Why did this not happen among the Danube and Eastern legions? How important was the leadership of an emperor, such as Vespasian, in civil war?

Lecture Twenty-Three
Flavian Frontiers and the Dacians

Scope: Vespasian, founder of Rome's second, Flavian, dynasty, was a pragmatic soldier who reorganized the imperial armies and frontiers. The upper Euphrates was fortified as a *limes*, or a system of highways and bridges based on the legionary fortresses of Satala and Melitene in Asia Minor. From hard experience, the Romans had learned to appreciate the threat of a Parthian invasion. In Britain and Germany, governors humbled barbarians who had sought to exploit the Roman civil war. Vespasian occupied and fortified the strategic Black Forest (Agri Decumates) in southern Germany. His son and successor, Domitian, waged a preemptive war against the Chatti, ancestors of the Hessians. Despite success, Domitian faced a deadly foe in Decebalus, who welded the Dacians of Rumania into an effective barbarian kingdom. Since the 2nd century B.C., the Dacians had created an urban civilization based on their gold mines and trade with the Greek world. Imposing taxes on his subjects and discipline on his warriors, Decebalus fielded a formidable army that inflicted three defeats on the legions of the lower Danube in 85–88 A.D. Domitian, fearful for this throne, purchased out of this frontier war by an unfavorable treaty and left the crisis to his successors.

Outline

I. No more pragmatic man ever came to the throne as emperor than Vespasian, and he was greatly appreciated by many members of the Roman Senate.

    A. By 70 A.D., the Senate comprised families who had risen in imperial service; most of the old republican senatorial families had died away. A new group of men, many of them equestrians, had been elected, and Vespasian came from the ranks of these men.

    B. Vespasian had two sons, Titus, who would have been 31 in 70 A.D., and Domitian, who was about 11 years younger than Titus. Domitian was a troubled man and really not fit to play the role of emperor, but Titus was extremely popular.

- **C.** Vespasian reorganized the military system after the civil war. Four legions that had defected during the rebellion were cashiered. Some of the men in these legions were then reassigned to create new legions.
    1. Vespasian appointed strong, aggressive governors on the frontiers to build up a sense of loyalty in the new units.
    2. The auxiliary units were also reformed. The Flavian emperors renewed the policy of posting auxiliary units away from their homelands.
- **D.** The Flavians took aggressive action on the frontiers to restore the majesty and image of Rome. The dynasty was desperate to earn a military reputation.
    1. Governors were ordered to conquer the island of Britain.
    2. Even more important were the punitive expeditions launched against the Germans; these were massive retaliatory strikes on the part of the Romans.
    3. Further, the Roman camps on the Rhine served as springboards for operations into the free German zone to incorporate more of Germany into imperial control.
    4. Vespasian initiated an advance into southern Germany with construction of a line of forts stretching from modern-day Mainz to Regensburg, including a region known in Latin as the Agri Decumates.
    5. The Flavians launched strikes into other regions of Germany. Notably, the emperor Domitian waged a war against the Chatti in Hesse.

II. Another important frontier was the Euphrates in the eastern section of Anatolia.
- **A.** Earlier, this frontier did not have adequate roads for logistical support, but it was reorganized under the Flavians.
- **B.** A strategic highway was constructed from Trapezus on the Black Sea to the cities of Melitene and Samosata, enabling travel into Mesopotamia, across the Euphrates, or into Syria. The rough terrain of the region would have made construction of forts and highways a daunting task.
- **C.** On this frontier, the Romans created a base from which to move in and impose Roman hegemony in Armenia and, if necessary, to

attack into Mesopotamia or farther east into Iran and pressure the Parthian king.
- **D.** In part, the construction on the frontiers paralleled other construction in the Roman world.
    1. From 70 to 235 A.D., the Romans essentially constructed the tourist industry of the Mediterranean world today. The period was one of great prosperity; the population increased; taxes rose; and the provinces became more Romanized.
    2. The roads, bridges, and fortifications built by the Romans were impressive structures, especially to the barbarians.

III. Although the Flavian emperors achieved success in northwestern Europe, Domitian faced a new barbarian threat along the 1,000-mile frontier of the Danube: the Dacians, who occupied modern Rumania.
- **A.** This region had been conquered by Augustus and his stepson Tiberius. The Balkan provinces were important for the strategic highways that linked Italy to the Greek world, as well as for the lucrative mines.
- **B.** Between the 1st and 2nd centuries A.D., the focus of Roman military power was shifted to the Danube and the East; eventually, 13 legions were posted in the Rhineland and 10 on the Euphrates and in Syria. Germany and Britain were handled by much smaller garrisons.
- **C.** In 85 A.D., Decebalus came to the throne of the Dacians, a group of tribes related to those living under Roman control in the Balkans. Although they were involved in different activities, the Dacians had a conscious identity as a group at least since the 2nd century B.C.
    1. The Dacians had learned to exploit their iron and gold mines in trade with the Greek world. Increasingly, these people moved toward an urban-based culture without Roman intervention. When the wars opened in 101 A.D. during Trajan's reign, the Dacians had been living in towns for a number of generations.
    2. The Dacians had also acquired a great deal of knowledge and technology from the Classical world, which they married with their own traditions. Above all, by the end of the 1st century B.C., the Dacians were already prized as warriors.

3. In 44 B.C., Julius Caesar had contemplated a war against the Dacians, because they had been united under King Burebistas and were raiding into Thrace and other regions.
4. The Roman conquest and development of the Balkan provinces probably altered patterns of trade and migration there. The Romans set up a political boundary along the middle and lower Danube, which ran through a line of communication and divided two zones that had been culturally related.
5. By 85 A.D., the Dacians again coalesced around a powerful king, Decebalus, and began to pose a military threat on the Danube. Further, through trade and contact with the Romans, the Dacians had learned to equip themselves more effectively, and because of their mineral wealth, they were able to hire large numbers of Germans and Sarmatian nomads to fight in the ranks of their army.

D. The initial attacks of Decebalus were treated as operations that could be handled by a single legion. The governors tried to carry out the preemptive strikes against the Dacians that had been used in Germany, but at least two legions were annihilated in these operations.

E. Domitian discovered that these opponents were not just raiding tribes; these were disciplined forces led by an effective king. The success of the Dacian attacks on the middle and lower Danube incited German and Iranian nomads to attack along the upper Danube.

F. Domitian came to terms with Decebalus in 92 A.D. by agreeing to pay the Dacians a subsidy and to provide Roman engineers and technical support to fortify Dacian towns. This king had forced the Romans to make concessions that no Roman emperor had previously made, and he would continue to press his advantage.

G. The trials with the Dacians brought forth the greatest of Roman emperors, Trajan, the *optimus princeps*, to carry out the first significant conquest since the invasion of Britain.

Readings:

Jones, B. W. *The Emperor Domitian*.

Levick, B. *Vespasian*.

Luttwak, E. N. *The Grand Strategy of the Roman Empire from the First Century A.D. to the Third.*

Questions to Consider:

1. Why did the Flavians extend so much effort on the frontiers and the imperial army? What lessons did they learn from the rebellions and civil wars of 69–70 A.D.? How significant were Flavian military victories over barbarian foes?

2. What were the advantages of the construction of permanent frontier fortresses, signal towers, and highways, known as the *limes*? How were these frontiers to be defended? Did the northern barbarians pose a threat that justified these measures?

3. What was the nature of the threat posed by the Dacians? How did Domitian compromise the Danube frontier by his treaty in 92 A.D.? Was a future war between Rome and the Dacians inevitable in 96 A.D.?

Lecture Twenty-Four
Trajan, the Dacians, and the Parthians

Scope: Trajan, the first Roman emperor descended from provincials, was hailed *optimus princeps*, "best emperor," for his victories over the barbarian foes, Dacians and Parthians. Twice, in 101–102 and 105–106 A.D., Trajan overran Dacia by a strategy of two columns totaling over 100,000 men that converged on Decebalus's capital, Sarmizegethusa. From the booty, captives, and profits from mining, Trajan funded an imperial patronage that secured his dynasty for the next century. In 115–117 A.D., Trajan deployed the same strategy against the Parthians with devastating effect. Although Hadrian relinquished Trajan's eastern conquests, Dacia proved a model in Romanization. At Rome, Trajan erected a commemorative column decorated with reliefs depicting his Dacian wars. This remarkable record, paralleled by literary sources and coins, reveals that Romans appreciated the nobility and tragic defeat of the Dacians. Trajan's reign was the climax of five centuries of confident Roman imperialism, but within a generation, perceptions and policies changed profoundly when Marcus Aurelius faced new barbarian challenges from Parthians and Germans.

Outline

I. The emperor Trajan (98–117 A.D.) was hailed as "the best of emperors" (*optimus princeps*); he was the first man of provincial origins to become emperor.

  A. With the death of Trajan in 117 A.D., Roman expansion was concluded. Trajan's conquests beyond the Euphrates are often viewed by modern historians as expensive and unnecessary but were immensely popular among the Romans themselves.

  1. Further, these wars paid off. The Dacian wars, for example, won the Romans 50,000 captives and 1.5 billion denarii.
  2. The Dacian wars financed an enormous building program in Italy and, indeed, funded the dynasty of the Five Good Emperors.

    B. Trajan also set the strategy for defeating the Parthian foe in the East.

II. Trajan inherited the problem of dealing with the Dacians from Domitian.
    A. Domitian had compromised imperial defense along the middle and lower Danube. His actions led to the massing of large numbers of forces on the Danube frontier and the development of highways in the Balkan provinces.
    B. In 101 A.D., Trajan massed more than 100,000 men to humble Decebalus, king of the Dacians. These forces were to operate in two columns, one coming from the west and one coming from the south.
        1. The two columns converged in western Dacia, ravaging the agricultural heartland of the kingdom and threatening to advance against the Dacian capital, Sarmizegethusa.
        2. The Roman army wintered on the imperial side of the frontier, then returned in the summer of 102 A.D.. This time, the southern column came into Dacia from the East, taking Decebalus by surprise.
        3. Decebalus surrendered and was probably required to return the skilled captives that he had negotiated from Domitian and pay reparations.
    C. Decebalus had been humbled but not defeated. As soon as the Roman forces withdrew, he reopened the war. Trajan reacted promptly, assembling a comparable force to return to Dacia within two years.
        1. Trajan used essentially the same strategy that he had in 101–102 A.D., but this time, the two columns converged on the Dacian capital in 105 A.D. and sacked it.
        2. By 106 A.D., resistance had collapsed, and Trajan decided to organize the former kingdom into a province. The nature of the conquest in Dacia led to rapid Romanization.
    D. The Dacian wars were hailed as a great triumph for Trajan, who reportedly penned a commentary similar to the one Julius Caesar had written describing the Gallic wars.
        1. The account no longer exists, but Trajan's Column, which today stands in Rome, gives us a remarkable insight into official attitudes toward barbarians in the high empire.

2. The marble column stands in Trajan's forum, a complex completed in 113 A.D. from the profits of the war. It rests on a square cube, in which the ashes of Trajan and his wife, Plotina, were later deposited in a golden urn, but this urn no longer survives.
   3. The column is constructed of 23 marble drums and faced with 400 marble slabs. It spirals up to 100 feet and is covered with reliefs that narrate the Dacian wars in pictures.
   4. The reliefs contain more than 2,500 figures and constitute the most detailed pictorial record available of the Roman army on campaign. The bridge of ships across the Danube is depicted, as well as scenes of rituals and the capture of cities and prisoners.
   5. Trajan is shown as a serene, resolved commander, often according clemency to the barbarian foes.

III. The victory in Dacia allowed Trajan to perfect the logistics and strategy necessary to take on the Parthian king.
   A. Part of Trajan's success rested on the Flavians' reorganization of the upper Euphrates frontier, although Trajan also contributed to the strengthening of the Eastern frontier.
   B. Trajan could have settled with the Parthian king by diplomatic agreement, as Augustus and Nero had done.
      1. In 112 or 113 A.D., the then-reigning Parthian king, Oroses, put his brother on the throne of Armenia without consultation with Rome.
      2. In response, Trajan moved east with large numbers of forces. By 114 A.D., Roman armies had overrun Armenia. The next year, two huge Roman columns moved into Mesopotamia and converged on the Parthian capital, Ctesiphon. The Romans stormed and sacked the city, and the Parthian kingdom broke out in civil war.
      3. With this victory, Trajan may have seen himself as a new Alexander the Great. Undoubtedly, the reports sent back to Rome were spectacular. Yet the victory resulted in no permanent annexations.
      4. Trajan was forced to pull back, in part because of rebellions among the Jewish populations in Mesopotamia and Cyrenica. He died unexpectedly on August 4, 117 A.D.

5. Hadrian faced opposition as Trajan's successor and had no taste for the Eastern war. He called a halt to the offensive against Parthia.

C. The successes of Trajan over the Dacians and Parthians gave later Roman emperors the winning strategy to defeat the eastern foe.
1. Several later Parthian wars took place. In 161–166 A.D., C. Avidius Cassius, the leading general of Marcus Aurelius, repeated the strategy of Trajan to humble Parthia.
2. The emperor Septimius Severus waged two Parthian wars, again employing the same tactics and logistics as Trajan.
3. In 199–200, Septimius Severus also organized the province Mesopotamia in northern Iraq that gave the Romans the bases to attack the Parthian political heartland ever after.

IV. The northern frontiers were not as quiescent as the eastern ones had become.

A. The last of the Five Good Emperors, Marcus Aurelius, faced the first serious Germanic incursions into the Roman Empire in 100 years.

B. Marcus Aurelius (r. 161–180 A.D.) was a Stoic philosopher and probably the noblest man to sit on the throne of Rome.

C. The emperor had waged a Parthian war with great success, but it was not a profitable war, and returning legions carried with them a plague. Perhaps 15 percent of the men in the army were killed by the plague in 166–169 A.D.

D. Both this Parthian war and the war against German invaders into the Balkans that came almost immediately afterward had to be financed by debasing the currency. The Romans had used this technique in the past to cover short-term needs for cash but had always restored the currency once the fiscal emergency had been met.

E. Historians are not sure what caused the invasions of the Germans. These may have been tribes moving up the Oder valley into Bohemia.
1. In 167–170 A.D., these tribes invaded the Balkan provinces, Italy, and Greece. Even tribes that had been long associated with Rome, such as the Sueves, started to raid into Roman territory.

2. Marcus Aurelius might have been planning a punitive strike against these Germanic tribes, but the Germans struck first.
3. By 171 A.D., Marcus Aurelius took the offensive and, for nine years, waged war north of the Danube. When he died in 180 A.D., the Romans were ready to incorporate these regions into the empire; however, the emperor's son and successor, Commodus, cancelled these plans.

F. Marcus Aurelius also commissioned a column, similar in construction to Trajan's Column, in celebration of the German wars. But the serenity and clemency of Trajan's Column are nowhere present in this one; the perceptions of the German wars are much more menacing and may have been even more significant than the victory.

Readings:

Bennet, Julian. *Trajan Optimius Princeps*. 2nd ed.

Lepper, F. A. *Trajan's Parthian War*.

Questions to Consider:

1. Why did Romans consider Trajan the greatest emperor since Augustus? How important were his victories over the Dacians and Parthians?
2. How do the reliefs of the columns of Trajan and Marcus Aurelius document a shift in perceptions of the barbarians? What accounted for these changes? How do the reliefs on the column of Marcus Aurelius mark a change in style and presentation in imperial arts?

Lecture Twenty-Five
Romanization of the Provinces

Scope: In Spain and Cisalpine Gaul, the Romans had learned the techniques of assimilating provincials. The Roman peace brought improvements in technology, transportation, and land management in former barbarian lands. The imperial army played a decisive role by constructing roads, bridges, and base camps. Archaeology documents expansion of the arable; development of viticulture; and manufacturing of ceramics, glass, leather goods, and textiles to supply the armies in the Rhineland and Britain. By the early 2nd century, some Gallic businesses were even exporting their wares in Italy. The Rhine and rivers of Gaul linked the cities of northern Italy with the North Sea—the primary axis of European civilization ever after. Dacia was Romanized soon after Trajan's conquest, as veterans, merchants, and miners flocked to mining boom towns and Roman colonies. Success in Dacia assured prosperity of the Balkan lands of Pannonia, Dalmatia, and Moesia. In eastern Asia Minor and on the desert frontiers of Syria and North Africa, archaeology documents similar patterns. In the 2nd century, wealthy provincials funded Roman-style municipalities, took imperial service, and even entered the Senate. In 212, the emperor Caracalla capped this process by granting citizenship to all free residents of the empire. But success carried responsibilities. Henceforth, the imperial government was committed to defending these vital provinces on the frontiers.

Outline

I. The Roman imperial army played a decisive role in Romanizing the frontier provinces of northern Europe and along the upper Euphrates and desert frontiers.

   A. The legionary bases we have discussed were more than just military strong points for launching expeditions against barbarian foes; they quickly became societies and cities in their own right, and these bases had to be supplied with foodstuffs, household goods, and equipment.

- **B.** The *limes*, the limits between the barbarian lands and Rome, came to rest in areas along lines of communication that allowed the armies to be supplied easily.
- **C.** Studies based on archaeology in northern Europe offer some interesting information on the economic and social impact of the army on these frontier zones.
    1. In the 1st century of the empire, for example, more than 100,000 soldiers of the Julio-Claudian army were stationed along the Rhine after the Varian disaster.
    2. These men would have required 7.5 million *modii* of wheat (50,000 tonnes) annually. The Roman army also issued generous rations in meat, wine, olive oil, and other types of commodities.
    3. The forces of the Rhine in the 1st century A.D. were supplied from production in northern Italy, especially Milan. The trade routes over the Alpine passes linked northern Italy to the Rhineland.
    4. One result of the presence of the Roman army on the Rhine was the transformation of Treveri (modern-day Trier) from a Celtic *oppidum* into a Roman city. Treveri became one of the centers for supplying the Roman army, producing wine in the 1st century A.D. and pottery and glass by the 2nd century.
    5. In supplying the army, the provincial zones experienced changes in their patterns of manufacturing and distribution of goods.
- **D.** By the 1st century A.D., cities in eastern Gaul emerged as major urban centers. In the 2nd century, villa farming and Roman agricultural methods took hold. Gallic notables adopted Roman tastes and mores.
- **E.** Even regions of Gaul not directly tied to supplying and equipping the army were profoundly changed.
    1. The Romans' ability to transport goods was equivalent to that seen in 18th-century Europe on the eve of the Industrial Revolution. Such movements of goods were accompanied by movements of attitudes, language, and identity.
    2. The modest Celtic settlement Lutetia (Paris), for example, was not directly tied to the army but enjoyed the advantages of its location on a major trade route.

3. The construction of highways prompted the relocation of Celtic populations from fortified hill forts to cities on the plains. In this way, the Celtic settlement of Bibracte declined as the population moved to the Roman city of Augustodunum (Autun).

F. Similar patterns of transformation also appeared in Britain, as well as in the Balkans, Dacia, eastern Turkey, and even along the desert frontiers of Syria and North Africa.

II. In the cities not directly along the frontier boundaries, the elites who led the process of Romanization were not Romans.

A. Many of these notables had earned their citizenship through service in Rome's auxiliary armies, and they took over the job of Romanizing the cities behind the frontier.

B. Again, Gaul serves as a good example of this pattern. The Gauls readily constructed amphitheaters and adopted the Roman tradition of gladiatorial games.

C. The practice of worshipping the spirit of the emperor (*genius*) had been established in the Roman army with Augustus and was transported to the provinces, where major shrines were erected.

D. The mining activities in the Balkans and Dacia gave a special dimension to that area.
   1. Gaul and Britain received the bulk of imperial attention and military presence in the 1st century; only in the 2nd century did the Balkans and Dacia experience this type of Romanization.
   2. In the reign of Nero, Dalmatia (Rumania) hit rich veins that produced 18,000 pounds of gold annually, or about 20 million *denarii*. Miners from Dalmatia were later lured into the Dacia mines under generous contracts.
   3. Mining towns mushroomed across Dacia and the Balkans that might include 5,000 miners, 10,000 laborers and slaves, and more than 15,000 civilians providing supplies and "entertainment."
   4. By 200 A.D., a network of mining towns existed, which in turn, fed business into the cities on the imperial highways. This combination of mining activities and military presence explains the rapid Romanization of Dacia.

III. Along the desert frontiers, the impact of Rome was not as remarkable.

- A. The Romans stationed their forces behind the boundaries of the desert, and much of the patrolling was done by Berber or Arab warriors.
- B. Nonetheless, these tribal groups were organized into ethnic Roman auxiliary units and stationed in Roman fortresses.
    1. One of the best examples of the mixed provincial culture that emerged in these situations comes from Dura-Europus, a base on the Euphrates that was the home of the XX cohort of Palmyrenes.
    2. The site was populated by a mix of Greek, Aramaic, and Latin speakers; excavations there have revealed a synagogue, as well as the earliest known Christian house church.
    3. Also found at Dura-Europus was the *Feriale Duranum* (c. 220s), the military calendar highlighting holidays in celebration of Roman war gods and victories.

IV. We close by touching on an area in Asia Minor, Anatolia, that may not immediately come to mind as a frontier zone.
- A. Some regions of Anatolia were thoroughly Hellenized, but the interior and eastern sections of Asia Minor (Turkey) constituted a Roman frontier province similar to those on the Rhine or the Danube. These regions were populated by "inner barbarians," tough mountain people, whom the Romans felt the necessity to control militarily.
- B. In what is today southwestern Turkey, in the Pisidiam highlands, near the modern town of Yalvaç, is an amazing Roman colony, Antiochia ad Pisidiam, founded by Augustus in 25 B.C.
- C. Perhaps 3,000–4,000 Roman veterans and their families were settled there and built a Roman city in the middle of a rugged Anatolian landscape. They immediately erected the impressive public buildings with which they were familiar in Italy.
    1. A series of monumental stairways and squares led to the great public center where the temple of Augustus was built.
    2. The city also had a series of fortification walls and an aqueduct, the arches of which still stand today. The aqueduct brought two-thirds of the city's water supply from mountain springs at 4,700–5,000 feet above sea level; it pumped 3,000 cubic meters of water a day and spanned over 6 miles.

©2004 The Teaching Company.

D. By 200 A.D., the *limes* had come to mark a political and cultural boundary. Further, the provincials, descended from the barbarian foes of Rome, were increasingly concerned about their security, which explains the expansion of the military system to defend these zones.
  1. This expansion began in the reign of Hadrian (117–138) and climaxed in the Severan age (193–235). This period marks a shift of military and fiscal resources away from the Mediterranean core to the provinces.
  2. In 212, the emperor Caracalla gave legal recognition to this cultural change by issuing the *Constitutio Antoninana*, extending citizenship to all free residents of the Roman Empire.

Readings:

Garnsey, Peter, and Richard Saller. *The Roman Empire: Economy, Society, and Culture*.

Whittaker, C. R. *Frontiers of the Roman Empire: A Social and Economic Study*.

Questions to Consider:

1. What was the impact of Roman military and fiscal demands on transforming frontier societies? How did these demands influence social, economic, and cultural change in provinces behind the military frontier?
2. What was the impact of building Roman colonies, highways, and fortresses? How did the Romans transform the urban landscapes of their empire? Why did these efforts have such a profound influence?

Lecture Twenty-Six
Commerce Beyond the Imperial Frontiers

Scope: The Roman peace witnessed an unparalleled expansion of regional and long-distance commerce beyond the imperial frontiers. In northern Europe, Rome fell heir to the trade routes of Celtic Europe emanating from Massilia (Marseilles), the Greek colony on the French Riviera, and the cities of northern Italy. Celtic merchants sailing to Jutland and the Danish islands sustained the growth of Roman cities in the Rhineland and Britain. Classical authors describe the routes and tribes of southern Scandinavia, and archaeological finds testify to the volume of Roman goods exported. The Germanic tribes of central Europe and Iranian nomads of the Russian grasslands were likewise drawn into the web of Roman markets. They all prized Roman luxuries, such as finely wrought jewelry and wine, but they also bought daily commodities with Roman coins. By 200 A.D., the northern lands beyond the *limes* from the western shores of Ireland to slopes of the Caucasus were linked to the Roman world by trade. To the far south, Berber caravans linked Roman North Africa to the kingdoms on the upper Niger. In the Far East, Alexandrine and Levantine merchants, versed in using the monsoons, sailed the Erythraean Sea (Indian Ocean) in an international luxury trade linking Rome to the distant ports of Axum (Ethiopia), Arabia Felix (Yemen), Taprobane (Sri Lanka), and India. This commerce enriched and reshaped the Roman and barbarian worlds alike.

Outline

I. From the mid-2nd century A.D., the barbarian peoples beyond the frontier experienced far more contact with Rome through the avenues of trade than through warfare. This lecture examines this trade and its role in the Roman economy.

II. The imperial peace of Rome transformed the volume of goods and the scale of trade on all frontiers.

    A. This aspect of trade in the Roman world is somewhat puzzling because the Romans themselves were not responsible for any

major innovations. Often the Romans borrowed existing technology, as for example, the carts and harnessing of the Celts.
- **B.** The imperial peace, and the resulting legal standards and common currency, created social conditions that facilitated the spread of trade and technology.
- **C.** Further, their cities on the frontier served as markets, stimulating trade both within the empire and into the barbarian lands. The trade contacts established by these cities in the 1st century were maintained well into the 5th, disrupted only by the fighting of the 3rd century.
- **D.** The Romans' contribution to these trade networks came in the form of a revolution in transportation.
    1. They made available technology in carts and harnessing and constructed all-weather roads, bridges, and canal systems.
    2. River transport was developed at least to the extent seen in northern Europe in the 17th and 18th centuries.
    3. The Romans also excelled in shipbuilding and built vessels using the shell and skeleton construction techniques.
    4. The Romans had both the motives to engage in long-distance trade and the means to carry it out on a hitherto unknown scale.

III. In the middle of the 1st century, trade between the Romans and the Germanic tribes increased considerably.
- **A.** This trade involved not only what is today western Germany but also Scandinavia and the lands around the Baltic in eastern Europe, as well as the Iranian nomadic areas.
- **B.** Most of this trade was carried out by provincial merchants of Celtic origin, who regularly sailed from Gallic and British ports into the North Sea and followed traditional routes into the Baltic.
- **C.** The Roman historian Tacitus and the geographer Strabo give us remarkably detailed information on the tribes dwelling in Jutland, the Danish islands, and Scandia (southern Sweden).
- **D.** Merchants also used river routes leading up the Lippe and the Main into western Germany, then picking up and following the Weser or Elbe to the North Sea.

1. An important route began at the legionary camp of Carnuntum, just to the east of what is today Vienna on the Danube.
2. This was the so-called Amber Route, which followed the Elbe and could cut over to the Vistula or Oder into the Baltic zone. Use of this route can be traced back to the late Bronze Age.
3. In the imperial age, the level of trade increased substantially.

E. Farther east, along the northern shores of the Black Sea, the city of Olbia, an ancient Greek colony, and Panticapeaum, the principal Greek city on the Crimean shore, had long contact with the peoples of the steppes.

IV. What went across the frontiers on these trade routes, and how did this trade change these societies?

A. Germania and Scandinavia exported raw materials, including timber, iron ore, flax, honey, amber, walrus ivory, and furs. Slaves, laborers, and recruits for the Roman army were another important commodity.

B. In turn, the Romans exported a host of finished goods, such as glass, pottery, and jewelry, as well as perishables, including textiles (silks, woolens, cottons), wine, and olive oil. Weapons and furniture were also manufactured in the empire for export to Germania.

C. A remarkable number of Roman coins have been found in the northern barbarian world, primarily the silver *denarius* used in payroll in the Roman army. In regions close to the Roman frontier in northern Europe, coins would have been used in exchanges for common Roman goods; in zones beyond the immediate frontier, coins would have been a curiosity brought in with other prestige goods.

D. The exchange of people, through immigration and the slave trade, was important to both sides of the frontier. The Romans needed the labor for construction of cities in the Rhineland. The existence of Gothic loan words from Latin and Greek for menial tasks and specialized goods documents the use of the Goths as servants and laborers.

E. This trade also allowed Germanic tribes to export excess population in a peaceful manner. Archaeology in villages shows continuity in population size and ways of life from the 1st century A.D. into the 4th century. This suggests that excess population was exported to the Roman world in the form of slaves, laborers, and soldiers.

F. The Roman imperial government tried to regulate trade, with limited success. For example, Roman emperors attempted to ban the export of weapons. They also attempted to enforce the return of captives and deserters who were skilled craftsmen and could establish manufacturing operations in frontier regions.

G. The prosperity that the barbarian peoples enjoyed from this Roman contact transformed their societies.

1. The Teutonic chieftains and nomadic khans acquired prestige goods and elevated themselves as rulers. Certain Roman products, such as silver bowls, coins, and glass, were used for gift exchange in this process.
2. Increased trade and Roman contacts also enabled these rulers to preside over larger political organizations by the end of the 2nd century A.D. To some extent, success in political organization and changing social patterns in the German world depended on the prosperity of the Roman Empire and the connections between the two worlds.

V. At the same time, the Romans engaged in impressive long-distance trade to the east and to the south.

A. The cities that the Romans established in North Africa and the security of Roman Egypt stimulated trade with contacts deep into Africa, especially for gold and exotic animals for the arena.

B. Trade in the east is well documented in the *Periplous* ("*Sailing Around*"), a manual for navigation. Several itineraries exist, outlining the caravan routes that started in the Roman world and moved east, crossing over to Mesopotamia, through Iran, and to the cities of central Asia or going south into Babylonia and taking the sea route to the Indian ports. There were also trade routes in the Indian Ocean.

C. All three of these major routes, again, owed a great deal to Roman organization, shipbuilding, and the stimulus of Roman markets.

1. In the time of Augustus, the trade down the Red Sea into the Indian ports probably increased fivefold.

2. The long-distance trade began as voyages of discovery but became long-term, consistent commercial development and exploitation.
- **D.** A good portion of the profits made in these transactions went to reinforce the imperial government through its customs duties or to the senatorial and equestrian families that backed the trading ventures. Profits were invested in land, as well as the spectacular building programs, social development, and festivals that characterized successful Classical civilization.
- **E.** Although Rome's economy is often classified as underdeveloped, immense profits from long-distance trade were netted by investors and the Roman state, and so contributed to the prosperity in the Roman world and the barbarian world beyond the imperial frontiers.

Readings:

Duncan-Jones, R. *Scale and Structure in the Roman Economy.*

Garnsey, P., K. Hopkins, and C. R. Whittaker. *Trade in the Ancient Economy.*

Questions to Consider:

1. How was trade promoted both within and beyond the Roman Empire by improvements in transportation, the spread of the use of coins, and rising demands for consumables by imperial cities? How did the trade circuits between Rome and the barbarian worlds beyond the frontier affect both trading partners?
2. How did the interaction resulting from trade change attitudes and perceptions of Romans and the foreign peoples (*gentes externae*)?

Lecture Twenty-Seven
Frontier Settlement and Assimilation

Scope: By 150, Romans could point to a definable *limes* that marked them off from the *gentes externae* ("foreign peoples") of the barbarian world. Rome did not halt as much as regulate barbarian movement. Fortresses and highways inhibited raiders along desert frontiers in North Africa or Syria. Along the great river frontiers or in Britain, legions and auxiliaries were stationed to intercept and destroy barbarian invasions. Simultaneously, the *limes* was a great mixing bowl of Romans, provincials, and barbarians from which emerged a distinct frontier society by 300. Favored tribes, such as the Batavians, were recruited into the army and gained citizenship. Other barbarians arrived as laborers, slaves, or immigrants. Latin loan words in the Gothic reveal the menial occupations of Germans on the frontiers. The term *colonus* came to denote peasant farmers, who by the mid-4th century, were veritable serfs and mostly barbarian captives in origin. Barbarian newcomers were dispersed and assimilated into Roman society. By the accession of Constantine, one out every five provincials in the frontier zones was of barbarian origin. In some ways, the *limes* was blurred as a common way of life emerged on both sides of the frontier. In another sense, the limits of Roman civilization extended beyond the political *limes*. But with Constantine, Christian emperors were to redefine this boundary and the relationship between Rome and barbarians.

Outline

I. By 200 A.D., the *limes*, the frontier, had become a political and cultural border, marking the extent of Roman political power and success in assimilating provincial peoples.

   A. The *limes* was not the same as a modern national border or a military barrier. At many points, the Roman frontier was unguarded, and people flowed across in both directions.

   B. One of the major sources of this flow was military recruits. For example, the Batavians, who lived in the marshlands of the lower Rhine (modern Holland), furnished at least 5,000 men to the

Roman army. This represented one-third of the tribe's adult male population. Other tribes, such as the Frisians, the peoples of the Agri Decumates, and the nomadic peoples of eastern Europe, were similarly recruited.

C. The movement of barbarians across the frontiers into Roman military units was constant and significant. The barbarians in these units learned Latin, were issued Roman-style weapons, and were moved into different areas of the empire. As discharged veterans, many of them settled in Roman territory and became provincial Romans.

D. Until the 4th century, barbarians served in auxiliary units. They were not allowed to use their own language, and none of them rose to a high position in the military structure or at court. They remained, essentially, soldiers, although their children and grandchildren would be assimilated into the general population.

E. The Romans sought to regulate the flow of immigration into the empire, rather than to halt it.
  1. Romans specifically took in populations that would be useful. Roman political and social institutions, such as the patron-client relationship, were at work in this kind of assimilation.
  2. Often, barbarian immigrants were dispersed once they arrived in Roman territory. For example, two exiled kings of the Marcomanni, Maroboduus and Vannius, along with their extensive retinues, were granted lands in the Balkan provinces.
  3. In a similar situation, Plautius Silvanus, legate on the lower Danube in 67 A.D., boasted that he settled 100,000 barbarians into the Balkan provinces, dispersing them into smaller communities.
  4. As late as 269 A.D., the emperor Claudius II defeated a huge horde of Goths, then settled them as *coloni* ("tenants"), again, in the Balkans.

F. The settlement of these barbarians in Roman imperial lands was done under specific arrangements. Tacitus tells of one situation in which a German tribe, the Ampsivarii, attempted to move into vacant lands in modern Belgium but was driven out by the Romans. At the same time, other tribes were allowed to settle in vacant lands so long as they asked permission and abided by certain agreements.

G. Roman coins, minted in 348–352, celebrated the long tradition of immigration by depicting a Roman emperor leading two barbarians out of their hut for resettlement in the empire.

H. Accurate statistics on the extent of this immigration are difficult to come by, but it is possible to make some educated guesses.
   1. In 429, King Gaiseric of the Vandals crossed from Spain into Africa, reputedly leading 80,000 Vandals, Sueves, and Alans. If this number is accurate, then these three barbarian tribes had 15,000 warriors.
   2. Classical authors grossly exaggerated the size of barbarian armies at 100,000 or 250,000, when most likely forces of 3,000 to 5,000 represented major forces. Many of the barbarian movements were probably also on this order of magnitude.
   3. Although these movements were relatively small, they were still significant in their impact on the frontier zones.
   4. By 300 A.D., probably one out of five provincials on the frontier of northern Europe was of recent barbarian origin.

II. We must also note that assimilation did not work in only one direction. The Roman army, administrative class, and elites to the immediate west or south of the military frontier acquired a great deal from the barbarian immigrants who settled among them.

A. By the end of the 1st century A.D. in northern Europe, soldiers of the Roman army began to wear hooded leather jackets that were common among the Celtic and Germanic peoples. They also adopted leggings and boots that were characteristic of the area in which they were stationed, as well as trousers and belts.

B. In some ways, the provincials in frontier zones also recalled their own traditions. In Gaul and Britain, from 200–300 A.D., jewelry, relief works, and textiles reflected a resurgence of older Celtic traditions.

C. The result of this mix was the emergence of a distinctly composite frontier culture. One feature that characterized this culture was that it was heavily military and marshal in its ethos.

- **D.** Archaeological work reveals that local and regional trade increased contact between the Romans and the barbarians without necessarily leading to settlement.
    1. The Roman army in Britain drew much of its meat from the tribes to the north of Hadrian's Wall.
    2. The same kind of provisioning went on in the lower Rhine. The Germanic tribes outside of Roman control provided hides and salted meat to the military forces stationed in that locale.

III. The barbarian tribes that were engaged in these activities and being absorbed into the Roman provincial system became increasingly important for the Roman army. They also became better armed and had a stronger identity of themselves.
- **A.** By the end of the 2nd century and the beginning of the 3rd, the literary sources describe larger and more clearly delineated tribal confederations among the barbarians; in the late 3rd and early 4th centuries, the sources name kings leading these confederations.
- **B.** The barbarians did not adopt city life or mining activities, but they did learn better military and political organization from the Romans. Ironically, Roman trade and military pressure caused this change on the other side of the frontier.
- **C.** This pattern is also seen along the southern and eastern frontiers. In the desert frontier of Syria, for example, the Romans and the barbarians experienced similar exchanges as those seen in northern Europe.
    1. From the early 2nd century A.D. on, the Romans began to incorporate Arab nomads into their auxiliary units.
    2. By 300 A.D., the Romans had to construct more forts and military highways to patrol this zone, and by the opening of the 4th century, Arab tribes were emerging with identities and institutions that they never had before.
    3. In the early Roman imperial age, it is difficult to track the movement and assimilation of these groups, but by the early 4th century, Arab confederations appeared that would ultimately fuse into Arab kingdoms by the end of the century.
    4. The same pattern also appeared in North Africa, with Berber tribes acquiring a sense of identity and greater political cohesion.

D. These barbarian tribes came into contact with the material culture of Rome and, especially, with the Roman army, which offered a hierarchy and organization that had been unknown to the barbarians.

E. The conversion of Constantine and the spread of Christianity enhanced the distinctive identities of the barbarians in the 4th and 5th centuries, which would become an important problem for Roman emperors as these barbarians became a critical military force in the later empire.

Readings:

Burns, Thomas. *Rome and the Barbarians, 100 B.C.–400 A.D.*

Thompson, E. A. *Romans and Barbarians: The Decline of the Western Empire.*

Questions to Consider:

1. How did barbarians settle in the Roman Empire? How important was military service? Did these means of exporting population to the Roman world act as a safety valve to Germanic societies in central Europe?

2. How did trade, travel, and military service enrich the material lives of barbarian peoples in central Europe? How did these same forces define the barbarians as ever more distinct from Romans? How did barbarians likely view the Roman world?

Lecture Twenty-Eight
From Germanic Tribes to Confederations

Scope: By commerce, immigration, and war, Germanic tribes transformed their world. Archaeology has revealed societies far more sophisticated by the 2nd century than the stereotyped images found in classical authors. The Suevic kingdom in Bohemia, for example, was a model of organization based on the achievement of the La Tène civilization and trade with Rome. Aerial photography has revealed widespread villa settlements by the mid-2nd century, which explains why the emperor Marcus Aurelius considered annexation of the kingdom. Early German warriors pledged loyalty to a lord and elected kings only in war; thus, Rome could seldom negotiate with a single leader. Any prince exalted by Roman gifts and friendship was compromised in the eyes of his fellow tribesmen. But by 200, the tribes of western Germany were coalescing into effective confederations: the Franks, Saxons, Alemanni, and Sueves. They were assisted by familiarity with Roman military organization and the prosperity from trade and cultural exchange. They had also learned to cooperate, because any tribe arousing Roman suspicions became a target. These German confederations posed a minor threat to Rome, but it was the sudden emergence of two new barbarian threats, the Goths and Sassanid Persia, along with succession crises and civil wars, that opened the Roman frontiers to an unexpected barbarian assault in the 3rd century.

Outline

I. This lecture deals with the relationship of Rome to various barbarian peoples during the crisis of the 3rd century.

  A. For historians, this is the era when Rome moved from its distinctly classical civilization into the period of Late Antiquity (300–750 A.D.).

  B. The barbarians are seen as major players in this transformation. The Roman world would be profoundly changed during this period, and the barbarian assault is seen as one of the key agents of that change.

II. The changes that took place are sketched out by two primary literary sources that describe Romans dealing with barbarians, Tacitus and Ammianus Marcellinus, "the last great historian of Rome."

    A. Tacitus was writing at a time when Rome was indisputably the superior partner in the Roman-barbarian relationship.

        1. He published his *Germania*, an ethnographic treatise on the Germans, in 98 A.D.. He also wrote the *Agricola*, an encomium to his father-in-law, Gnaeus Julius Agricola, governor of Britain from 78 to 85 A.D.

        2. These two works together reflected the views of one segment of the Roman upper classes about barbarians in the year 100 A.D.

        3. Tacitus's account can be compared against archaeological evidence, but it also clearly represents the prejudices of a Roman political elite that had an idealized and unchanging vision of Germanic society. The Germans described by Tacitus in 100 A.D. are the archetype of the noble savage that reappears throughout Western literature.

        4. Tacitus also uses the Germans to measure the extent to which the Roman political elites had lost their freedom under despotic rulers. Tacitus tells us a good deal more about his view of the Roman imperial monarchy than about the barbarians.

    B. Ammianus Marcellinus served in the army of the late Roman Empire; his history begins in the time of Tacitus and concludes with the Battle of Adrianople (378).

        1. Ammianus's account accepts the fact that German barbarians moved freely through the military high commands. The easy intermixing of Romans and barbarians on the frontier is taken for granted, even by the highest ranks of Roman society.

        2. This significant change grew out of the crisis of the 3rd century.

III. We begin our examination of this crisis with a look at the Roman army.

    A. *The Grand Strategy of the Roman Empire* is a controversial work by E.N. Luttwark describing how the Romans defended their empire. The value of Luttwark's book was to refocus scholarship on the fact that Roman soldiers were stationed on the frontiers to defend the empire from barbarian foes.

- **B.** By the 2nd century A.D., there were significant changes in the positioning of the Roman army and imperial goals. Further, the legions on the frontiers were no longer being recruited primarily from Romans and Italians. By the reign of Hadrian, most legionaries came from regions in which they were stationed.
- **C.** With the emperor Hadrian, the Roman army also began to erect stone fortifications instead of wooden structures. Legions were no longer concentrated in large forces; each legion was tied to a separate camp, which resulted in some loss of mobility.
- **D.** The emperor Septimius Severus instituted a number of laws that are also seen as affecting the ability of the Roman army to wage wars of conquest. For example, Severus removed the laws forbidding soldiers to marry, which made some soldiers reluctant to embark on far-flung expeditions.
    1. Roman military policy used detachments of units (*vexillationes*), usually composed of younger, unmarried men, in offensive operations, while older, more settled soldiers were left in the garrison to hold the position on the frontier.
    2. This policy became prominent in the 3rd century, fostering a sense of detachment between field armies moving with the emperor and forces stationed on the frontier.
    3. Over the course of the 3rd and 4th centuries, the Roman civil administration became militarized, and an increasing number of soldiers became detached from military service for use in tax collection and administration of justice. Indeed, one of the ways in which the army lost its professional edge was by becoming too involved in the business of civilian government.
- **E.** These social changes in the army—the ethnic origins of the soldiers, the purposes for which the soldiers were used—led to the demise of the traditional Roman army by 300 A.D.

IV. At the same time that the Roman army was changing, the Germanic kingship emerged as a result of pressure from, and contact with, the Romans themselves.
- **A.** Early Germanic tribes and Iranian nomads were organized in villages based on kinship groups, but the Romans sought leaders for these groups with whom they could make agreements.
- **B.** The kings who emerged in these tribes probably came from aristocratic groups in which they had competitors. They received

gifts from the Romans and could, in turn, pass on prestige goods to their warriors. Through their influence, tribal kings could affect the decisions of tribal assemblies.

C. The Romans never fully understood that any one of these kings who was identified with Rome could easily be overthrown by rivals.

V. The level of fighting between barbarians and Romans increased significantly in 235 A.D.

A. One reason we know that the fighting was serious is that the imperial government could not pay for the wars. The Romans had to debase their silver currency to the point that their fiscal institutions were compromised.

B. Further, in 235, when the fighting intensified on the frontiers and the empire began to be plagued by civil wars, traditional legions responded, but over the course of the crisis, the army changed significantly.

C. In 235, the emperor Severus Alexander was assassinated by a clique of his army officers on the Rhine frontier. This put in power the Thracian Maximinus I.

D. The murder of Maximinus in 238 led to a succession of emperors from the high aristocracy who failed to contain the attacks in the east and the north. When the last of these emperors was assassinated in 268, a line of tough soldier-emperors came to the throne. These emperors halted barbarian attacks, restored Roman imperial authority on the frontiers, and carried out monetary and administrative reforms.

E. The northern provinces, Gaul, the upper Danube, and Britain, were hit hard by the crisis, starting from the mid-3rd century. At this point, new coalitions of Germans appeared, including the Saxons in northern Germany, who began to raid the island of Britain.

F. The imperial government failed to protect the coasts of Britain. In 287–288, military forces in Britain raised a rebellion and put their own man, Carausius, on the throne.

G. Likewise in Gaul, Postumus, commander of the Rhine army, rebelled in 260. From 260–274, a Gallo-Roman emperor ruled Britain, Gaul, and parts of Spain from Trier.

H. The barbarian attacks came principally from West Germanic tribes who had acquired better organization and discipline from the Romans; the result was political fragmentation in the empire. The Germanic barbarians had become a serious threat, along with the Sassanid shahs of Persia and the Goths, whom we shall meet in the next lecture.

Readings:

Luttwark, E. N. *The Grand Strategy of the Roman Empire from the First Century A.D. to the Third.*

MacMullen, Ramsay. *Roman Government's Response to Crisis, A.D. 235–337.*

Questions to Consider:

1. What were Roman perceptions of the northern peoples in the 1st and 2nd centuries? How does Tacitus reflect the prejudices and perceptions of the Roman upper classes?

2. How significant were the Germanic attacks in transforming the Roman West? How did they lead to the secessionist empires in Gaul (260–274) and Britain (287–296)? How was provincial and barbarian life transformed by the crisis of the 3rd century?

Lecture Twenty-Nine
Goths and the Crisis of the Third Century

Scope: Between 150 and 200, East Germanic peoples migrated from their Baltic homelands into eastern Europe. Foremost were the Goths from southern Sweden, who followed the river routes of Russia later used by the Vikings. The Goths, who settled to the north of the Black Sea, learned horsemanship from the Sarmatian nomads. In the 230s and 240s, Goths under Kniva invaded Dacia and Pannonia. They were followed by other Germans of Scandinavian origin (Vandals, Gepidae, and Herulians), as well as Sarmatian tribes. These migrations, in turn, pushed the West Germanic confederations into Gaul and northern Italy. Civil wars and the campaigns against Sassanid Persia distracted the legions. In 251, the emperor Trajan Decius was defeated and slain by the Goths in the Dobrudja. For nearly two decades, the Goths terrorized the Balkan provinces, while Herulians entered the Aegean world, sacking the environs of Athens and Ephesus in 262. Failure to contain the Goths discredited the Severan senatorial elite. In a coup in 268, the first of the soldier emperors risen from the ranks, Claudius II, seized the throne. He and his successors, Aurelian and Probus drove back the Goths and defeated the rival secessionist Roman states in Gaul and Syria. But Rome paid a high price for victory. Diocletian, who ended a half century of civil war and invasion, faced new conditions along the frontier and barbarian foes who had been bested but hardly defeated.

Outline

I. This lecture looks at a new barbarian threat, the Goths, a Germanic-speaking people who originated from Sweden. They are closely associated with the political and military crisis that Rome suffered after 235 A.D.

  A. This lecture also examines the Roman situation—the civil wars and the wars against the foe in the East, the Sassanid shahs of Persia.

B. Finally, we look at how the Romans surmounted the threat of the Goths, primarily under the leadership of a new breed of soldier-emperors.

II. The Goths seem to have spoken an East Germanic dialect, akin to the Scandinavian languages of the north. The Goths who came to settle in eastern Europe retained close ties with the Baltic world.

A. The homeland of the Goths was said to be the island of Gotland or the southern Swedish districts of Gautland. In the late 2nd century, the Goths crossed from their Swedish homeland into central Europe.

B. By the first quarter of the 3rd century, the Goths had reached their new homes in eastern Europe and were pressing south and southwest against Sarmatian and Germanic tribes that, in turn, raided the Roman frontiers.

C. The main direction of Gothic attacks was along the middle and upper Danube, so that the Goths had to cross Dacia. In the mid-240s, this province came under heavy pressure from the Goths and was abandoned by the Romans in 271.

III. By the mid-240s, the Goths were attacking the Roman Empire directly from their settlements in eastern Europe. Their timing was fortuitous, because the empire was preoccupied with other problems.

A. As mentioned earlier, the emperor Severus Alexander was murdered in 235. He was the last emperor of a dynasty that had ruled Rome since 193 A.D. and the last representative of political stability for Rome for the next 50 years.

B. During this 50-year period, each of the three regional armies—the Rhine, the Danube, and the Eastern army—put their candidates on the throne. Rome lost the political stability of the Augustan solution, because no dynasty was in place to take over after Severus Alexander was murdered.

C. The Rhine army put Maximinus I on the throne, a Thracian from humble origins who was known for his great strength. Maximinus was unpopular and was murdered by his own soldiers in 238 in a civil war.

D. Civil war in 238 put on the throne a young emperor named Gordian III, who was a member of the older Roman aristocratic elite. From 238–268, although most of the emperors seized power through the regional armies, they originated from the high senatorial and equestrian classes.

    E. These emperors failed to contain the Gothic threat, in part because they faced serious pressure on the Eastern frontier from the Sassanid Persians. Large numbers of military forces on the Danube had to be transferred to the East to meet the Persian threat.
        1. Roman emperors were compelled to defend the Eastern provinces where two-thirds of the population and wealth were located.
        2. In the 3rd century, the locus of imperial power shifted to the Eastern provinces, symbolized by the founding of Constantinople as the "New Rome."

IV. The Goths attacked in tandem with other Germanic peoples from Scandinavia.

    A. In the mid-240s, the literary sources mention new German tribes, notably Vandals, Gepidae, and Herulians. By the early 4th century, we hear of the Rugians, Lombards, and Burgundians, who would play important roles in the early Middle Ages.

    B. Only a single Gothic king, Kniva, is mentioned as coordinating Gothic raids in the 240s and early 250s.

    C. The Goths were assisted by the Roman civil wars. The emperor Gordian III was murdered by his army in 244, and Philip I, "the Arab," seized the throne. Philip battled the Goths on the middle and lower Danube with limited success.

    D. In 249, Trajan Decius, as governor of Moesia, defeated the Goths and was declared emperor by the Danube legions. The legions marched into northern Italy and killed Philip, leaving the Danube unprotected.

    E. The Goths thereupon attacked Dacia and the Danube provinces. In 251, Trajan Decius fell fighting the Goths at Abrittus in Lower Moesia—a humiliating defeat.

    F. The new emperor, Trebonnianus Gallus, concluded a hasty treaty with the Goths and returned to Rome to secure his position. As a result, the Goths were still free to operate along the frontier.

    G. In 253, the legions of the Lower Danube again declared their commander, Aemilian, emperor. Aemilian defeated and slew

Trebonnianus Gallus, but Aemilian, in turn, was defeated and killed by Valerian, the candidate of the Rhine army.

1. Within a decade, the Romans fought three major civil wars, and on each occasion, the Danube legions were withdrawn from the frontiers.
2. The civil wars compromised defense and drove the imperial government to debase the silver currency, thereby precipitating a monetary and fiscal crisis by the 260s.

V. The emperor Valerian, and his son and co-emperor Gallienus, battled assaults from three directions: from the Germans in the north, the Goths in Dacia and the Danube provinces, and the Persians in the east.

A. The situation worsened after 260 for two reasons. First, Valerian was captured by the Persian shah Shapur. Second, the legions of the Rhine declared as emperor Postumus, who ruled an independent regional state in the Roman West based at Treveri. Postumus gained legitimacy in the eyes of Western provincials by checking the Franks and Alemanni.

B. Gothic attacks climaxed with devastating raids in 262 and 267, when the Goths sacked the suburbs of Athens. Goths also burned the Artemisium of Ephesus, the greatest city of Asia Minor.

C. In the 280s and 290s, Gaul experienced destructive and widespread attacks by the Franks and Alemanni.

D. Gallienus was murdered in 268 by his Illyrian officers, who acclaimed Claudius II as emperor. Claudius was the first of the soldier-emperors who would halt the crisis in Rome.

E. In 268, the empire fragmented into three rival states—one in the east, opposed to Persia; the Central Empire (comprising Italy, Africa, the Danube provinces, and Asia Minor); and the northwestern provinces under the Gallo-Roman emperors.

F. Claudius died of plague after winning a significant victory against the Goths in the Balkans in 269. His successor, Aurelian, was hailed as the restorer of the Roman world. Aurelian halted the attacks on the Danube and pulled Roman forces out of Dacia; he also ended the Palmyrene and Gallo-Roman empires.

G. With the accession of the last of the soldier-emperors, Diocletian, the boundaries of Rome had been restored. Diocletian himself ended the civil wars at Rome.

©2004 The Teaching Company.

H. In the course of battling these barbarian foes in the 3rd century, the Romans had lost some strategic provincial zones in southern Germany and Dacia, and the barbarians had gained confidence and better organization to face the Romans in the 4th century.

Readings:

Burns, T. R. *A History of the Ostrogoths*.

———. *Rome and the Barbarians, 100 B.C.–400 A.D.*

Questions to Consider:

1. How humiliating were the defeats suffered at the hands of the Goths, notably the death of the emperor Trajan Decius? How destructive was the fighting from the 240s to 280s? What accounted for the success of Roman arms after 268?

2. In what ways did the barbarian threat contribute to the imperial crisis of the 3rd century? How were state and society transformed by this crisis?

Lecture Thirty
Eastern Rivals—Sassanid Persia

Scope: In 227 A.D., Ardashir, Sassanid shah of the Persians, overthrew the Parthians. The Sassanid shahs proclaimed themselves heirs of the Achaemenid Empire and condemned the Parthians and Arsacid kings as barbarian interlopers. In large part, Rome had contributed to the success of this political revolution, because repeated imperial victories had shattered Parthian power. Shahs Ardashir and Shapur I built a Near Eastern bureaucratic state exalted by the reformed monotheism based on the teachings of Zoroaster. They also overthrew the Kushans, thereby acquiring access to the nomadic horse archers, silver mines, and caravan cities of central Asia. Sassanid shahs, who fielded armies with siege and supply trains, declared their intent to expel the Romans from Asia. In 229–232, the emperor Severus Alexander had to take the field to defend the Eastern provinces. His inconclusive Persian war cost him his throne and political stability in Rome for the next half century. In 260, Shapur scored his greatest success by capturing the emperor Valerian and plundering eastern Asia Minor and Syria. Sassanid armies won victories as a result of imperial blunders. The legions and cities of the Roman East rallied and expelled the Persians. Briefly, Odenathus, caravan prince of Palmyra, and his wife, Zenobia, made their city the capital of an Eastern Roman state. In 273, Aurelian restored unity to the Roman world, and his successors humbled the Persians by 300. Henceforth, however, Rome faced a rival empire, rather than a barbarian foe, in the East.

Outline

I. The Sassanid state was the creation of two shahs, Ardashir (227–241) and Shapur I (241–272). These rulers built an effective bureaucratic state based on the traditions of the Hellenistic world, as well as the earlier Persian and Near Eastern empires.

    A. To some extent, the Persian shahs owed their success to the Romans, especially to the emperor Trajan and his strategy for defeating the Parthians. The weakening of the Parthian kings by the Romans enabled their overthrow by the Persian shahs.

- **B.** Further, the Sassanid rulers had legitimacy in the eyes of the majority of Iranians. The shahs adopted the symbols and traditions of Persian monarchs from the 6th century B.C. and sponsored Zoroastrianism, which served as one of the pillars of Sassanid power and eventually became a state religion.
- **C.** The bureaucratic state of the shahs, based on the support of the Iranian landed elites, replaced the loose hegemony that the Parthian kings had exercised over the various peoples of Iran.
- **D.** The Sassnid army was accompanied by disciplined infantry, war elephants from India, and siege and supply trains. The shahs had far greater financial and military resources to field such armies than the Parthian kings.

II. Zoroastrianism, the religious ideology of the shahs, explains why they were so determined to go to war with Rome.
- **A.** According to the literary sources, in 229, Ardashir I sent a message to the then-reigning emperor of Rome, Severus Alexander, that the Romans could have peace with Persia if they withdrew from Asia. The Persian shah demanded that the Romans relinquish control of Asia Minor, Armenia, the Syrian provinces, and Egypt—the locus of financial strength in the Roman world.
- **B.** The Persians had visions of restoring the empire of Cyrus the Great from the 6th century B.C. When the Romans refused, war erupted, and Severus Alexander had to take the field.
- **C.** Persian expeditions were expensive and difficult. The Persians attacked imperial territory in 230, but the Romans were not in a position to launch a counteroffensive for another two years. Severus Alexander had limited success in this first Persian war. In 232, he was forced to negotiate with Ardashir in order to return west and face Germanic attacks on the Rhine.
- **D.** The ensuing frontier and civil wars allowed the new shah, Shapur, to reopen the offensive against the Roman Eastern provinces. Shapur waged three great campaigns, which are recorded on a monumental inscription in southern Persia.
    1. Shapur's first efforts were directed toward the Roman fortresses in Mesopotamia, which had been organized into a

network in 198–200. The fortresses ultimately repelled the Sassanids' efforts to capture Syria and Asia Minor, but the attacks were serious.

2. In 242, Gordian III had to take the field but was murdered before his army could go into action. His successor, Philip the Arab, arranged a truce with Shapur and agreed to pay him 20,000 gold aurei to break off the operation.

3. Roman civil war in 253 allowed Shapur to renew his offensive and, according to his monumental inscription, he sacked Antioch, third city of the Roman Empire.

4. The emperor Valerian waged an inconclusive Persian campaign in 254–256. When Shapur launched a third campaign in 258, Valerian again took the field, but he was captured near Carrhae in 260. The demoralized Eastern legions failed to check the Persians from sacking cities of Syria and Asia Minor.

5. The Eastern army rallied under two new emperors, Macrianus and Quietus, and drove the Persians out, but Shapur retained his booty and captives and celebrated the third campaign as a victory.

E. In 260, the Roman Eastern frontier was disorganized, but Shapur could not exploit his victory because Rome commanded the loyalty of the city elites of the East.

III. In 260, an enigmatic figure, Odenathus, emerged to save the Roman East.

A. Odenathus was a merchant prince from the city of Palmyra, which had dominated the caravan trade running into the Sassanid Empire. By the middle of the 2nd century, Palmyra had adopted Greek civic-style institutions.

B. Odenathus, a product of this composite provincial society, commanded operations against the Persians, launching an offensive against Ctesiphon that compelled Shapur to sue for peace by 264.

C. Odenathus, down to his death in 266/7, never aspired to rule as emperor, for he, and later his wife Zenobia, lacked legitimacy among the elite classes of the Roman East.

D. At his accession in 270, Aurelian refused to accept Vaballathus, the son of Zenobia, as an imperial colleague. In 271, Palmyrene

forces moved to secure Egypt and Asia Minor, but in 272, Aurelian swept across Asia Minor and capture Palmyra.
- **E.** Aurelian reorganized the Eastern frontier, and Diocletian constructed the line of desert forts and highways known as the *Strata Diocletiana*.
- **F.** In 298–300, Galerius, the Caesar of Diocletian, wrested from Shah Narses strategic fortresses on the Upper Euphrates that closed the fighting of the 3rd century.

Readings:

Isaac, Benjamin. *The Limits of Empire: The Roman Army in the East.*

Watson, A. *Aurelian and the Third Century.*

Questions to Consider:

1. How did the first shahs, Ardashir, Shapur, and Narses, use war against Rome as a means to advance their dynasties and personal reputations? Why did they fail to conquer the Eastern Roman provinces? How important was the opposition of the Armenians to Sassanid Persia?
2. What accounted for Roman setbacks and defeats on the Eastern frontier after 230? How did these Eastern wars transform the Roman state and society? What accounted for the ultimate success of Roman arms in the East?

Lecture Thirty-One
Rome and the Barbarians in the Fourth Century

Scope: At the opening of the 4th century, barbarian invasion and civil wars had militarized life in the frontier provinces. Many Romanized provincials had fled threatened zones, while German and Sarmatian barbarians were settled in depopulated districts. The *limes* bristled with fortifications and signal towers constructed to inhibit movement of barbarian invaders within the empire, rather than to act as bases for strikes across the frontier. The emperor Constantine stationed field armies near imperial capitals, while the frontiers were manned by second-class formations (*limitanei*). Henceforth, frontier wars were fought on Roman soil. Consequently, provincial society experienced repeated raids, even though trade and cultural exchange resumed. Two major changes in Roman society dictated future relations between Romans and barbarians. Diocletian restored order by exalting the power of the emperor and forged the late Roman autocracy known as the *Dominate*. Thereafter, honor and rank were defined by service to the emperor, rather than patriotic service to one's native city. In 324, Constantine founded Constantinople, "New Rome," and sponsored Christianity as the favored religion of his court. As a result, all barbarians, who were treated as dreaded foes in official iconography, could become civilized imperial servants by embracing Christianity and professing loyalty to the emperor. Barbarian peoples could, thus, enter the Roman world without acquiring a Roman identity.

Outline

I. This lecture explains the changes that occurred in the Roman world as a result of the civil and frontier wars of the 3rd century.

   A. Two emperors were fundamentally involved with these changes. One was the last of the pagan emperors, Diocletian (284–305), and the other was Constantine (306–337), the first Christian emperor.

   B. These two emperors are often seen as creating the style of late-Roman government known as the *Dominate*. In this government, the emperor was an autocrat, styled as *dominus noster*, "our lord."

The government was also associated with the exaltation of imperial power, the construction of a new bureaucracy of civil officials, the reorganization of the army, and the establishment of new policies concerning the barbarian peoples.

C. In many ways, Constantine built on the tradition of Diocletian, but the two emperors fundamentally differed. Diocletian came from a generation of soldier-emperors and looked to Augustus as his model. Constantine, as the first Christian emperor, created an imperial order.

II. Diocletian was a tough Balkan soldier who understood that the extent of the barbarian threat required an imperial presence on each of the key frontiers.

A. Diocletian shared imperial power with three colleagues, and the four emperors reigned together in an arrangement known as the *Tetrarchy* ("rule of four").

1. In 285, Diocletian elevated his comrade-in-arms Maximianus to rule as Augustus of the West, residing in the city of Milan. Diocletian himself ruled from his capital at Nicomedia (in modern Turkey), close to the Danube frontier.

2. In 293, Diocletian and Maximianus adopted sons to serve as junior emperors (Caesars), Galerius (293–305) in Antioch and Constantius I Chlorus (293–305) in Trier.

B. The Tetrarchy gave Rome a measure of stability for 20 years and allowed Diocletian to return the government to a sound monetary footing. Under this arrangement, efforts were also made to rebuild cities and frontier fortifications and to revive the ancient gods.

C. Unfortunately, civil war erupted in just over a year after the retirement of Diocletian and Maximianus.

1. Galerius and Constantius assumed power in 305 and, in turn, appointed their own junior emperors.

2. The appointments passed over Constantine I, the son of Constantius, who died while campaigning in Britain in 306. The Western army immediately declared Constantine I as emperor.

3. Constantine accepted the position and, in doing so, condemned the Roman Empire to another round of civil wars.

- **D.** These civil wars ended in 324, when Constantine defeated his last opponent Licinius and united the empire under his sole authority. These wars also differed from those in the 3rd century.
    1. First, the empire was not assaulted by the same barbarian threats that had taken advantage of the civil wars in the 3rd century.
    2. Further, in the 4th century, emperors ruled regional states and waged long-term civil wars. The control of Rome was needed for legitimacy so that command of powerful regional armies was essential.
- **E.** These changes transformed the Roman monarchy and society.

III. Constantine overhauled the civil and military administration of the empire.
- **A.** The Senate was no longer important to the central administration of the government. Emperors distanced themselves from members of the aristocracy, preferring the services of bureaucrats who could collect taxes and enforce the emperor's will in the provinces but would not offer any challenges.
- **B.** The size of imperial administration was greatly increased. In 200 A.D., the Roman imperial government might have had 3,000 high officials; in 320 A.D., there were at least 35,000.
    1. A new palace administration was created around the person of the emperor. Many of the key positions were staffed by eunuchs, who posed no threat to the emperor.
    2. The civil and military administration was divided. Provincial administration was reorganized into three tiers. Instead of 35 provinces, 125 were recognized; these provinces were grouped into regional districts known as *dioceses*. The dioceses were further grouped into four *prefecturates*.
    3. Notions of honor, as well as the client-patron relationship, were inverted in the new government. In the early empire, an individual had to have high status and honor to serve the state. Under Constantine and later emperors, high status was the reward for serving the state, which resulted in mismanagement and corruption.
    4. Finally, under Constantine, it behooved officials to convert to Christianity. After 324, Christians had control of the court, the administration, and the army. In 325, at the Council of Nicaea,

Constantine defined Christianity and created the imperial church.
- **C.** The army, the other pillar of imperial power, was reforged by Constantine.
    1. Diocletian premised his army on the traditions of the legions, although these were divided into garrison units and vexillations, or battle units. More cavalry were recruited, but the imperial army relied primarily on infantry until the 6th century.
    2. In the 4th century, the mission of the army had changed from defending the frontiers to defending the emperor.
    3. The *Notitia Dignitatum*, army roles compiled in 406–423, tells us that imperial forces were classified into the privileged *comitanensis*, the "comrades" who comprised the emperor's field army, and the *limitanei*, who guarded the frontier. This division probably came out of the regional civil wars, in which the emperor needed an effective field army to battle his rivals.
    4. Both the field and the frontier armies were increasingly being manned by barbarians. There were few ethnic units in the 4th century, but many in the officer corps carried Germanic names. The army was a route for social mobility for the barbarians in a way that it had not been in the 3rd century.
    5. This change was the result of the bloodletting in the civil wars of the 3rd century, because few veterans survived to train recruits for the new wave of civil wars in the early 4th century. The lack of adequate training also explains changes in Roman arms and tactics, such as simplification of the armor and helmets and the replacement of the *gladius* with a thrusting spear.
    6. The division of the army into garrison and field units also led to a steady erosion of frontier territories over the course of the 4th century. By the mid-4th century, the Roman armies no longer launched deep strikes into barbarian lands; the fighting took place on imperial territory.
    7. The impact of Christianity on the imperial army's fighting ability is still an open question. Most soldiers probably saw the new imperial standard, the *labarum*, as a talisman of the house of Constantine, rather than a Christian symbol. But with

the end of the traditions of the legions and the shift in religious loyalties, Roman soldiers no longer had the certainty in their divine protectors that they had in the Principate.
8. The late Roman army lacked the discipline and traditions of the camp of Hadrian. In the late 4th century, members of the literate class called for a return to the *antiqua legio* ("ancient legion") to defeat the barbarians, but those appeals failed.

Readings:

Jones, A. H. M. *The Decline of the Ancient World.*

Matthews, John. *The Roman Empire of Ammianus.*

Questions to Consider:

1. What were the significant changes in the Roman state and society that transformed the relationship with barbarians in the 4th century? In what ways did the emperors Diocletian and Constantine reshape this society of the Dominate?

2. How did the changes in the imperial army and frontier defense compromise the integrity of the Roman world? Why did emperors pursue new military and frontier policies? What were the primary threats and concerns of emperors down to the reign of Valens?

Lecture Thirty-Two
From Foes to Federates

Scope: During the reign of Constantius II, the Goths and their East Germanic kin embraced Arian Christianity through the efforts of Ulfilas, "the apostle to the Goths." Ulfilas adapted the Greek alphabet to the Gothic language to translate the Bible and created a literary culture. The Goths, whose society was transformed by the booty and captives taken in raids of the 3rd century, acquired an ethnic identity. From the mid-4th century on, Goths, Franks, and Alemanni came to monopolize imperial military commands. Constantius II recruited more tribal regiments of barbarians, known as "federates" (*foederati*), into imperial field armies. Federates, who served under their own leaders and used their own weapons and tactics, were settled in depopulated frontier lands. The new arrangements carried dangers. In 350–353, the Western army revolted under the usurper Magnentius, an officer of barbarian origin. The ensuing civil war opened the frontiers to barbarian migrations for the next 15 years; these served as the dress rehearsal for the collapse of the Roman West in the 5th century. In 375, the emperor Valens admitted 100,000 Goths into the Balkans as federates, refugees from a terrifying new nomadic race, the Huns, who had just overthrown the Gothic kingdom—an event long remembered in Scandinavian epic. Corrupt imperial officials drove these Goths into rebellion. On August 8, 378, the Gothic rebels annihilated the Eastern Roman field army and slew the emperor Valens at Adrianople. For the second time, the Goths plunged the Roman Empire into a political crisis.

Outline

I. In this lecture, we shall discuss the relationship between the barbarian foes of Rome and the new imperial order created by Constantine in the early 4th century.

    A. The northern barbarians were eventually transformed into *federates*, or allies. Specifically, the term *foederati* refers to German tribes who were recruited as ethnic military units to fight under contract for the Roman emperor.

B. This lecture also looks at how well the Dominate coped with barbarians in the East, that is, the Sassanid shahs of Persia, and in the north, the Germanic barbarians who were now organized into confederations led by kings. In this Germanic group we include the Goths, who at the time, were a dominant power in eastern Europe.

II. We begin with the Persians. The late Roman army reformed by Constantine was tested in a war against Persia in the generation after Constantine's death—and found wanting.

    A. Shah Shapur II (309–379) challenged three Roman emperors: Constantius II (337–361), Julian (360–363), and Valens (364–378). They fought the Persians with an imperial army suffering sundry problems.

    B. In the 350s, Shapur reopened the wars of conquest against Rome and besieged the cities of Mesopotamia; these operations climaxed in 359 with the capture of the fortress of Amida in southeastern Turkey.

        1. The successes of Shapur forced Constantius II to mount a major eastern expedition. As in the 3rd century, such a campaign required the withdrawal of large numbers of forces from Europe and posed a heavy financial burden for Rome.

        2. As Constantius was engaged in fighting the Persians, the army of the Rhine rebelled and declared Julian the Apostate as emperor in 360. Julian had been reared as a Christian but had later secretly converted to paganism.

        3. In 361, Constantius died of illness, and Julian as sole emperor inherited the Persian war so that, ironically, he withdrew forces from the West.

    C. In spring 363, Julian led his main column down the Euphrates, but he failed to capture Ctesiphon or to draw Shapur into decisive battle.

        1. To some extent, the blame can be placed on Julian's own failure in leadership. He timed the campaign poorly, and his army suffered from lack of provisions and water. Julian was forced to withdraw, and he was killed in a skirmish on June 26, 364.

      2. Jovian, elected emperor, evacuated the army under truce whereby he surrendered to Shapur the strategic fortresses of Roman Mesopotamia.

  D. This defeat of the Eastern field army proved significant. Rome relinquished the provinces gained in 300, and in 385–386, Theodosius I agreed to an unfavorable partition of Armenia whereby Persia gained most of the former kingdom. From 400 on, Persia was occupied in dealing with nomadic barbarians on its own frontiers and could not pursue further operations against Rome.

III. Defeat in Persia, however, had repercussions across the empire and seriously affected the northern frontiers.

  A. By 300 A.D., the Germans had gained a great deal of confidence, along with better organization and equipment, from their fighting in the 3rd century.

      1. In addition, ever more Germans were recruited into the reorganized Roman army and served in the *comitanensis*, not in auxiliary units. These soldiers retained their German identity far more strongly than they did in the old imperial army.

      2. We read in the history of Ammianus Marcellinus that many of the German officers retained their tribal names. There was also an alarming tendency for these leaders to operate on both sides of the frontier, as both Germanic kings and Roman officers.

      3. These changes in the army might have been partly to blame for Julian's failure. The field forces did not perform to standard and were unable to carry out effective siege warfare.

  B. The defeat in Persia also compromised the northern defenses.

      1. In 350, the Western army rebelled under Magnentius in response to the imperial policy of halting sacrifices.

      2. Magnentius was, by origin, a barbarian and retained ties to his kinsmen. He recruited Franks and Alemanni from the other side of the frontier for the rebellion.

      3. The rebellion forced Constantius to suspend his Persian war and to march west in 352–353. With the defeat of Magnentius, Constantius returned to the East.

- **4.** With the departure of Constantius, the Western frontiers collapsed. From 355 on, barbarians surged into Roman territory, penetrating deep into Gaul.
- **5.** Constantius sent his cousin Julian to restore the West. In 357, Julian won a decisive victory over the Alemanni near Strasbourg. He claimed to have defeated a coalition of 35,000 men led by 7 kings.
- **6.** Julian reorganized the defenses of Gaul by settling Franks as federates on the lower Rhine.

C. The frontier of the Danube also showed some of the same changes that can be documented in the Rhineland.
- **1.** The Danube frontier changed as a result of a decision made by the emperor Valens in 375. Valens and his brother, Valentinian, had been elected jointly by the army in 364; Valentinian ruled in the West, and Valens took charge of the East and the lower Danube.
- **2.** In 375–377, Valens admitted 100,000 Goths who had petitioned for refuge from the Huns in the empire. The Goths had been settled in eastern Europe as members of a confederation.
- **3.** Between 370–375, the Gothic king and his army were annihilated by an attack of two nomadic peoples, the Alans and the Huns. The Goths fled before these invaders to the banks of the Danube.
- **4.** Valens accepted the Goths into the empire and settled them in the old province of Moesia. The Roman authorities, however, could not feed or house such large numbers of immigrants; abuses by corrupt officials and starvation drove the Goths into rebellion in 377.
- **5.** As Goths plundered the Balkans, Valens had to suspend his eastern operations. On August 9, 378, Valens engaged the Goths near the city of Adrianople.
- **6.** The Roman army became entangled in assaulting the Gothic infantry, and so lost cohesion when the Gothic cavalry surprised the Roman army in the rear. The emperor Valens was killed, and 20,000 Roman soldiers fell.
- **7.** Gratian, the surviving emperor in the West, appointed Theodosius I in the East. Theodosius came to terms with the federates and returned them to their territory. By 382, the

Goths had been given land and terms and enrolled in the Eastern army, but they had learned an important lesson: Rebellion was effective in extorting concessions from Rome.

Readings:

Elton, Hugh. *Warfare in Roman Europe, A.D. 350–425.*

Lenski, N. *Failure of Empire: Valens and the Roman State in the Fourth Century A.D.*

Questions to Consider:

1. How did the clash between Rome and Sassanid Persia in the early 4th century influence changes in Roman policy on the frontiers? What weaknesses in the late Roman army were revealed by the failure of the emperor Julian's eastern expedition in 363?

2. Why did the Germanic confederations pose a more powerful threat to Rome after 300? In what ways did the imperial government promote the formation of these tribal identities and rise of tribal kings? Why did the Roman emperors come to rely ever more on tribal federate armies for their field forces?

Lecture Thirty-Three
Imperial Crisis and Decline

Scope: Theodosius I, elevated as emperor in the East following Adrianople, received the submission of the Goths, who were restored to their lands on promise of military service. Roman field armies were steadily filled with barbarian mercenaries tied by personal loyalty to the emperor. The East Germans, devoted to Arian Christianity, were divided further from other Christians after Theodosius upheld the Nicene confession in 381. On Theodosius's death, the courts of his sons, Arcadius at Constantinople and Honorius at Milan, clashed. Stilicho, commander of the Western army, intrigued to dominate the two courts and marry into the imperial family. Stilicho advanced his personal ends by exploiting the threat of Alaric and his Gothic federates, who raided the Balkans in 395–397. In 400–402, Alaric and his Goths migrated across the Balkans and entered Italy. Stilicho, who preferred to humble, rather than destroy, Alaric, withdrew field armies from Gaul to Italy. In the winter of 408, Germanic tribes migrated en masse across the frozen Rhine, overrunning the northwestern and Iberian provinces. Honorius, who ordered the execution of Stilicho, was powerless to prevent a Gothic sack of Rome in 410. Alaric's Goths, henceforth known as Visigoths under his successors, were granted an independent kingdom in Aquitaine with rights to collect taxes and assign lands. Within a generation, the Western Roman Empire was dismembered by similar treaties into Teutonic kingdoms, while the imperial court at Ravenna fell into the hands of barbarian generalissimos who played the role of king makers.

Outline

I. This lecture examines the implications of the Battle of Adrianople in 378, in which the Goths defeated the Eastern Roman field army.

  A. The defeat at Adrianople proved decisive in retrospect, as a result of the arrangements that followed immediately afterward.

  B. In 379, the emperor Theodosius was commissioned by his colleague, the emperor Gratian, to take charge of the Eastern provinces and come to terms with the rebel Goths. Theodosius's solution was to renegotiate the military contracts of the Goths, settle them back in their quarters along the Danube, and ensure that they received sufficient provisions.

C. Under Theodosius, the Goths became one of the major elements of the Roman imperial field army. They were recruited in tribal regiments and usually fought under their own kings.

D. In 392, the Western army staged yet another revolt, perhaps in response to Christian legislation. Theodosius marched west with an army that included 20,000 Goths and won a total victory against the Western army at the Battle of Frigidus. This was seen as a vindication of both Theodosius and the Christian God.

E. At Frigidus, two talented officers of Theodosius served: Alaric, the future Goth king who would sack Rome, and Stilicho, a Vandal-Roman provincial who would defend Rome. By 395, Stilicho was supreme commander (*magister militum*) under Theodosius.

F. Theodosius was a charismatic soldier-emperor who commanded the loyalty of the Germanic kings and officers. Without such an emperor, German warriors could transfer their loyalty, as many were to do in the crisis after 395.

G. The bureaucratic elites, who were denied command of armies, employed German tribal armies in rebellions from the imperial governments, but in so doing, they allowed the Germans to carve out their own kingdoms.

II. Theodosius died in January of 395 and was succeeded by two sons, Arcadius (395–408) and Honorius (395–423). The succession crisis that ensued revealed the institutional and military weaknesses of the late Roman state.

A. Arcadius was 17 years old and ruled the wealthier half of the Roman Empire from Constantinople. The emperor in the West was Honorius, who was 11 years old. Both young emperors were in the hands of ministers.

B. The Eastern court was divided into factions, while in the West, Stilicho had at his command virtually all the field armies of the Roman world. Stilicho also claimed that Theodosius had named him regent for the two brothers.

- **C.** The Eastern court was not inclined to be dominated by the barbarian Stilicho, who was determined to link himself to the imperial family through marriage.
- **D.** Stilicho had an opportunity to intervene in the East, because the Eastern government had alienated Alaric, a talented officer in the army and king of the Visigoths.
    1. When Alaric was passed over for command of the Eastern army, he attacked Thrace, Macedonia, and Greece in 395-397. The Eastern government summoned Stilicho and the Western army for salvation.
    2. In handling this crisis, Stilicho revealed that his primary motivation was personal ambition. He could have destroyed the Goths on several occasions but, instead, decided to negotiate.
    3. In 397, Stilicho gave Alaric the position of commander of a regional army (*dux*) and settled the Goths as federates in Epirus.
    4. This arrangement revealed that a tribal army by rebellion could force terms from the Roman imperial government.

III. In 400 A.D., the civil aristocracy in Constantinople reasserted itself in a popular riot against the Gothic soldiers quartered in the city by Stilicho. At the same time, the Eastern government encouraged the Goths to move west as a way of embarrassing Stilicho and the Western government.

- **A.** In 404, the Goths entered Italy through the Julian Alps. Again, Stilicho chose not to destroy the Goths in northern Italy, because he hoped to negotiate. He did, however, withdraw large numbers of field forces from the Rhine and upper Danube, many of whom were Germanic soldiers.
- **B.** The northern provinces were left open to German migration. On New Year's Eve in 406, the Rhine froze and barbarians moved across in great numbers. The frontier defenses collapsed, and Stilicho was discredited with the ruling classes at Rome.
- **C.** Honorius decided to remove the Western court from Milan to Ravenna on the east coast of Italy. This move underlined the fact that the Western government was unable to defend its vital frontier provinces.

D. In 408, Honorius had Stilicho arrested and executed. Most of the field army consisted of barbarian tribal regiments who owed their loyalty to Stilicho; as a result of his death, these regiments defected.

E. Alaric, as leader of the only military force left in Italy, pressured the imperial government by attacking Rome.
  1. From 408–410, Alaric conducted three different blockades of Rome. His goal was to gain a command from the government so that he could legitimize his tribal regiments as a Roman army and reward his followers with land or money.
  2. Honorius refused to deal with Alaric, who captured and sacked Rome on August 24–26, 410. The Goths retired into southern Italy where Alaric died in late 410.
  3. Athaulf, Alaric's brother-in-law, led the Goths (henceforth known as Visigoths) out of Italy as imperial federates who were to clear Gaul of the barbarian invaders who had immigrated there in 406-407.

F. In 406–407, Franks had migrated into northern Gaul; Burgundians settled in central Gaul; and Vandals, Sueves, and Alans entered Spain. As imperial power broke down in these regions, the cities reacted in various ways. Some of them bought off the Germans with food; others hired them on as soldiers in local rivalries.

G. The only effective field army in the Western Empire after 406 was in Britain. This army rebelled in 407 and crossed over into Gaul, leaving Britain unprotected. The Roman administration there broke down over the next generation.

H. In 411–418, the Visigoths restored order in Gaul and Spain. They became federates and were rewarded with territory in southern Gaul that would today be the Aquitaine.
  1. Under an imperial treaty (*foedus*), the Goths were to receive one-third of the tax revenues from surrounding Roman provinces to support themselves as a field army.
  2. In effect, the Visigoths were settled as an armed nation, and the foundation was laid for the creation of a territorial kingdom.

I. At the death of Honorius in 423, the Western court had lost its possessions beyond the Mediterranean core. In 425, Valentinian III, nephew of Honorius, ruled under the tutelage of a new *magister militum*, Aetius. To control German federates residing in the Western Empire, Aetius called in a frightening new barbarian ally, the Huns.

Readings:

Burns, T. S. *Barbarians within the Gates of Rome: A Study of Roman Military Policy and the Barbarians, ca. 375-425 A.D.*

Heather, Peter. *Goths and Romans, 332–489*.

Questions to Consider:

1. What was the frontier and military situation faced by the two imperial governments in 395? Could a charismatic soldier-emperor have met the crisis? How responsible were the weak-willed emperors Arcadius and Honorius in precipitating a crisis? What institutional weaknesses contributed to the crisis?

2. What were the ambitions of Stilicho and Alaric, and was it a matter of historical irony that they were cast in the roles of defender and sacker of Rome? How did the migration of the Visigoths and their settlement in Gaul transform them into a nation?

Lecture Thirty-Four
Attila and the Huns

Scope: The Huns were the first steppe nomads from central Asia who arrived in eastern Europe to play a pivotal role in the course of medieval history. They were to be followed, in turn, by Avars, Bulgars, Khazars, Pechenegs, Cumans, and Mongols. In 370, Huns migrated westward from their homes north of the Caspian Sea. They were one of many Turkic-speaking tribes who displaced the Iranian-speaking nomads on the Eurasian steppes between the 4th and 6th centuries. The Huns smashed the Gothic kingdom, whose legendary king, Ermanaric, committed suicide. By 380, the Huns dominated the southern Russian grasslands and had subjected the barbarians of central Europe. Rome initially employed the Huns as allies to keep German federates in check. In 437, on imperial orders, Huns annihilated Burgundians settled around Worms—an incident remembered in Germanic legend. Attila, once sole king of the Huns, launched devastating raids into the Balkan provinces of the Eastern Empire in 441–443 and 447. The raids gained Attila the sobriquet "Scourge of God," as well as captives and booty. Foremost, Attila dictated treaties to the court at Constantinople requiring tribute in gold and abandonment of the Danubian *limes*. In 451, Attila invaded Roman Gaul, to the dismay of the Western court and its commander, Aetius, who had premised imperial policy on an alliance with the Huns. At Châlons, Aetius and Visigothic federates checked the Huns. The next year, Attila halted his invasion of Italy on an appeal of Pope Leo I, and Attila's premature death led to the collapse of the Hun Empire. But the fury of the Huns ensured that the Germanic kingdoms of the West would succeed to Rome.

Outline

I. This lecture deals with the Huns and their most famous king, Attila, the "Scourge of God." Ironically, the Huns never conquered the Roman Empire, but they played an important role in shaping the political and cultural landscape of the world that came immediately after the breakup of the Western Empire.

- **A.** The Romans and Germans saw the Huns as a new people who were outside the stereotypes of barbarians that the Romans had passed on for centuries.
- **B.** The Huns are first mentioned in the accounts of Ammianus Marcellinus. Writing in the 380s–390s, he describes them as "abnormally savage." Based on this account and scant archaeological evidence, the Huns are believed to be the first Turkomen to enter eastern Europe.
- **C.** Some modern scholars have attempted to identify the Huns with a group known as the Hsiung-nu in Chinese sources. Other than the similarity in names and the fact that both groups were Turkish speakers, there is no evidence to support this identification.
    1. The Hsiung-nu are found in Chinese accounts from the 2nd century B.C. to the 2nd century A.D., in the Han dynasty, which was roughly contemporary with the late Roman Republic and early Roman Empire.
    2. The construction of the Great Wall and migration of the Hsiung-nu to the west are often erroneously cited as explanations for the fall of the Roman Empire.
    3. As mentioned earlier, most of the Great Wall as it stands today was constructed in the 17th and 18th centuries. In antiquity, the Great Wall was a set of ditches and fortifications, comparable to what the Romans were building in Britain and Dacia.
    4. The Chinese became adept at handling these nomads by mounting cavalry, usually recruited from Turkic or Mongolian allies, in combination with infantry armed with crossbows. These military formations were far more effective in controlling nomadic warriors than the wall.
    5. Indeed, the Hsiung-nu as a coalition had disintegrated by 150 A.D., but the Chinese efforts to control half of the Silk Road caravan trade probably did assist in the ethnic transformation of central Asia.

II. In 375, the Huns were comparatively recent arrivals on the eastern steppes between the Don and Volga Rivers. They allied with Iranian Alans to crush the Goths.

- **A.** These Huns were probably related to other Turkomen groups, such as the Hephthalites ("White Huns") who attacked the Persian Empire.
- **B.** The Hun victories in 375 sent the first wave of Gothic migration into the Balkan provinces.
- **C.** By 395, the Huns had subjected the Alans of the southern Russian steppes. They then poured over the Caucasus and attacked into the Near East. St. Jerome, writing in Bethlehem, identifies the Huns with the Four Horsemen of the Apocalypse.
- **D.** At first, the Romans used the Huns as allies to pressure German tribes. By 400 A.D., the Huns had settled into the lower Danube and expanded the range of their attacks.
    1. The Huns were a nomadic warrior elite who exacted tribute from the agriculturalists, the people in the Russian forest zones, and the Dacians involved in mining operations. They also subjected a number of Germanic tribes, including several groups of Goths.
    2. In 422, the then-reigning king of the Huns, Ruga (also Rua or Rugila), crossed the lower Danube, devastated Thrace, and exacted 350 pounds of gold from the imperial government. This was the first serious attack of the Huns into imperial territory, and it came just as the Western Empire was collapsing.
    3. Ruga was succeeded by two of his nephews, Attila and Bleda. Attila murdered his brother, seized the kingship, and welded the Hun tribes together as a *khan*.

III. Before Attila, the Huns had been primarily interested in blackmailing the Roman Empire and had hired themselves under contract as federates for the Romans. Indeed, the entire military force of the Western imperial government was premised on this alliance with the Huns from 425–450.

- **A.** Attila did not seek to conquer the Roman Empire, but he instead wished to extend the sway of his domains. He also milked the Roman government in the east for gold.
- **B.** In any military operation, Attila had speed and surprise on his side and was skilled in gathering intelligence from merchants, diplomats, and envoys. He timed his invasions carefully, generally when the imperial field armies were fighting elsewhere.

- **C.** Unlike the Goths, the Huns learned siege warfare. In 441–443 and 447, Attila commanded devastating raids into the Roman Balkans and captured cities with siege equipment. In constructing such equipment, it is clear that Attila augmented his army with the skills of his captives and subjected peoples.
- **D.** In their attacks, the Huns were checked by the Theodosian Walls, which had been constructed by the Praetorian prefect Anthemius as the defense of Constantinople.
    1. The first obstacle in these fortifications was a moat (*fossa*), 60 feet wide and 25 feet deep. Next came the outer walls, which were 25 feet high and 10 feet thick and were guarded by towers of about 40 feet high. The inner walls were 40 feet tall, guard by towers that were 60 feet tall.
    2. Attila discovered that the capital could not be taken. The Theodosian Walls cut off the peninsular triangle of Constantinople, forming an island that could be supplied by sea.
- **E.** When Theodosius II died in 450, he was succeeded by his sister, Aelia Pulcheria, who married Marcian, a tough general from the Balkans. Marcian refused to deal with Attila.
    1. Simultaneously, Honoria, the elder sister of Valentinian III, appealed to Attila to "rescue" her in the West. Attila interpreted this as a marriage proposal and demanded half of the Roman Empire as a dowry.
    2. When Valentinian refused, Attila invaded Gaul with a huge barbarian army. The only way that the Roman commander, Aetius, could oppose this onslaught was to appeal to the Visigoths in southern Gaul for assistance.
    3. In 451, the two armies collided at the Battle of Châlons. The king of the Goths, Theoderic, fell, but the Huns were checked. Attila retreated to his capital, but in the next year, he invaded Italy.
    4. In 452, two senior senators and Pope Leo I were sent as emissaries to meet Attila on the banks of the Po. Attila was persuaded to retire, but he vowed to come back and settle with the Romans.
    5. Attila returned to his capital near Budapest and married a new wife, Ildico. In celebration of this marriage, he drank to

excess, burst a blood vessel, and died. His new wife was accused of murdering Attila and immediately killed.

F. With Attila's death, the Hun Empire quickly collapsed. This had been a great barbarian state, but it was held together by a charismatic ruler and had no institutional basis to sustain it. The experience of Attila, however, proved decisive.

1. This experience confirmed that the Germanic territorial kingdoms that were emerging with the death of Honorius would succeed to the Western Roman world.
2. In 454, Valentinian was murdered, bringing to an end the line of legitimate Western emperors. The last of the Western emperors would be deposed in 476; with one exception, they were nothing more than figureheads of the *magister militum*.

Readings:

Gordon, C. D. *The Age of Attila: Fifth-Century Byzantium and the Barbarians.*

Maencehn-Helfen, O. J. *The World of the Huns: Studies in their History and Culture.*

Questions to Consider:

1. What were the aims and achievements of Attila the Hun? How much did Attila owe his success to the indifferent leadership of Theodosius II and Valentinian III? Did Attila deserve his reputation as the "Scourge of God"?
2. In what ways did Attila determine the course of the barbarian world that followed the collapse of the Western Roman Empire?

Lecture Thirty-Five
Justinian and the Barbarians

Scope: With the collapse of the Hun Empire, Germanic federates consolidated kingdoms in the Western Roman Empire. Anglo-Saxons overran Britain, driving Celtic provincials into Wales, Cornwall, and Brittany. Franks and Burgundians occupied northern and eastern Gaul, respectively. The Visigoths conquered Spain; the Vandals founded a kingdom in North Africa. In 476, Odoacer, barbarian generalissimo in Italy, deposed the last Western emperor, Romulus Augustus. At Constantinople, Roman emperors, who ruled over the wealthy Greek-speaking provinces of the East, treated these barbarian kingdoms as their allies. Hence, the emperor Zeno commissioned Theoderic and his Ostrogoths to replace Odoacer in Italy in 489–491. Justinian, the last great Roman emperor, pursued a policy of reconquest to reverse the military decisions of the 5th century. A consummate diplomat, Justinian inherited a full treasury and a professional army. He also had a brilliant commander in Belisarius, who destroyed the Vandal kingdom in 533–534. His stunning victories over the Ostrogoths promised equal success in Italy. But a Persian invasion in 540, the outbreak of plague, and the rally of the Goths by Totila prolonged the fighting in Italy. The Gothic war ruined Classical Italy, bankrupted the imperial treasury, and ended plans of recovering the Western provinces. Within a generation, Justinian's restored Roman world was shaken by new migrations of barbarians that ended the Classical world.

Outline

I. This lecture covers the political and cultural situation that emerged in the former Western Empire at the end of the 5th century and beginning of the 6th. We will also look at the Eastern emperor Justinian (527–565), who dominated the 6th century.

    A. Justinian's efforts to reverse the political and military decisions of the 5th century and retake the Western provinces were ultimately unsuccessful, but in these efforts, he transformed the Mediterranean world and northwestern Europe.

- **B.** After Justinian's death in 565, the empire contracted to only the Anatolian and Greek core, centered on Constantinople. The role of Rome as the major intermediary with the barbarian peoples ended.
- **C.** In 476, the last Western Roman emperor, Romulus Augustus, was deposed by the German Odoacer, who ruled Italy as a representative of Emperor Zeno in Constantinople. The events that followed were billed as a reunification of the Roman Empire, even though the Western provinces were out of the hands of imperial administration.

II. From Justinian's viewpoint in 527, the changes in the Roman Empire might not have seemed as dramatic as they do to us today.
- **A.** Except in Britain, the Germanic tribes had settled in the former Western provinces and Italy under legal treaties with either the Western or Eastern imperial government.
- **B.** Britain was an exception for several reasons. First, it was a remote island province and had been brought in late to the Roman political and cultural order. Further, Britain suffered no major Germanic attacks until late in the 3rd century. It was subject to coastal raids but had a sophisticated system of naval defenses.
    1. In 410, however, as a result of the usurpation of Constantine III, Britain was left without an effective Roman military presence, and the Roman administration disappeared within 20 years.
    2. After 430, Romano-Celtic warriors began to assert themselves as dynasts to impose order on the island. By 450, Germanic tribes began to arrive in the province in great numbers.
- **C.** At this time, southern Gaul was controlled by the Visigoths as federates under a treaty with Rome. The Goths had to compete with the Burgundians in central Gaul and the Franks, who had expanded across the Rhine into northern Gaul.
    1. The Franks, under Clovis, subjected the Burgundians and drove the Visigoths into Spain.
    2. Clovis passed on a loose Frankish state to his sons. He had also inherited some of the Roman administration in his territories by taking over the church and converting to Catholic Christianity.

- **D.** The Visigoths in Spain, the Ostrogoths in Italy, and the Vandals in North Africa were all descended from East Germanic peoples and had converted to Arian Christianity.
    1. The Visigoths created a territorial kingdom in Spain, converted to Catholicism, and issued codes based on Roman common law. They were overthrown by an Arabic conquest in 711–713.
    2. In 439, the Vandals occupied Carthage, so that they ruled as a naval power over the provinces of Africa and Numidia as well as Sardinia and Corsica.
    3. The Ostrogoths were the most successful of the Germanic immigrants in the late Roman state. In 489–491, the king of the Ostrogoths, Theoderic, conquered Italy on the orders of the Eastern government and substituted himself as ruler, defeating and slaying Odoacer.
    4. The successor states that followed the collapse of the Western Empire, then, showed a great deal of cultural continuity with the Roman world. The peculiar martial society that had been created on the Roman frontiers from the 2nd century B.C. to the 4th century A.D. had simply migrated into the interior and taken over.

III. Justinian was determined to reverse this political change.
- **A.** Justinian was unpopular, in part because his wife, Theodora, a former prostitute, as well as his able ministers of low origin, outraged the elites of Constantinople.
    1. Justinian also surrounded himself with talented "new men," notably the general Belisarius, who was responsible for the military reconquests of the Western provinces.
    2. Justinian needed victories to gain prestige with the army and to intimidate the elite classes. This may have been one reason for conducting the wars of reconquest.
    3. The other reason was that Justinian strongly believed in the need to restore the immutable Christian Roman order.
- **B.** Although the wars of reconquest cost the empire dearly, Justinian initially had sufficient money and manpower if the wars were quick and decisive.

1. In 532, Justinian bought off Shah Chosroes I by Perpetual Peace, but the security of the Eastern frontier was compromised..
2. In 533, Justinian was free to send an expeditionary force under Belisarius who decisively defeated and overthrew the Vandals in two battles. Roman rule returned to Africa.

C. Justinian then turned to Ostrogothic Italy under the pretense of intervening on behalf of his former ally, Queen Amalasuntha, who had been murdered by her consort, Theodahad.
   1. Initially, this war also went well. In 536, Belisarius landed in Campagna and swept aside resistance, occupying Rome, but the Goths regrouped under an able king, Wittigis, who besieged Rome in 536–537.
   2. Belisarius raised siege and resumed the offensive, capturing Ravenna, along with Wittigis and his court, in 540.
   3. Belisaurius, however, was recalled to check a Persian attack into Syria, and so the Goths rallied under Totila who waged a war of attrition. In 552, Justinian's eunuch general Narses decisively defeated and slew Totila, but imperial victory came at the price of Italy's devastation.

D. The Eastern Empire was ravaged by a plague in 542–543. This was the first of a series of pandemics that destroyed populations in the Near East and Europe and led to a demographic collapse. Together with rebellions in Africa and Spain, the plague put an end to the idea of reconquering the West.

E. By the time of Justinian's death in 565, he had recovered the Mediterranean lands of the former Western Empire, but these provinces were in no position to pay for the restored imperial government. Further, these Germanic states were evolving into distinct local societies with no ties to the old imperial administration.
   1. The wars of reconquest had seriously sapped the military and financial resources of the Eastern Empire.
   2. New barbarians migrated into Italy and the Balkans, while the Persians renewed their wars of conquest.
   3. Within a decade of Justinian's death, the empire was fighting for its life. The wars and migrations that followed Justinian shattered the Roman state; transferred the Roman political legacy to Constantinople; and saw the arrival of new

barbarians who shaped the destinies of Western Europe, Eastern Europe, and the Islamic world.

Readings:

Cameron, Averil. *The Mediterranean World in Late Antiquity, A.D. 395–600.*

Moorhead, J. *Justinian.*

Questions to Consider:

1. What were the strengths and weaknesses of the East Germanic kingdoms of the Visigoths, Ostrogoths, and Vandals? Did an alliance of these kingdoms pose a threat to Constantinople?
2. Why did Justinian seek the reconquest of the Western provinces? How well did he comprehend conditions in the former Western provinces? Why did the reconquests of Africa and Italy prove so difficult?

Lecture Thirty-Six
Birth of the Barbarian Medieval West

Scope: The dissolution of Justinian's Mediterranean-wide empire resulted in the birth of the medieval world. The Lombards, fierce pagan federates, settled in the Balkans, crossed the Alps in 568, and overran northern and central Italy. Henceforth, imperial rule was confined to the coastal cities, islands, and far southern regions. Slavic-speaking tribes crossed the Danube and settled in the Balkan provinces, thereby isolating Constantinople from Western Europe. The emperors in Constantinople were put on the defensive battling, first, the Persians, then the armies of Islam. These Eastern Roman or Byzantine emperors came to rule over a Hellenic state based in Anatolia. In the West, the papacy fell heir to the Roman legacy. Pope Gregory the Great initiated the alignment of the Roman church with the Celtic and Germanic peoples of Western Europe. Clovis, Merovingian king of the Franks, made the Franks the political heirs of Rome in the West. Clovis welded the Germanic peoples and Roman provincials of Gaul into the first Catholic Christian kingdom of the barbarian west. Anglo-Saxon kings in England followed Clovis's example by embracing Catholic Christianity in the next century. North of the Alps in the old Celtic heartland, barbarian newcomers and Roman provincials constructed a new order based on Christian, Roman, and Germanic traditions that produced the Carolingian Empire and, thus, medieval Christendom in the 8th century.

Outline

I. This lecture concludes the 900 years covered in our examination of the relationship of Rome and the barbarians.

II. We shall begin with a look at the successor societies in the East and move west.

   A. The Byzantine Empire reinvented itself in the 7th century as a medieval kingdom dedicated to the Roman political legacy but Greek in speech and Orthodox in faith.

B. The reign of the emperor Heraclius (610–641) marked an important transition into the Byzantine period.

C. The eastern half of the Roman Empire was attacked by sundry new peoples.

    1. The Turkomen tribe known as the Avars moved into eastern Europe in the later years of Justinian's reign and constructed a steppe empire. They plagued both the Byzantine successor state and the Frankish kingdom down to the 8th century.

    2. The Avars were accompanied by Slavic-speaking subject tribes, who moved into the Balkans and settled in great numbers as the authority of Constantinople over its provinces weakened. From the 6th century to the 8th century, the region of the Balkans was ethnically and linguistically transformed by these peoples.

    3. This region saw a return to the pattern that existed before the Romans, with Hellenized urban cities along the shores and village life and stock raising in the interior.

D. The Sassanid shahs of Persia nearly won the age-long struggle with the Byzantines. Heraclius achieved a significant victory over the Persians, but this final Persian war, which ran from 602–628, weakened both empires.

E. The ultimate winners of this conflict were the Arabs, who would overrun the Sassanid Empire and the Roman provinces of Syria, Palestine, Egypt, and Libya in 634–642.

F. The emergence of the Avars, the Slavs, and the Muslim-Arab caliphate marked a significant break from the Classical Roman order.

III. We usually think of the barbarian legacy in terms of Western Europe, primarily because the people who settled there were the archetypes of barbarians to the Greeks and Romans.

    A. The Germanic-speaking tribes were the groups that ultimately toppled the Roman Empire. In 375, when the Goths first arrived in the Roman world, Rome was clearly losing the ability to assimilate these barbarians. Further, the Romans had contributed a great deal to creating tribal identities among these invaders and enabling them to form new territorial kingdoms.

- **B.** The wars of Justinian opened Italy to a new Germanic people, the Lombards.
    1. In 568, the Lombards were settled as imperial federates in Pannonia. They fought as auxiliaries in the later campaigns of Justinian's wars to bring the Goths to heel in Italy.
    2. Within three years of Justinian's death, as many as 200,000 Lombards migrated to northern Italy. They quickly took over the regions that had once been Cisalpine Gaul.
    3. Lombard society is well illuminated in charters and law codes; these documents reveal that the Lombards settled as a military elite. With this society, the Roman institutions that had survived broke down, and Italy entered a medieval world. The Lombards brought a martial ethos and assimilated to the Roman elite.
    4. Essentially, Italy returned to the world before 264 B.C., when it was characterized by a host of different societies and linguistic groups that were unified slowly by the Romans in the course of the 4th and 3rd centuries B.C.
- **C.** The same pattern can be seen in England, France, and Spain.
    1. In England, for example, the Anglo-Saxons who arrived were pagans, and they destroyed what little progress Christianity had made.
    2. The Franks took over the Celtic heartland of Gaul and quickly assimilated the aristocratic elite of the Gallo-Roman population. The Merovingian kings based their administration on the church for civil matters and gave real power to regional counts (*comites*). Therefore, in the course of the 5th–7th centuries, the society of Gaul became privatized and broke up into local identities.
    3. As far as we know from literary sources, the pattern in Visigothic Spain was similar. Members of the Visigothic aristocracy rallied after Muslim conquests in the 700s and reinvented themselves as the Christian princes of the Reconquista.

IV. To some extent, it can be argued that the 900-year history of Roman ascendancy was an interlude in local barbarian societies.

- **A.** But Rome was a powerful memory for these societies. All the territorial kingdoms that emerged in Western Europe looked to the papacy in Rome for guidance in the use of Christianity for their political aims.

B. Foremost, the example of Rome endured. All Germanic kings styled themselves as Roman rulers. They put value in the literary culture, and they saw the need for cities or the issuing of law codes. As Christian monarchs, these Germanic kings looked to Rome as their model.

C. These kingdoms did not represent merely a return to La Tène civilization; they were new societies. The impact of the Roman legacy is revealed in the fact that, by 800, these Germanic kingdoms had a new sense of identity as Latin Christendom.

Readings:

Arnold, C. J. *Roman Britain to Saxon England.*

Geary, P. J. *Before France and Germany: The Creation and Transformation of the Merovingian World.*

Goffart, Walter. *Barbarians and Romans, A.D. 418–584: The Techniques of Accommodation.*

Questions to Consider:

1. How did the failure of Justinian's reconquests ensure the success of new barbarians and the end of the Roman Mediterranean world in the 7th century? What was the impact of the Avars and Slavs? How did the Arabs fall heirs to the late Roman imperial order?

2. Why did the image of Rome exercise such a powerful influence on the later Germanic kings? How did their emulation of the vision of Rome lead to the birth of Latin Christendom?

Maps

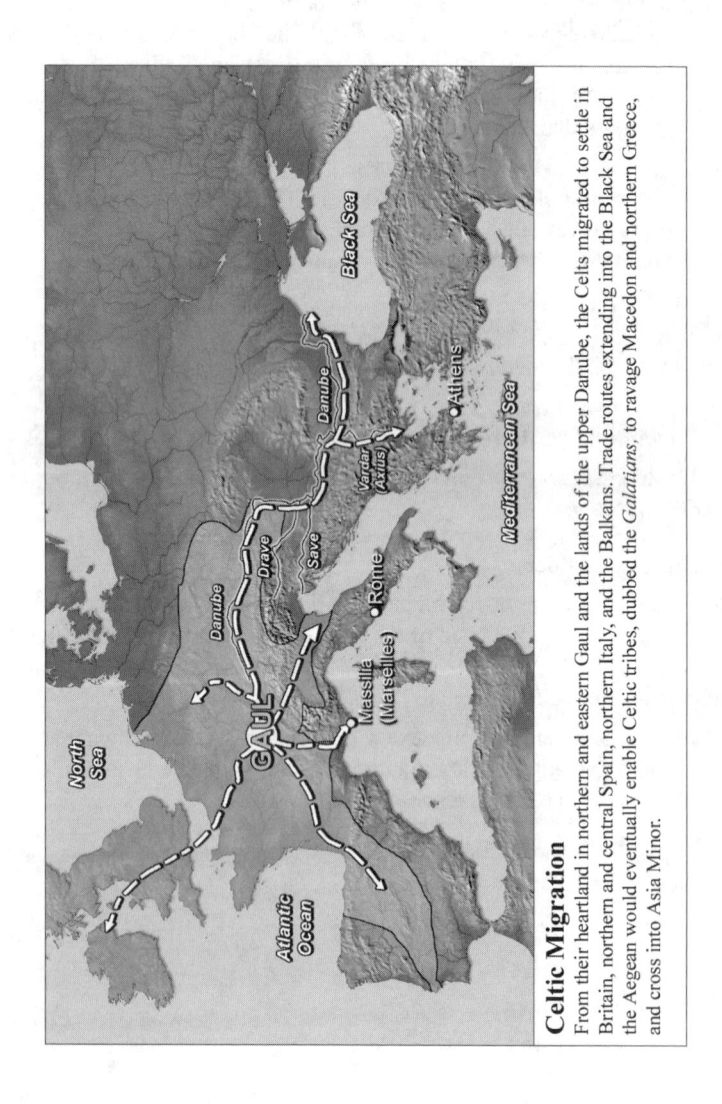

Celtic Migration

From their heartland in northern and eastern Gaul and the lands of the upper Danube, the Celts migrated to settle in Britain, northern and central Spain, northern Italy, and the Balkans. Trade routes extending into the Black Sea and the Aegean would eventually enable Celtic tribes, dubbed the *Galatians*, to ravage Macedon and northern Greece, and cross into Asia Minor.

Organization of Roman Italy, 264 B.C.

- Romans
- Latins
- Italian Allies

In 264 B.C., the population in peninsular Italy was divided into four categories. Romans were divided into citizens, and citizens without the franchise, who had been incorporated from areas more distant from Rome. Latins enjoyed a "half-citizen" status, but could attain full citizenship upon completing military obligations and coming to Rome. Italian allies owed military service to Rome but retained their own institutions.

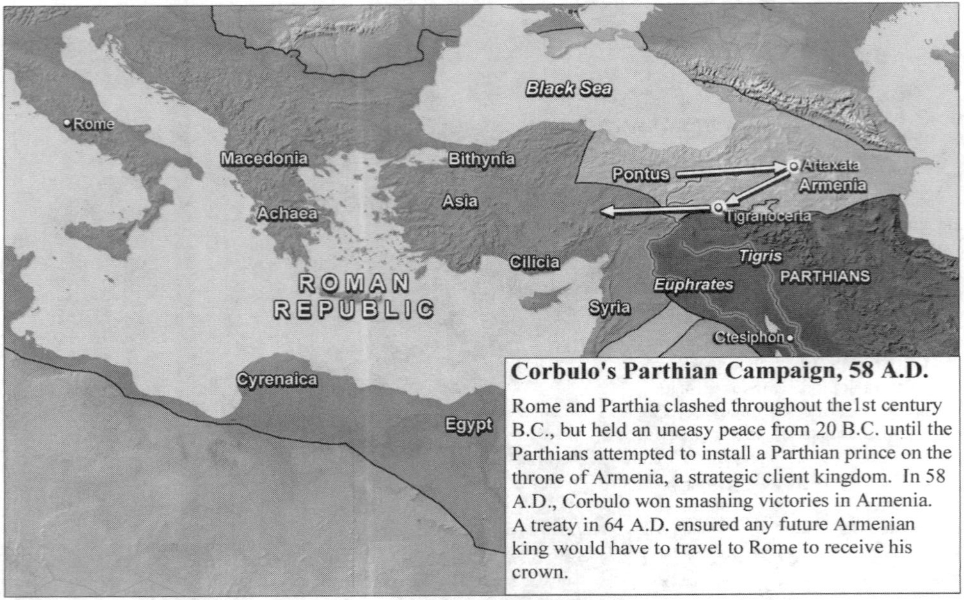

Corbulo's Parthian Campaign, 58 A.D.

Rome and Parthia clashed throughout the 1st century B.C., but held an uneasy peace from 20 B.C. until the Parthians attempted to install a Parthian prince on the throne of Armenia, a strategic client kingdom. In 58 A.D., Corbulo won smashing victories in Armenia. A treaty in 64 A.D. ensured any future Armenian king would have to travel to Rome to receive his crown.

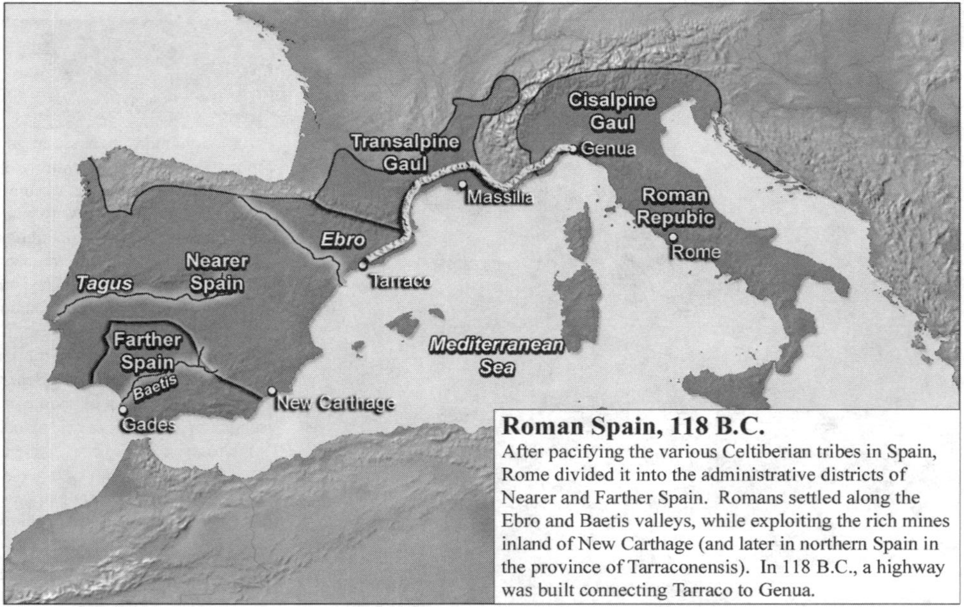

Roman Spain, 118 B.C.

After pacifying the various Celtiberian tribes in Spain, Rome divided it into the administrative districts of Nearer and Farther Spain. Romans settled along the Ebro and Baetis valleys, while exploiting the rich mines inland of New Carthage (and later in northern Spain in the province of Tarraconensis). In 118 B.C., a highway was built connecting Tarraco to Genua.

Caesar's Conquest of Gaul, 59-52 B.C.

Since 121 B.C., security of Roman Gaul had rested on alliances between Romans and tribal leaders in Gaul. The Suebi, a Germanic people, along with the Helvetians, threatened to destabilize this arrangement, and Caesar took action, defeating the Helvetians at Bibracte in 58 B.C., as well as threats from the Eburones, Carnutes, the Nervii, and the Averni. One of his greatest victories came over Vercingetorix of the Averni at the siege of Alesia in 52 B.C. These victories, as well as his defeats of the Catuvellauni in Britain, secured Caesar his great reputation.

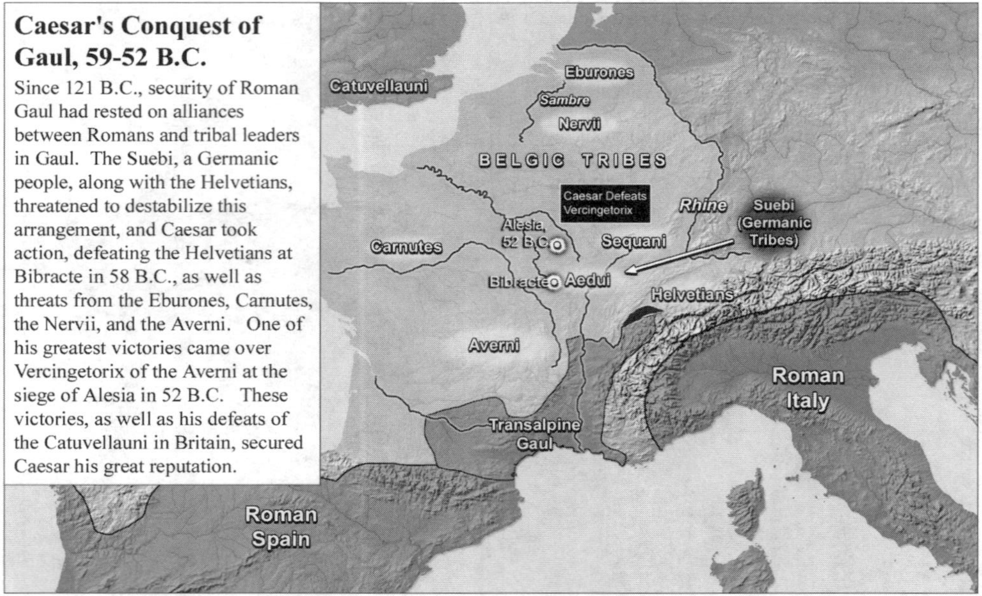

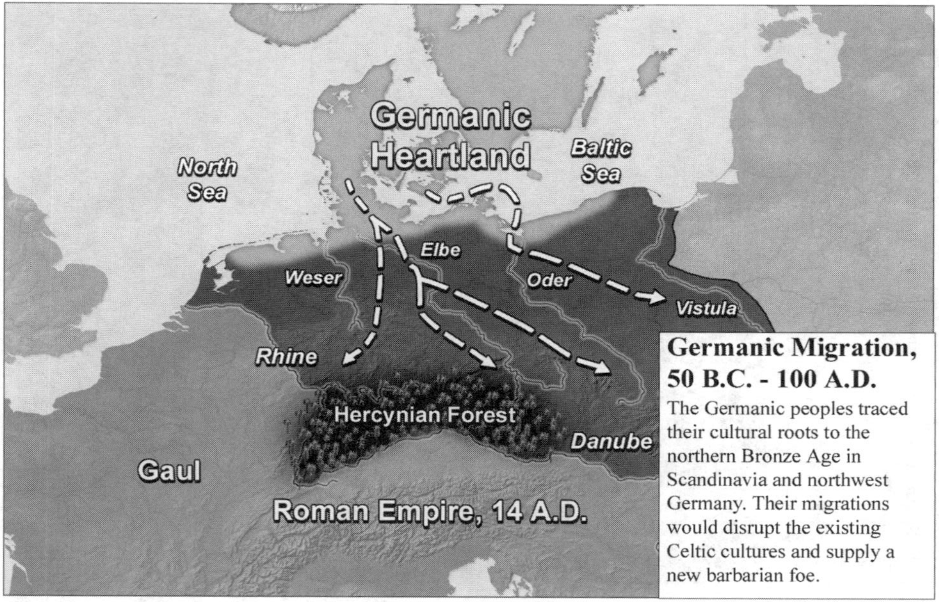

Germanic Migration, 50 B.C. - 100 A.D.

The Germanic peoples traced their cultural roots to the northern Bronze Age in Scandinavia and northwest Germany. Their migrations would disrupt the existing Celtic cultures and supply a new barbarian foe.

Roman Britain, 139 A.D.

The Romans erected the Antonine Wall in northern Britain, but ultimately withdrew their frontier to the line marked by Hadrian's Wall, due to the difficulties in provisioning troops posted as far north as the Antonine Wall, where the populace was primarily engaged in stock raising and could not feed an army from their agricultural output.

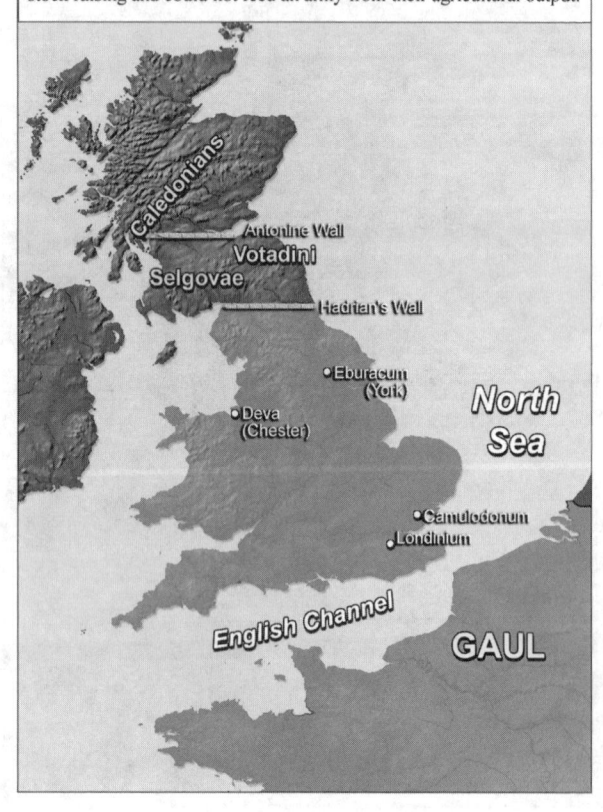

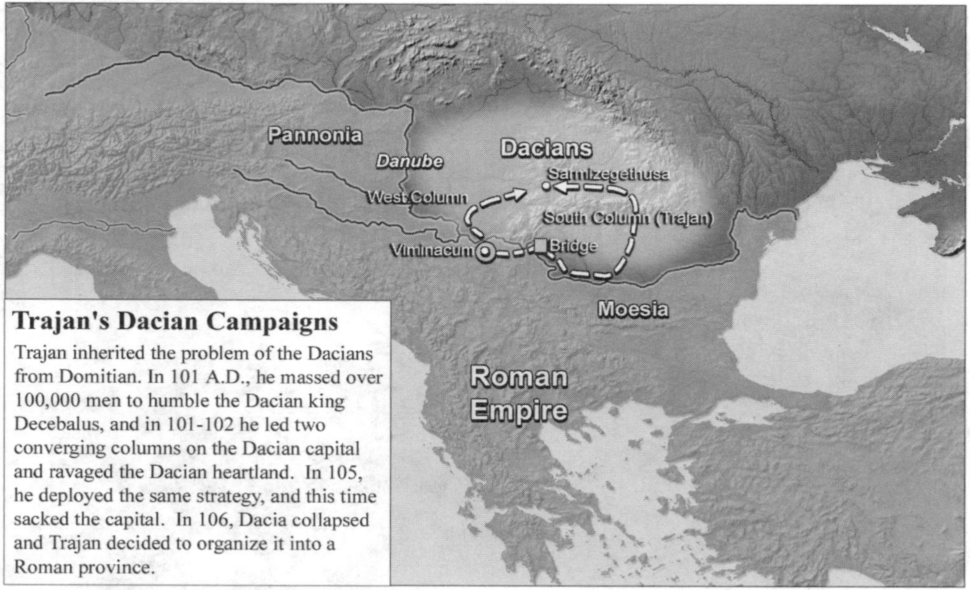

Trajan's Dacian Campaigns

Trajan inherited the problem of the Dacians from Domitian. In 101 A.D., he massed over 100,000 men to humble the Dacian king Decebalus, and in 101-102 he led two converging columns on the Dacian capital and ravaged the Dacian heartland. In 105, he deployed the same strategy, and this time sacked the capital. In 106, Dacia collapsed and Trajan decided to organize it into a Roman province.

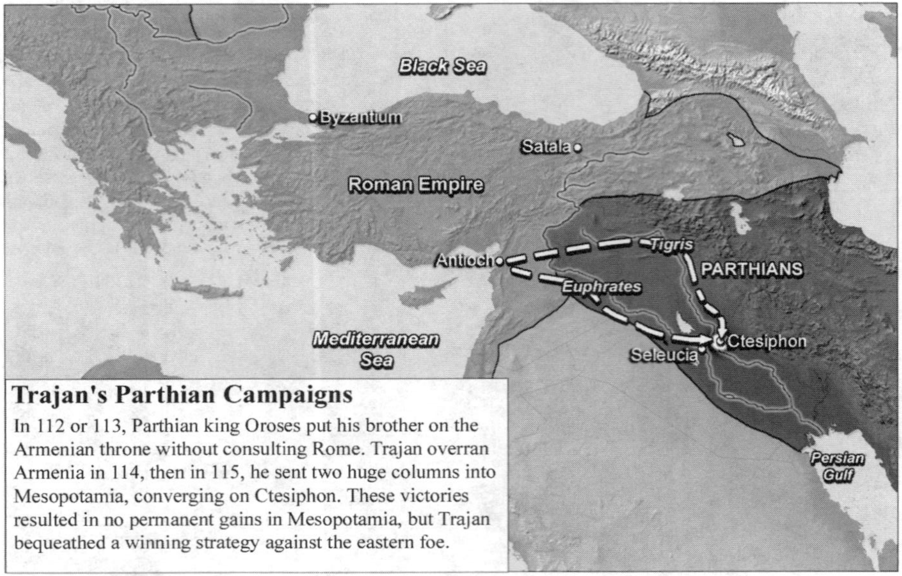

Trajan's Parthian Campaigns

In 112 or 113, Parthian king Oroses put his brother on the Armenian throne without consulting Rome. Trajan overran Armenia in 114, then in 115, he sent two huge columns into Mesopotamia, converging on Ctesiphon. These victories resulted in no permanent gains in Mesopotamia, but Trajan bequeathed a winning strategy against the eastern foe.

The Goths:

Between 150 and 200, East Germanic peoples migrated from their Baltic homelands into eastern Europe. Foremost were Goths from southern Sweden who followed the river routes of Russia. Settling near the Black Sea, they raided Roman territory in the 230s, and by the 240s, they were pressing hard on the frontier. They attacked in tandem with other tribes, including the Vandals, Gepidae, Herulians, Rugians, and Burgundians. These tribes would carve out successor kingdoms in the Roman world.

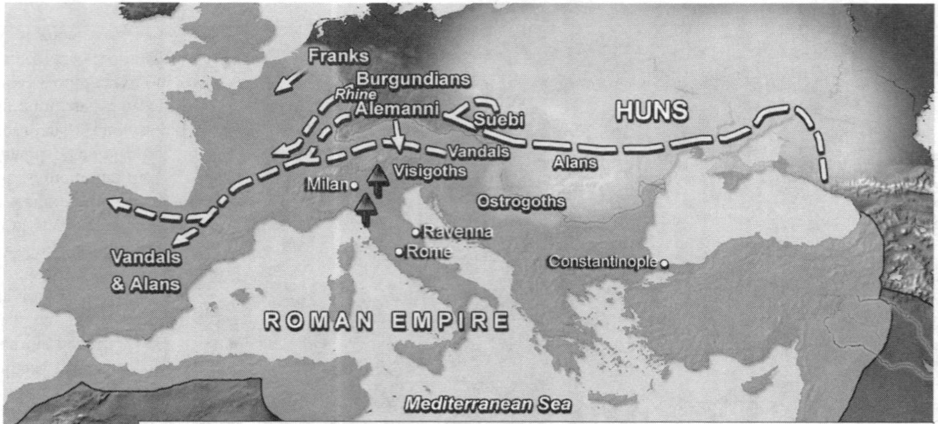

Barbarians Overrun the West

In 402, the Visigoths entered northern Italy under the leadership of Alaric. Stilicho moved field armies from the Rhine and Danube to counter them, leaving the frontier unprotected. When the Rhine froze on New Year's Eve, 406, Franks, Alans, Suebi, Burgundians, Alemanni, and Vandals poured over the frontier. Roman weakness was confirmed by Honorius's craven decision to move the court from Rome to Ravenna, a city protected by swamps and marshes.

The Byzantine Empire, 636

The emperor Justinian had considerable success in restoring the Roman Empire by recovering Italy, North Africa, and southern Spain, but many of these territorial gains had been lost by 636. Slavic tribes settled in the Balkans and the interior of Greece. Lombards controlled much of Italy. The Visigoths would hold Spain until the Muslim conquest, and Britain was now firmly under the control of the Anglo-Saxons.

Timeline

ca. 814 B.C.	Foundation of Carthage by Phoenicians.
ca. 800–450 B.C.	Hallstatt (Early Iron Age) civilization in Celtic Europe; emergence of Iranian-speaking steppe nomads, Scythians.
775–650 B.C.	Greeks colonize southern Italy (Magna Graecia) and Sicily; Phoenicians colonize western Sicily and Sardinia; emergence of Etruscan city-states in central Italy.
753 B.C.	Legendary foundation of Rome by Romulus.
ca. 600 B.C.	Foundation of Greek colony of Massilia (Marseilles).
509 B.C.	Proclamation of the Roman Republic.
500–400 B.C.	Gauls overrun Etruscan cities in the Po valley; emergence of Germanic civilization in Scandinavia and northern Germany.
494–287 B.C.	Conflict of Orders between patricians and plebians.
ca. 450–50 B.C	La Tène (Late Iron Age civilization in Celtic Europe); migrations of Celts into the British Isles, Spain, and northern Italy.
396 B.C.	Capture of Veii; Roman Conquest of southern Etruria.
390 B.C.	Battle of Allia—Gauls under Brennus sack Rome; Roman Conquest of Latium and central Italy.

367 B.C.	*Lex Licinia-Sextia*—Consulship opened to plebians; restriction on possession of public land (*ager publicus*); rise of expanded political class of nobles (*nobiles*).
ca. 350–200 B.C.	Migration of Dacians from Balkans into Dacia (Rumania).
343–341 B.C.	First Samnite War.
340–338 B.C.	Latin Revolt—reorganization of Roman alliances in Italy.
334–323 B.C.	Alexander the Great conquers Persian Empire.
326–304 B.C.	Second Samnite War—Rome emerges as leading power in Italy.
ca. 325 B.C.	Pytheas of Massilia visits northern Europe.
323 B.C.	Death of Alexander the Great; Partition of Macedonian Empire; Ptolemy I establishes Ptolemaic dynasty in Egypt; emergence of Hellenistic World.
312 B.C.	Seleucus I establishes Seleucid monarchy in Asia.
298–290 B.C.	Third Samnite War—pacification of southern Italy.
283–282 B.C.	Roman victories over Gallic Boii and Senones on lower Po.
281–279	Galatians invade Macedon and Greece; Antigonus II Gonatas defeats Galatians; establishment of Antigonid Dynasty of Macedon.
280–275 B.C.	War of Rome against King Pyrrhus.
279–277 B.C.	Galatians cross into Asia Minor.

264 B.C.	Outbreak of First Punic War.
ca. 250–230 B.C.	Parthians migrate into northern Iran.
241 B.C.	Surrender of Carthage—end of First Punic War; Rome annexes Sicily as province.
238 B.C.	Roman seizure of Corsica and Sardinia from Carthage.
237–230 B.C.	Hamilcar Barca founds Carthaginian empire in Spain.
232 B.C.	*Lex Flaminia*—Romans settle confiscated Gallic lands.
226 B.C.	Treaty of the Ebro defines Roman and Carthaginian spheres in Spain.
225 B.C.	Battle of Telamon—defeat of last Gallic invasion of Italy.
223 B.C.	Accession of Philip V, Antigonid King of Macedon; accession of Antiochus III, King of Seleucid Empire.
221 B.C.	Hannibal assumes command in Carthaginian Spain.
218 B.C.	Outbreak of Second Punic War; founding of Latin colonies at Placentia and Cremona; invasion of Italy by Hannibal; rebellions of Ligurians and Celts in northern Italy.
217–211 B.C.	Publius and Gnaeus Cornelius Scipio battle Carthaginians in Spain.
216 B.C.	Battle of Cannae—Hannibal defeats two consular armies; rebellion against Rome in Campania and southern Italy.
215 B.C.	King Philip V declares war on Rome; outbreak of First Macedonian War.

210 B.C.	Scipio Africanus arrives in Spain with proconsular *imperium*.
209 B.C.	Scipio Africanus captures New Carthage.
205 B.C.	Election of Scipio Africanus consul with command in Africa.
204 B.C.	Scipio Africanus invades Africa.
202 B.C.	Battle of Zama—Scipio Africanus defeats Hannibal.
201 B.C.	Surrender of Carthage—end of Second Punic War; Masinissa confirmed as King of the Numidians.
200 B.C.	Outbreak of the Second Macedonian War; Battle of Panium—end of Ptolemaic power; Antiochus III restores Seleucid power in Asia Minor.
200–187 B.C.	Roman conquest of Cisalpine Gaul and Liguria.
197 B.C.	Battle of Cynocephalae—defeat of Philip V of Macedon; outbreak of First Celtiberian War; organization of provinces of Nearer and Farther Spain.
195–194 B.C.	Marcus Porcius Cato, the Elder, campaigns in Nearer Spain.
192 B.C.	Outbreak of Asian War against King Antiochus III.
190 B.C.	Battle of Magnesia—Scipio Asiaticus defeats Antiochus III.
188 B.C.	Treaty of Apamea—Antiochus III cedes lands west of Taurus mountains; consul Gnaeus Manlius Vulso breaks power of Galatians; Attalid kings of Pergamum rules western Asia Minor

	as Rome's client; rise of Bithynia, Pontus, and Cappadocia in Asia Minor; rise of the Parthians in Iran.
180–178 B.C.	Tiberius Sempronius Gracchus secures peace in Spain; growth of cities and Roman exploitation of mines in Spain.
175–129 B.C.	Han emperors of China subject Hsiung-nu (putative ancestors of Huns).
173 B.C.	Grants of public land *viritim* in Aemilia.
172 B.C.	Outbreak of Third Macedonian War against King Perseus.
171 B.C.	Court *de repetundis* investigates administrative abuses in Spain.
169 B.C.	Refounding of Latin colony of Aquileia, in Venetia.
168 B.C.	Battle of Pydna—Lucius Aemilius Paullus defeats King; Perseus of Macedon; reorganization of Macedon into four client republics; foundation of Corduba (Cordova) in Spain.
154 B.C.	Outbreak of Lusitanian War.
153 B.C.	Outbreak of Second Celtiberian War; fiscal reforms in Spanish provinces.
150 B.C.	Servius Sulpicius Galba massacres Lusitanians; Viriathus rallies Lusitanians and wages guerilla war; Sarmatians extend control over eastern European steppes.
149 B.C.	Outbreak of Third Punic War; outbreak of Macedonian revolt led by pretender Andriscus;

Lex Calpurnia—permanent courts *de reputundis* against provincial abuses.

148 B.C. .... Annexation of province of Macedonia; Romanization of Transpadana, Venetia, and Liguria; death of King Masinissa of Numidia; accession of Micipsa.

147 B.C. .... Scipio Aemilianus elected consul with command against Carthage.

146 B.C. .... Scipio Aemilianus sacks and razes Carthage; annexation of provinces of Africa and Achaea (Greece).

145 B.C. .... Quintus Fabius Maximus Aemilianus recruits volunteers for war in Spain.

143 B.C. .... Outbreak of Third Celtiberian (Numantine) War.

140 B.C. .... Parthian conquest of Iran and Mesopotamia.

141 B.C. .... Rejection of Spanish treaty of consul Quintus Pompeius.

137 B.C. .... Defeat and humiliation of Gaius Hostilius Mancinus by Numantines; political trials over Spanish War at Rome; popular agitation over draft and land reform.

134 B.C. .... Scipio Aemilianus, consul, besieges Numantia.

133 B.C. .... Tribunate and death of Tiberius Sempronius Gracchus; failure of land reform at Rome; beginning of Roman Revolution; Scipio Aemilianus captures Numantia—end of Third Celtiberian War; Roman annexation of province of Asia.

129 B.C.	Legal recognition of equestrian order (*ordo equester*).
125 B.C.	Massilia appeals to Rome against Salluvian prince; Tourtomotulus; Romans conquer southern Gaul.
124–122 B.C.	Tribunates of Gaius Sempronius Gracchus—second land reforms; agitation of Latins and Italians for Roman citizenship; Equestrians secure fiscal exploitation of Asia.
121 B.C.	*Popularis* demonstrations at Rome over repeal of reforms; riots and murder of Gaius Sempronius Gracchus; Lucius Domitius Ahenobarbus organizes province of Gallia Transalpina; accession of King Mithridates VI Eupator of Pontus.
120–115 B.C.	Migration of Cimbri and Teutones from Jutland into Central Europe; decline of La Tène towns (*oppida*) in southern Germany.
118 B.C.	Death of King Micipsa—civil wars in Numidian kingdom; repeal of agrarian legislation of Gaius Gracchus.
113 B.C.	Cimbri defeat consul Gnaeus Papirius Carbo at Noreia; Cimbri and Teutones disrupt eastern and southern Gaul.
112 B.C.	Jugurtha reunites Numidia; outbreak of Jugurthine War.
111 B.C.	Defeat and humiliation of consul Lucius Calpurnius Bestia by Jurgurtha.
110–109 B.C.	Gaius Mamilius Limetanus investigates senatorial corruption in conduct of Jugurthine War.

109–107 B.C.	Quintius Caecilius Metellus campaigns against Jugurtha; Gaius Marius intrigues for the command in Africa.
107 B.C.	Marius elected consul and recruits landless volunteers.
106 B.C.	Capture of Capsa by Marius; flight of Jugurtha; surrender of Jugurtha to Lucius Cornelius Sulla.
105 B.C.	Battle of Arausio—Cimbri and Teutones destroy two Roman armies; election of Gaius Marius as consul; alliance of Marius with radical *popularis* Lucius Appuleius Saturninus.
104–103 B.C.	Marius reorganizes and trains Roman army.
103 B.C.	*Lex Appuleia*—Roman veterans settled in Africa.
102 B.C.	Battle of Aquae Sextiae—Marius defeats Teutones in southern Gaul.
101 B.C.	Battle of Vercellae—Marius annihilates the Cimbri.
100 B.C.	Collapse of coalition between Marius and *populares*; Marius suppresses disorder in Rome; arrest and murder of radicals Saturninus and Glaucia; Optimates assert authority of the Senate.
100–50 B.C.	Romanization of Liguria, Transpadane Italy, and Venetia; Romanization of Transalpine Gaul (Narbonnesis).
99 B.C.	Accession of Tigranes I, the Great, of Armenia.

94–93 B.C.	Publius Rutilius Rufus reforms administration in Asia.
93 B.C.	Alliance of Mithridates VI and Tigranes.
92 B.C.	Trial and exile of Publius Rutilius Rufus; Sulla, governor of Cilicia, receives submission of Parthian envoys; Tigranes I conquers Media and Mesopotamia.
91 B.C.	Tribunate and assassination of Marcus Livius Drusus the Younger.
90 B.C.	Outbreak of the Social War.
89 B.C.	*Lex Plautia-Papiria*—enfranchisement of Latins and Italians; *Lex Pompeia*—Latin status extended to residents of Cisalpine Gaul; outbreak of the First Mithridatic War; Mithridates overruns Roman Asia Minor; cities of Greece revolt against Rome.
88 B.C.	Sulla's march on Rome—first civil war; proscriptions and exiles of Marians; Mithridates VI orders the massacre of Romans in Asia.
87 B.C.	Marius and *populares* reoccupy Rome and purge optimates; death of Marius, consul VII; Lucius Cornelius Cinna reforms Rome; Sulla, as proconsul, defeats Pontic armies in Greece.
85 B.C.	Treaty of Dardanus between Sulla and Mithridates VI.
82 B.C.	Battle of Colline Gate—Sulla occupies Rome; Quintus Sertorius organizes *populares* exiles in Spain.

82–78 B.C.	Dictatorship of Sulla at Rome—proscriptions and exiles of Marians; Sulla reforms Roman constitution.
77 B.C.	Death of Sulla.
76 B.C.	Pompey assumes command in Spain against Sertorius.
ca. 75–60 B.C.	Migration of Belgic tribes from Gaul into southeastern Britain.
74 B.C.	Outbreak of Third Mithridatic War.
73 B.C.	Lucius Licinius Lucullus defeats Mithridates at Cyzicus; Lucullus invades and conquers Pontus.
72 B.C.	Murder of Sertorius—collapse of *popularis* cause in Spain; Pompey reorganizes Spanish provinces.
70 B.C.	Consulships of Pompey and Marcus Licinius Crassus; Lucullus reforms administration of Asia.
69 B.C.	Battle of Tigranocerta—Lucullus defeats King Tigranes I of Armenia; mutiny of legions and recall of Lucullus.
67 B.C.	*Lex Gabinia*—Pompey commands war against Cilician pirates.
66–63 B.C.	Pompey commands war against Mithridates VI of Pontus; Pompey imposes Roman hegemony over Armenia; Tigranes relinquishes his conquests in Media, Mesopotamia, and Syria; Parthians extend control to Upper Euphrates.
63 B.C.	Suicide of King Mithridates VI; Pompey annexes Syria and organizes the Roman East.

60 B.C.	Formation of First Triumvirate (Pompey, Crassus, and Julius Caesar); Burebistas forges first Dacian kingdom.
59 B.C.	Consulship of Julius Caesar—*popularis* reforms at Rome.
58 B.C.	Caesar, proconsul of Cisalpine and Translpine Gaul and Illyricum, defeats the Helvetians and Ariovistus, king of the Suevi.
57 B.C.	Julius Caesar campaigns against the Belgic tribes; Battle of Sambre—Caesar defeats Nervii; Caesar pacifies central and southern Gaul; outbreak of civil war in Parthian Empire.
56 B.C.	Consul of Luca—renewal of First Triumvirate; extension of proconsulship of Caesar; election of Pompey as consul.
55 B.C.	Election of Crassus as consul; first British and first German expedition of Julius Caesar.
54 B.C	Second British expedition of Julius Caesar; revolt of Nervii and Eburones in northeastern Gaul.
53 B.C.	Second German expedition of Julius Caesar; outbreak of the Gallic Revolt under Vercingetorix; Battle of Carrhae—defeat and death of Crassus by Parthians; Pompey renews political links with optimates.
52 B.C.	Siege of Alesia—surrender of Vercingetorix to Caesar.
49 B.C.	Outbreak of civil war—Caesar versus Pompey and optimates; Roman

	citizenship extended to Liguria, Transpadana, and Venetia.
48 B.C.	Battle of Pharsalus—Julius Caesar defeats Pompey; flight and death of Pompey in Egypt.
46 B.C.	Battle of Thapsus—Caesar defeats optimates in Africa; annexation of Numidia and refounding of Carthage as Roman colony.
44 B.C.	Assassination of Julius Caesar by Liberators; clash between Mark Antony and Octavian; Liberators organize forces in provinces.
43 B.C.	Formation of Second Triumvirate (Octavian, Mark Antony, Lepidus); proscriptions and executions of optimates in Italy.
42 B.C.	Liguria, Transpadana, and Venetia incorporated into Italy; Battle of Philippi—Mark Antony and Octavian defeat Liberators.
41–37 B.C.	Mark Antony reorganizes the Roman East; Octavian reforms Rome and settles Roman West.
40 B.C.	Marriage of Mark Antony and Octavia (sister of Octavian).
38 B.C.	Marriage of Octavian and Livia Drusilla.
37 B.C.	Marriage of Antony and Cleopatra VII, Ptolemaic Queen of Egypt.
36 B.C.	First Armenian Expedition of Mark Antony.
34 B.C.	Second Armenian Expedition of Mark Antony.

32 B.C.	Outbreak of civil war between Mark Antony and Octavian.
31 B.C.	Battle of Actium—Octavian defeats Antony and Cleopatra.
30 B.C.	Suicides of Antony and Cleopatra; Octavian annexes Egypt and reorganizes Roman East.
27 B.C.	First Constitutional Settlement—legal definition of powers of Augustus; Octavian reigns as first emperor Augustus.
25 B.C.	Marriage of Julia, Augustus' daughter, and Marcus Claudius Marcellus; outbreak of Cantabrian War in northwestern Spain; founding of colony at Antiochia at Pisidiam
23 B.C.	Second Constitutional Settlement of Augustus; death of Marcus Claudius Marcellus; Agrippa pacifies northwestern Spain.
21 B.C.	Marriage of Marcus Vispanius Agrippa and Julia.
20 B.C.	Augustus concludes settlement with King Phraates IV of Parthia; secures return of standards of Crassus's legions; Macromanni under Maroboduus migrate to Bohemia.
16 B.C.	Augustus reorganizes Gaul and the Rhine frontier; Tiberius and Drusus annex Raetia; Roman frontier (*limes*) organized on Upper Danube.
14–9 B.C.	Roman conquest of Illyricum (Dalmatia and Pannonia).
12 B.C.	Death of Agrippa in Illyricum.

12–9 B.C.	Campaigns of Tiberius and Drusus in Germany and Illyricum.
11 B.C.	Death of Octavia; rise of Livia Drusilla; marriage of Tiberius and Julia.
9 B.C.	Death of Drusus the Elder in Germany; imperial cult at Cologne founded for German province.
6 B.C.	Tiberius retires from public life to Rhodes.
2 B.C.	Lucius Domitius Ahenobarbus, legate of Illyricum, crosses Elbe.
4 A.D.[1]	Return of Tiberius to Rome and adoption as heir by Augustus; Tiberius adopts Germanicus as his heir.
6	Outbreak of revolts of the Batones in Pannonia and Dalmatia; annexation of Moesia and establishment of *limes* on Lower Danube.
9	Germans rebel under Arminius, Prince of Cherusci; P. Quinctilius Varus and three legions slaughtered in Teutoburg Forest; Tiberius campaigns in Germany and secures Rhine frontier.
ca. 10–40	Cunobelinus extends power of Catuvellauni over southeastern Britain.
14	Death of Augustus, and accession of Tiberius; mutinies among legions in Germany and Pannonia.
14–16	Germanicus campaigns in Germany.

---

[1] Henceforth all dates are A.D.

Year	Event
19	Death of Germanicus; Maroboduus, exiled by subjects, received into Roman Empire.
20	Overthrow and murder of Arminius, Prince of Cherusci.
37	Murder of Tiberius and accession of Caligula.
39	German and abortive British expeditions of Caligula.
41	Murder of Caligula and Praetorians salute as emperor Claudius.
42	Annexation of Mauretania (Morocco and western Algeria).
43	Claudius leads Roman invasion of Britain.
45–64	Kujula Kadphises establishes Kushan Empire in Central Asia.
46	Annexation of Thrace as province.
48	Claudius secures admission of Gallic nobles into Senate.
50	Jazyges, Sarmatian nomads, settle in Theiss basin; Roxolani settle in Wallachia and Moldavia; Cologne (Colonia Agrippinesis) elevated to Roman colony; development of trade with Germanic and Sarmatian tribes.
51	Accession of King Vologaeses I of Parthia.
53	Tiridates I, brother of Vologaeses, accepted as king by Armenians.
54	Murder of Claudius and accession of Nero; outbreak of Parthian War over Armenian succession; Gnaeus

	Domitius Corbulo, legate of Cappadocia, commands Roman forces in Armenia.
58	Corbulo captures the Armenian capitals Artaxata and Tigranocerta; Tiridates flees to Parthia; war between Hermandurii and Chatti.
59	Armenia restored as client kingdom under Tigranes V.
60	Gaius Suetonius Paullinus, legate of Britain, captures Mona; revolt of Boudicca in Britain; recall of Corbulo and Suetonius Paullinus.
62	Tiridates I recovers Armenia and expels pro-Roman Tigranes V.
63	Corbulo, legate of Syria, campaigns in Armenia; Tiridates submits to Roman hegemony.
66	Peace between Rome and Parthia over Armenia; Tiberius Plautius Silvanus, legate of Moesia, secures Danube *limes*; outbreak of First Jewish War.
68	Revolt of Gaius Julius Vindex in Gaul; Galba proclaimed emperor in Spain; suicide of Nero—end of Julio-Claudian Dynasty.
69	Civil war—The Year of the Four Emperors; Rhine legions hail Vitellius emperor; murder of Galba at Rome; Praetorian Guard hail Otho as emperor; Danube legions recognize Otho—outbreak of civil war; raid of Roxolani into Moesia; First Battle of Bedriacum—defeat and suicide of Otho; Senate receives Vitellius as

emperor; eastern legions hail as emperor Vespasian, legate of Judaea; Gaius Julius Civilis raises revolt of Batavians in Rhineland; Danube legions recognize Vespasian and invade Italy.

69 (cont) .... Queen Cartimandua of the Brigantes exiled by Venutius; Second Battle of Bedriacum—defeat of Vitellian legions; Julius Civilis declares *Imperium Galliarum* ("Empire of the Gauls"); capture of Rome by Flavian legions; murder of Vitellius; Senate recognizes as emperor Vespasian—founding of Flavian Dynasty.

70 .... Quintus Petilius Cerealis crushes revolts in Rhineland; Julius Civilis and Batavians surrender on terms; Titus captures Jerusalem; Vespasian initiates reform of army and frontiers; growth of Trans-Saharan trade.

71 .... Triumph of Vespasian and Titus at Rome; Petilius Cerialis, legate in Britain, campaigns against Brigantes.

72 .... Reorganization of Anatolian provinces and frontier on Upper Euphrates; legionary bases established at Satala and Melitene; Alans, Sarmatian nomads, invade Armenia and Iran.

74–77 .... Sextus Julius Frontinus, legate of Britain, pacifies northern Wales.

78–85 .... Gnaeus Julius Agricola, legate, conquers northern Britain.

79 .... Death of Vespasian, and accession of Titus.

81	Death of Titus, and accession of Domitian.
83–84	Domitian campaigns against the Chatti; the *limes* of Upper Germany and Agri Decumates fortified.
85	Battle of Mount Graupius—Agricola defeats Caledonians under Calgacus; recall of Agricola and Roman withdrawal from Caledonia; accession of Decebalus, King of the Dacians; Dacians raid Moesia and defeat legate Oppius Sabinus.
86	Domitian campaigns against the Dacians.
87	Dacians annihilate army under Cornelius Fuscus in Vulcan Pass.
88	Domitian concludes unfavorable treaty with Decebalus; Domitian campaigns against Marcomanni, Quadi, and Jazyges.
96	Murder of Domitian—end of Flavian Dynasty; proclamation of Nerva as emperor; era of Five Good (or Adoptive) Emperors.
98	Death of Nerva, and accession of Trajan; Cornelius Tacitus composes his *Agricola* and *Germania*.
101–102	First Dacian War—Trajan imposes Roman hegemony over Decebalus.
105	Outbreak of the Second Dacian War.
106	Capture of Sarmizegethusa and suicide of Decebalus; annexation of Dacia as Roman province; annexation of Arabia

	Petraea and organization of desert *limes* in Syria.
112	Dedication of forum, column, and markets of Trajan.
113–117	Outbreak of the Parthian War.
114	Trajan conquers and annexes Armenia as province.
115	Trajan conquers and annexes northern Mesopotamia; outbreak of Jewish Revolt in Cyrene.
116	Trajan captures Ctesiphon; conquest of Lower Mesopotamia; Jewish Risings in Cyprus and Egypt compel withdrawal of Trajan to Syria.
117	Death of Trajan, and accession of Hadrian; Hadrian surrenders conquests east of the Euphrates; Armenia restored as Roman client kingdom.
122	Aulus Platorius Nepos, legate of Britain, constructs Hadrian's Wall along Tyne-Solway line.
123	Hadrian visits the Syrian and Cappadocian *limes*.
128	Hadrian reorganizes *limes* of North Africa.
135	Flavius Arrianus repels Alan invasion into Cappadocia.
138	Death of Hadrian, and accession of Antoninus Pius.
139–141	Construction of Antonine Wall in northern Britain.
ca. 150–235	Goths migrate from Sweden to eastern Europe; disintegration of

	Confederation of Hsiung-nu; westward migration of Turkomen tribes across Asian steppes.
161	Death of Antoninus Pius, and joint accession of Marcus Aurelius and Lucius Verus; outbreak of Parthian War.
162	Gaius Avidius Cassius, legate of Syria, commands Eastern expedition.
164	Avidius Cassius captures Ctesiphon; Roman withdrawal from Antonine to Hadrian Wall in Britain.
166	Peace between Rome and Parthia.
167	Outbreak of German Wars.
169	Death of Lucius Verus; collapse of Roman defenses on Upper Danube; Roxolani attack across the Lower Danube into Moesia.
170	German tribes ravage the Balkan provinces; Marcommani besiege Aquileia in Italy.
171–75	Marcus Aurelius invades homeland of Marcomanni and Quadi.
ca. 174/5	Battle of Rain Miracle—Roman victory over Quadi.
176	Dedication of Column of Marcus Aurelius at Rome.
177	Commodus hailed co-Augustus.
178–80	Renewed fighting against Germans and Sarmatians; Marcus Aurelius organizes provinces of Marcomannia and Sarmatia.

Year	Event
180	Death of Marcus Aurelius, and accession of Commodus; Commodus abandons Marcomannia and Sarmatia.
192	Assassination of Commodus—end of Antonine Dynasty.
193	Sucessive proclamations and murders of Pertinax and Didius Julianus; civil war among Didius Julianus, Septimius Severus, and Pescennius Niger, respective commanders of the Western, Danube, and eastern armies.
195	Septimius Severus establishes Severan Dynasty; apex of imperial civilization.
198–200	Parthian War—Septimius Severus sacks of Ctesiphon; organization of Roman province of Mesopotamia.
208–211	British campaign of Septimius Severus.
211	Death of Septimius Severus; joint accession of Caracalla and Geta.
212	Caracalla murders his brother Geta; *Constitutio Antoniniana*—Roman citizenship granted to all free residents.
214–217	Parthian War of Caracalla.
217	Murder of Caracalla by his Praetorian Prefect Macrinus; eastern army hails Macrinus as emperor.
218	Elagabalus declared emperor by Syrian legions; defeat and death of Macrinus in civil war—restoration of Severan dynasty.
222	Murder of Elagabalus, and accession of Severus Alexander.

227	Shah Ardashir I overthrows Parthians and establishes Sassanid Empire.
230–233	Inconclusive Persian-Roman War.
235	Murder of Severus Alexander and Julia Mamaea; Maximinus I Thrax proclaimed emperor by the Rhine army; beginning of Political and Military Crisis.
238	Senatorial revolts in Africa and at Rome against Maximinus; Maximinus murdered by mutinous soldiers at Aquileia; accession of Gordian III.
241	Accession of Shah Shapur I; extension of Sassanid rule into Central Asia.
242	Outbreak of Persian War against Shah Shapur I.
244	Murder of Gordian III instigated by Praetorian Prefect Philip I; Philip I hailed emperor and purchases peace from Shapur.
246–249	Goths attack Dacia, Pannonia, and Moesia; Franks and Alamanni attack the Rhine frontier; Saxon pirates raid the shores of Britain and Gaul.
249	Danube legions hail as emperor Trajan Decius; Trajan Decius defeats and slays Philip I in civil war.
251	Battle of Abrittus—Goths defeat and slay Trajan Decius; Danube legions declare as emperor Trebonnianus Gallus
253	Shah Shapur invades Syria, sacking Antioch; Danube legions declare as emperor Aemilian; Trebonnianus

	defeated and slain by Aemilian in civil war; Valerian, legate of Raetia, defeats and slays Aemilian; joint accession of Valerian I and Gallienus.
253–256	First Persian Expedition of Valerian.
258–260	Second Persian Expedition of Valerian.
260	Valerian captured by Shah Shapur I; Persians overrun Asia Minor, Mesopotamia, and Syria; Postumus founds Gallo-Roman Empire in west; Revolt of Macrianus and Quietus in east; Odenathus of Palmyra assumes command of eastern frontier.
ca. 260–300	Consolidation of Germanic confederations of Franks, Saxons, Alemanni, Sueves, and Goths; migration of East Germanic Vandals, Gepidae, Herulians, Rugians, Lombards, and Burgundians into central Europe.
262	Goths ravage Aegean world, burning Artemisium of Ephesus; Odenathus captures Ctesiphon and imposes peace on Shapur I.
267	Herulians invade Balkans, sacking suburbs of Athens; murder of Odenathus—Queen Zenobia directs policy of Palmyra.
268	Assassination of Gallienus by Illyrian officers; accession of Claudius II Gothicus, first of soldier emperors.
269	Battle of Naissus—Claudius II Gothicus defeats Goths.

270	Aurelian hailed as emperor by Danube legions; Zenobia of Palmyra aspires to rule Roman East.
271	Aurelian withdraws from Dacia and Agri Decumates; fortification of Rome by Aurelian.
272	Aurelian captures Palmyra and restores imperial rule in east.
274	Aurelian conquers Gallo-Roman Empire and reunited Roman Empire.
276–282	Reign of Probus—end of Gothic Threat; Franks and Saxons attack northwestern provinces.
282–283	Persian Expedition of Carus—sack of Ctesiphon.
284	Accession of Diocletian—creation of the Dominate; reforms of army and administration.
285	Diocletian nominates Maximianus as Augustus of the west; formal division of the Roman Empire.
287	Rebellion of Carausius—creation of Romano-British Empire.
293	Galerius and Constantius I proclaimed Caesars of the east and west; creation of the Tetrarchy ("rule of four").
296	Constantius I recovers Britain—end of Romano-British Empire.
298–300	Galerius wages Persian War.
300	Shah Narses cedes to Rome Mesopotamian fortresses on Upper Tigris; construction of *Strata*

	Diocletiana along desert frontier in Syria.
305	Abdications of Diocletian and Maximianus; Galerius and Constantius I succeed as Augusti; Maximinus II Daia and Severus II hailed Caesars.
306	Death of Constantius I in Britain; western army proclaims as Augustus Constantine; Praetorians and Senate at Rome hail as emperor Maxentius; outbreak of civil wars.
308	Galerius summons Council of Carnuntum to settle political crisis; Licinius elevated by Galerius as Augustus of the west.
311	Death of Galerius, and Licinius rules as Augustus in Balkans.
312	Constantine defeats and slays Maxentius at the battle of Milvian Bridge; conversion of Constantine to Christianity.
313	Alliance of Constantine and Licinius; "Edict of Milian" extends toleration to Christians; Licinius defeats Maximinus II, and conquers Roman East.
323–324	Constantine defeats Licinius and reunites the Roman Empire.
330	Dedication of Constantinople (Byzantium) as New Rome.
337	Accession of sons of Constantine—Constantine II, Constans, and Constantius II.

340	Constantine II defeated and slain by Constans in civil war; Constans rules henceforth the entire Roman West.
342–311	Bishop Ulfilas converts Goths to Arian Christianity.
355–364	Shah Shapur II wages war against Rome.
350–353	Revolt of Magnentius in Gaul and murder of Constans; civil war between Constantius II and Magnentius.
355–357	Franks, Alemanni, and Saxons overrun northern frontiers.
357–360	Caesar Julian defeats Alemanni, and settles Franks as federates in Brabant.
360	Proclamation of Julian II as emperor by western army.
361	Death of Constantius II; Julian as sole emperor restores paganism.
363	Abortive Persian expedition and retreat of Julian II; death of Julian and accession of Jovian.
364	Jovian cedes eastern Mesopotamian fortresses to Persia; eastern army proclaims as emperors the brothers Valentinian I in west and Valens in east.
367	Saxons overrun imperial defense of Britain; Count Theodosius restores order in Britain.
375	Death of Valentinian, and accession of Gratian in West; Huns and Alans defeat Goths; suicide of King Ermanaric; Goths admitted into Roman Empire by Valens; Huns

	extend sway over steppes of eastern Europe.
378	Battle of Adrianople—Goths defeat and slay Valens.
379	Theodosius I created Eastern Emperor by Gratian.
382	Theodosius resettles rebel Goths as federates on Lower Danube frontier.
383–388	Western army rebels under Magnus Maximus.
ca. 386	Rome and Persia partition Armenia.
391–392	Theodosius I issues laws against paganism.
392–394	Revolt of Western army led by *magister militum* Arbogast.
394	Battle of the Frigidus—Theodosius I reunites Roman Empire.
395	Death of Theodosius I; division into Eastern and Western Roman Empires; Accession of Aracdius and Honorius; Alaric and Visigoths invade Thrace.
396–397	Stilicho, *magister militum* of west, intervenes against Alaric in Greece; Stilicho settles Alaric and Visigoths in Epirus.
400	Alaric and Visigoths migrate to Italy.
402	Alaric and Visigoths invade Italy; Honorius removes the Western court to Ravenna.
406	Great Barbarian Migration across Rhine; Saxons, Franks, and Burgundians overrun northern and

	eastern Gaul; Sueves and Alans overrun Spain.
408	Accession of eastern Theodosius II in east; Honorius executes Stilicho; collapse of imperial defense in Italy.
410	Usurper Constantine III and field army of Britain invade Gaul; Alaric and Visigoths sack Rome; death of Alaric in southern Italy.
411	Athaulf leads Visigoths as federates in Aquitaine.
413	Burgundians settled as federates at Worms in Rhineland; construction of walls of Constantinople.
423	Death of Honorius—dynastic crisis in Roman West.
425	Accession of Western Emperor Valentinian III; Aetius as *magister militum* dominates imperial policy in the west.
429	Vandals, Alans, and Sueves under Gaiseric invade Africa.
ca. 430–450	Emergence of Romano-Celtic warlords in Britain; Saxons, Angles, and Jutes raid shores of eastern Britain.
433	Accession of Attila as king of the Huns.
439	Vandals capture Carthage.
441–443	Attila ravages Balkan Provinces.
442	Valentinian III acknowledges by treaty the Vandal Kingdom (Africa, Sardinia, and Corsica).

443	Attila imposes annual tribute on Theodosius II; Collapse of Roman Frontier on Upper and Middle Danube; Burgundians secure federate treaty in eastern and southern Gaul.
444	Attila murders his brother Bela and seizes sole power of Hun Empire.
447	Attila imposes new tribute (6,000 pounds of gold) on Theodosius II.
450	Accession of Marcian in east; Marcian ends annual tribute to Attila; Empress Honoria appeals to Attila; Anglo-Saxon migration into southern and eastern Britain.
451	Attila invades Western Roman Empire; Battle of Châlons—Aetius and Visigoths check Attila in eastern Gaul.
452	Attila invades northern Italy and is halted at Po by Pope Leo I; retreat and death of Attila.
454	Valentinian III orders execution of Aetius.
455	Death of Valentinian III—dynastic crisis at Ravenna; Gaiseric and Vandals sack Rome.
456	Ricimer, *magister militum*, king maker in Roman West; imperial court at Ravenna loses control over remaining western provinces.
457	Death of Marcian, and accession of Leo I as Eastern Emperor.
466	King Euric II initiates Visigothic conquest of Spain.

474	Accession of Zeno as Eastern Roman Emperor.
476	Odoacer, *magister militum*, deposes Romulus Augustulus; Zeno confirms Odoacer as *magister militum* and patrician; end of the Western Roman Empire.
482	Accession of Clovis as Merovingian king of the Franks.
486	Clovis conquers the Romano-Gallic kingdom of Soissons.
496	Conversion of Clovis to Catholic Christianity; submission to Clovis of Burgundians, Alamanni, and Thuringians.
489–491	Ostrogoths under Theoderic defeat Odoacer; foundation of Ostrogothic Kingdom (Italy, Sicily, Dalmatia, and Provence).
491	Death of Zeno, and accession of Anastasius I.
507	Battle of Vouillé—Clovis expels Visigoths from Aquitaine.
518	Death of Anastasius I, and accession of Justin I.
523	Accession of King Hilderic—crisis in Vandal kingdom.
526	Death of King Theoderic of the Ostrogoths; accession of Athalaric under regent Queen Amalasuntha; outbreak of Persian War.
527	Death of Justin I, and accession of Justinian I.

530	Battle of Daras—Belisarius defeats Persian army; Gelimer deposes Hilderic—crisis in Vandal Kingdom.
532	Perpetual Peace—Justinian pays 11,000 pounds of gold to Chosroes I.
533	Belisarius conquers the Vandal Kingdom.
534	Death of Athalaric, and Marriage of Amalasuntha and Theodahad.
535	Revolts and Moorish attacks in Africa; Theodahad murders Queen Amalasuntha—Justinian declares war; Belisarius conquers Sicily from Ostrogoths.
536	Ostrogoths depose Theodahad and elect Wittigis as king Belisarius reoccupies Rome.
537–538	First Ostrogothic Siege of Rome.
540	Belisarius captures Wittigis and Ostrogothic court; organization of Byzantine administration at Ravenna; outbreak of Second Persian War.
541	Belisarius assumes command of eastern army; Ostrogoths elect Totila king and overrun Italy.
542–543	Outbreak of Plague in Mediterranean world, Europe, and Near East; beginning of Pandemics—demographic collapse.
544	Belisarius assumes command in Italy.
545–547	Second Ostrogothic Siege of Rome.
552	Battle of Busta Gallorum—defeat and death of Totila; end of Ostrogothic

	Kingdom and restoration of imperial rule in Italy.
554	Justinian issues Pragmatic Sanction to reorganize Italy.
562	Justinian concludes Fifty Year Treaty with Chosroes.
565	Death of Justinian I, and accession of Justin II.
568	Migration of Lombards under Alboin into northern Italy.
572	Outbreak of Persian War.
578	Death of Justin II, and accession of Tiberius II.
582	Death of Tiberius II, and accession of Maurice Tiberius; imperial recovery in the Balkan provinces.
591	Maurice Tiberius restores Shah Chosroes II to Sassanid throne and concludes peace with Persia.
602	Phocas overthrows and murders Maurice Tiberius; outbreak of Persian War; collapse of the frontier on Lower Danube; Slavs and Avars migrate into the Balkans.
610	Overthrow of Phocas, accession of Heraclius; administrative, military and fiscal reforms.
622	The "Flight" (Hegira) of Muhammad from Mecca; Heraclius launches offensive against Persia.
630	Muhammad received in Mecca—unification of Arabia; under Islam;

	Heraclius received in triumph at Jerusalem.
634	Accession of Caliph Umar I; creation of Islamic Empire (Caliphate).
636–639	Muslim conquest of Mesopotamia, Syria, Palestine; collapse of Eastern Roman frontier.
639	Battle of Qadisiya—Muslim conquest of Sassanid Empire.
641	Death of Heraclius—succession crisis at Constantinople; Muslim conquest of Egypt.

Glossary

Achaemenid: The dynasty of Persian kings (559–330 B.C.) who ruled the Near East during the classical age.

adlection (Latin *adlectio*): The right of the Roman emperor to nominate worthy men to the Senate at the rank of a curule magistrate.

Africa: The Roman designation of the region settled by Phoenicians in Tunisia and along the shores of western Libya; annexed as the province of Africa in 146 B.C.

ager publicus ("public land"): Land appropriated by Roman people from defeated foes. Those occupying the land, designated *possessores*, paid a rent to the Roman state. *Populares* reformers after 133 B.C. proposed to redistribute such land on long-term leases to poorer citizens.

Agri Decumates ("Tithe Lands"): Comprising Germany between the Main and upper Danube, this region was annexed by Rome in 73–161 A.D. It was abandoned circa 260–271 A.D. and subsequently occupied by the Alemanni.

ala (pl. *alae*; "wing"): Auxiliary unit of cavalry (512 men).

Alans: Iranian-speaking nomadic Sarmatians dwelling on the steppes between the Black and Caspian Seas from the 2nd century B.C. to the 4th century A.D.

Alemanni: A confederation of southern Germanic tribes united in the 3rd century A.D., who pressed along the upper Rhine and Danube frontiers.

Amber Route: A network of trade routes across central Europe that linked the Mediterranean world with the lands of the Baltic Sea.

amicitia ("friendship"): Denoted either cooperation between Roman politicians or informal diplomatic relations between Rome and a client power.

Anglo-Saxons: Germanic tribes of northern Germany and Jutland who migrated to Britain in 450–550 A.D., thereby establishing England.

aquila (pl. *aquilae*; "eagle"): The legionary standard that was believed to have sacred power (*numen*). From the time of Gaius Marius, each legion carried a distinct eagle.

Arsacid dynasty: Founded by King Arsaces (r. c. 246–210 B.C.); ruled the Parthian Empire in 246 B.C.–227 A.D.

Asia: The western third of Asia Minor (modern Turkey); annexed as a Roman province in 133–130 B.C.

assemblies: Roman citizens voted in four different assemblies based on property or residence. The Centuriate Assembly (*comitia centuriata*), based on centuries that favored age and wealth, elected the senior magistrates (censors, consuls, and praetors). The *imperium* for these magistrates was voted in the Curiate Assembly. The Tribal Assembly (*comitia tributa*) passed law (*lex*; pl. *leges*). See ***concilium plebis*** for the fourth assembly.

assiduus (pl. *assidui*): A Roman citizen of propertied class eligible for draft.

auctoritas ("influence"): The personal qualities and patronage of a Roman that commanded respect and loyalty, as opposed to the legal power, or ***imperium***, voted by an assembly.

auxilia: Any allied forces serving in the Roman army under the republic. The emperor Augustus organized the auxiliaries into professional units of provincials commanded by Roman officers.

barbarian (Greek *barbaros*; pl. *barbaroi*; "foreigner"): In the Classical age, this term designated non-Greeks who did not live under the rule of law. Romans turned the term into a cultural designation for those outside their civilized world.

Batavians: A Germanic people dwelling in the lower reaches of the Rhine (modern Holland) allied to imperial Rome; furnished soldiers to the auxiliary army.

Belgae: Related Celtic-speaking tribes of northeastern Gaul and southeastern Britain who were regarded as the fiercest Gallic warriors.

bellum iustum ("just war"): Declared by Rome according to the fetial rite; the origin for the later medieval and modern religious war.

beneficiarius (pl. *beneficiarii*): Roman soldiers on detached service.

Bibracte: In eastern Gaul; the site where Julius Caesar defeated the Helvetians in 58 B.C.

Burgundians: East Germanic people dwelling in the upper Main valley in the 4th century; migrated into eastern and southeastern Gaul in the 5th century A.D.

Caledonia: The Scottish highlands—regions never conquered by Rome.

canabae: Civilian settlements near a legionary base; *canabae* evolved into cities.

castra: A legionary camp; passed into English as the word *chester*. The *castellum* (pl. *castella*; "castle") was a fort garrisoned by an auxiliary unit.

cataphractus (pl. *cataphracti*): A lancer wearing chain mail or lamellar armor. Parthians, Persians, and Sarmatians based their armies on this heavy cavalry. From the reign of Hadrian (r. 117–138), the Romans fielded comparable units of *cataphracti*, who became the elite forces of the early Byzantine age.

Celt (Greek *Keltos*, pl. *Keltoi*): A speaker of related Indo-European languages in the British Isles and western and central Europe. See also **Gauls**.

Celtiberians: Descendants of Celtic immigrants and native Iberians, who dwelled in central and southwestern Spain and Portugal.

censor: One of two magistrates, elected at intervals of five years, who revised the census and the membership of the Senate, let out public contracts, and ruled on public morals. Censors held no *imperium*, but they held office for 18 months and were regarded as the most senior magistrates in the republic.

Centuriate Assembly: See **assemblies**.

centurion (Latin *centurio*; pl. *centuriones*): A noncommissioned officer who commanded a century. There were 60 centurions in the post-Marian legion.

century (Latin *centuria*; pl. *centuriae*): The basic tactical unit of a legion. Initially, 100 men formed a century; in the imperial army, the number was 80 men.

civis Romanus (pl. *cives Romani*; "Roman citizen"): A citizen with full legal and political rights. See *ius Latinum*.

civitas (pl. *civitates*): An urban-based community under Roman law in the imperial age.

civitas sine suffragio ("citizenship without the suffrage"): A citizen accorded only private rights of Roman citizenship. All members of this class had been promoted to full citizens by 188 B.C.

cohort (Latin *cohors*; pl. *cohortes*): A tactical unit of the legion. Initially of 600 men, the cohort of the imperial age was fixed at 480 men. Auxiliary units of infantry were also organized into cohorts.

collegium (pl. *collegia*): A burial society and guild of craftsmen, cults, or professions.

colonia (pl. *coloniae*; "colony"): One of two self-governing communities under military obligation to Rome. Initially, colonies comprising settlers of Latin status were founded in Italy from the 4th through the 2nd centuries B.C. After 88 B.C., colonies were founded in the provinces and were usually of Roman legal status.

colonus (pl. *coloni*; "cultivator"): A dependent tenant in later Roman imperial law.

comes (pl. *comites*; "count"): A commander of a regional field army under the Dominate.

comitatenses: Units of the imperial field army in the Dominate; the senior service; see also **limitanei**.

comitatus: The Roman designation for a retinue of dedicated Germanic warriors; these warriors have been compared to the *beserkers*, "frenzied warriors," in later Scandinavian legend.

concilium plebis: A meeting of only the Roman plebians (without patricians present), organized in voting units identical to the Tribal Assembly and presided over by a tribune of the plebeians. This assembly passed *plebiscitia* (plebiscite), which had the power of law (*lex*) since 287 B.C. This was the assembly preferred by *popularis* reformers in the late republic.

Constitutio Antoniniana: Edict issued by the emperor Caracalla in 212 A.D. that granted citizenship to all free inhabitants of the Roman Empire.

consul: One of two senior curule officials of the Roman Republic annually elected by the Centuriate Assembly and with *imperium*, the right to command armies. Consul became a senior administrative post under the Roman Empire.

cuneus ("wedge"): An attack in dense column, favored by Germanic warriors.

curule magistrates: Any senior official elected (censor, consul, praetor, quaestor) who had a chair of office (*sella curulis*). Such officials were eligible for membership in the Senate.

Dacians: A Geto-Thracian-speaking peoples dwelling in modern Rumania (Dacia), who were conquered by Trajan in the Dacian Wars (101–102, 105–106 A.D.).

de repetundis ("on corruption"): Courts at Rome, first reported in 171 B.C., that investigated and punished Roman magistrates for corruption in the provinces. In 149–70 B.C., the composition of juries was a political issue between senators and equestrians.

dedictii: Defeated foes who surrendered unconditionally; in the imperial age, such barbarians were often settled as *coloni* in imperial provinces.

denarius (pl. *denarii*): The Roman silver coin, minted at 84 to the Roman pound from 214 B.C. to 64 A.D. (3.83 gr.); used to meet fiscal obligations. Twenty-five denarii were exchanged to a gold coin (*aureus*). The debasement of the denarius to meet rising costs after 235 A.D. resulted in inflation and fiscal instability.

dictator: An official with overriding *imperium*, elected in a emergency, who could serve only six months. The office was discontinued after the Second Punic War (218–201 B.C.). In 82–78 B.C., Lucius Cornelius Sulla was the first of the great *imperatores* of the late republic who revived the office to legitimize an extraordinary position in civil war.

dilectus: The Roman draft, for which all citizens of propertied status (*assidui*) were eligible in the Roman Republic.

diocesis (pl. *dioceses*): The administrative unit of several provinces under the Dominate. Constantine (r. 306–337 A.D.) organized the imperial Christian church by dioceses.

Dominate (284–476 A.D.): Refers to the late Roman imperial government after Diocletian (r. 284–305), who dropped republican symbols and styled himself an autocrat or lord (*dominus*).

donative (Latin *donativum*): The money given to veterans by a Roman commander at his triumph; in the imperial age, the donative became a regular bonus to the entire army.

Druids: Members of the Celtic priestly caste who reportedly headed resistance to Rome.

dux (pl. *duces*; "duke"): The commander of a garrison in the later Roman Empire.

epigraphy: The study of inscriptions.

equestrian order (Latin *ordo equester*; "knights"): The propertied class below the senatorials. In the 2nd century B.C., the equestrians amassed fortunes and, thus, legal rank from careers in justice, the military, banking, and commerce.

Erythraean Sea: The Roman designation of the Red Sea and Indian Ocean.

ex formula togatorum ("from the formula of togated peoples"): The obligation of Latin and Italian allies to provide soldiers on demand by the Roman Republic.

fascis (pl. *fasces*): The bundle of rods carried by lictors as symbols of the power of life and death held by Roman republican magistrates elected with *imperium*.

Feriale Duranum: Military calendar discovered at the Roman fortress of Dura-Europos on the Euphrates, in Syria, dating from the reign of Severus Alexander (r. 222–235 A.D.).

Five Good Emperors (96–180 A.D.): Nerva (96–98 A.D.), Trajan (98–117 A.D.), Hadrian (117–138 A.D.), Antonius Pius (138–161 A.D.), and Marcus Aurelius (161–180 A.D.), whose collective reigns marked the height of the Roman peace (*pax Romana*).

Flavian dynasty (69–96 A.D.): The second imperial dynasty of Rome ruled by the emperors Vespasian (r. 67–79 A.D.) and his two sons, Titus (r. 79–81 A.D.) and Domitian (r. 81–96 A.D.).

foederatus (pl. *foederati*; "federates"): Barbarians serving in tribal armies under contract to Rome. In 417–418 A.D., the emperor Honorius settled the Visigoths in Aquitaine as federates; they were the first Germans to gain a kingdom in the Western Roman Empire.

foedus: A formal treaty issued by Rome to any ally. Such treaties bound Italian allies to the Roman Republic. In the 5th century A.D., emperors issued such a treaty to Germanic tribal armies who were quartered in the provinces.

Franks: A coalition of tribes in northwestern Germany between the Rhine and the Weser, which emerged as a power in the late 3rd century A.D. The Franks, under King Clovis (r. 482–511 A.D.), conquered most of Roman Gaul.

Frisians: Kin of the Batavians; occupied the shores of Holland; entered into alliance with Rome; and supplied the Roman army of the lower Rhine with hides, meat, and dairy products.

Galatians: The Celts who settled in western Asia Minor in 279–255 B.C.

Gallia Comata ("Long-Haired Gaul"): The three Gallic regions (later the provinces of Aquitania, Belgica, and Lugdunesis) beyond the Roman province in southern Gaul, Narbonensis, organized in 121–118 B.C.

Gallomachy: A monumental relief depicting the combat of Greeks and Gauls.

garum: A fish sauce devised and marketed from Gades (Cadiz) in southern Spain.

Gauls (Latin *Gallus*; pl. *Galli*): The Latin designation of Celtic speakers and, more specifically, of those Celts dwelling in Gaul proper (Transalpine Gaul) and northern Italy (Cisalpine Gaul).

genius (pl. *genii*): The spirit of a Roman emperor that was deified on his death.

gens (pl. *gentes*): The extended Roman clan, as opposed to a *familia* ("family"), which was a branch of the *gens*. The second name (*nomen*) of a Roman male denoted the *gens*; the third name (*cognomen*) designated the family. Female names were based on the *nomen*.

Gepidae: An East Germanic peoples of the 4th and 5th centuries A.D. who headed the revolt that ended the Hun Empire in 454 A.D..

Germania: The Roman designation for central and northern Europe east of the Rhine and north of the upper Danube, where German-speaking peoples dwelled.

gladius (pl. *gladii*): The cutting and thrusting sword of the legionary.

Hallstatt civilization (c. 800–450 B.C.): The early Iron Age civilization of Celtic peoples in central Europe.

Hellenes, Hellas: Proper Greek names for Greeks and Greece.

Hellenistic (323–31 B.C.): The "Greek-like" civilization in the Near East and Mediterranean world after the death of Alexander the Great (r. 336–323 B.C.).

Hercynian Forest: Roman name for the Black Forest (Schwartzwald).

Herulians: An East Germanic people who headed the invasion of Greece in 267 A.D.

Hibernia ("land of winter quarters"): The Roman name for Ireland.

Hispania (Spain): The Roman name for the Iberian peninsula (modern Spain and Portugal).

Huns: The first Turkish-speaking nomads to enter Europe circa 375 A.D.; under King Attila (r. 434–452 A.D.), they dominated the barbarian world.

imago (pl. *imagines*): The Roman death mask images of ancestors displayed in the atrium of a Roman house. The term later designated the official portrait of the Roman emperor.

imperator (pl. *imperators*): A Roman commander who had been saluted by his soldiers for a major victory. The term designated the extraordinary commanders of the late republic (88–31 B.C.) and, later, the Roman emperor.

imperium: The right to command an army accorded to senior magistrates. The magistrates were elected by the Centuriate Assembly, but the *imperium* was voted by the Curiate Assembly.

Imperium Galliarum ("Empire of the Gauls"): Proclaimed by the Gallic and German insurgents under Gaius Julius Civilis in 69–70 A.D.

itinera ("itineraries"): Schematic maps and directions for overland travel.

ius Italicum ("Italian right"): The exemption from direct taxation awarded to favored Roman colonies in the provinces.

ius Latinum ("Latin status"): A legal category created by Rome in 338 B.C. for those Romans and allies settled in colonies in Italy. Each self-governing

Latin colony enjoyed rights of marriage and contract with Rome. Latins had the right to migrate to Rome and acquire Roman citizenship. Latin status was, thus, defined as midway between full citizenship and allied status.

Jazyges: Sarmatian nomads who settled in the Theiss valley (eastern Hungary) in the 1st and 2nd centuries A.D.

kurgan: Monumental Scythian burial barrows erected on the southern Russian steppes between the 6th and 2nd centuries B.C.

La Tène civilization (c. 450–50 B.C.): Late Iron Age culture of the Celtic peoples of central and western Europe characterized by the settlements known as *oppida*.

laetus (pl. *laeti*): Barbarians (either captives or immigrants) settled in communities within the Roman Empire during the 4th century A.D.

Late Antiquity (c. 300–750 A.D.): The late classical and early medieval periods; the term is used to designate cultural continuity.

Latins, Latin status: See *ius Latinum*.

legatus (pl. *legati*; "legate"): A lieutenant of a Roman republican magistrate with *imperium*. In the Principate, governors of senatorial rank ruled provinces as legates of the emperor, with either proconsular or propraetorian rank.

legio (pl. *legions*): The legion (5,200 men) was the Roman strategic fighting unit capable of independent operations. Under the republic, each consul typically commanded two legions of citizens and two of allies.

lex Appuleia (103 B.C.): Law passed by the tribune Lucius Appuleius Saturninus that granted leases of public land in Africa to veterans of Gaius Marius.

lex Pompeia (89 B.C.): Law of consul Gnaeus Pompeius Strabo that granted Latin status to the provincials of Cisalpine Gaul.

lex Sempronia (133 B.C.): The law of the tribune Tiberius Sempronius Gracchus that granted leases of public land in Italy to poor citizens. The law was suspended in 129 B.C.; it was reactivated by Gaius Sempronius Gracchus in 123 B.C.

libertus (pl. *liberti*): A freedman of a Roman citizen. Freedmen acquired Roman citizenship and became clients of their former masters.

lictor: The official who carried the *fascis*, the symbol of *imperium*. A dictator was accompanied by 24 lictors; consuls, by 12 lictors; and praetors, by 6 lictors.

limes ("limit"): Originally designated any Roman military encampment that marked a border. In the imperial age, the term designated the political-cultural boundary between the Roman and barbarian worlds.

limitanei: Units of the Roman frontier or garrison army in the 4th and 5th centuries; see *comitanenses*.

Lombards (Langobardi): An East Germanic people who migrated into northern Italy in 568 and shattered Byzantine control over the peninsula.

Luca (56 B.C.): The scene of the conference where Julius Caesar, Pompey, and Crassus renewed their alliance, the First Triumvirate. Caesar received a five-year extension of his proconsulship in Gaul; Pompey and Crassus stood for the consulship of 55 B.C.

Lusitanians: Celtic-Iberian tribes in Portugal and southwestern Spain.

magister militum ("master of the soldiers"): The supreme commander of late Roman field armies. The position was held by Stilicho (395–408 A.D.), Aetius (425–454 A.D.); Ricimer (457–472 A.D.); and Odoacer (476–491 A.D.).

maniple (Latin *manipulus*; pl. *manipuli*): The principal legionary tactical unit, comprising two centuries, from the 4th through the 2nd centuries B.C. The large cohort replaced the maniple in the late republican and imperial ages.

Mare Nostrum ("Our Sea"): Roman designation of the Mediterranean Sea.

Merovingian dynasty (458–751 A.D.): The family of Clovis (r. 482–511 A.D.), who ruled the early Frankish kingdom.

Moors (Latin *Mauri*): The Berber-speaking nomads of North Africa.

mos maiorum ("custom of the ancestors"): Expressed Roman reverence for tradition over change (*res novae*, "new things").

Nabataeans: Arabic nomads who formed a kingdom east of the Jordan, based at Bostra and Petra. The region was annexed as the Roman province of Arabia Petraea in 106 A.D.

nobilis (pl. *nobiles*; "noble"): Those of Roman families (either of patrician or plebian order) whose members had held a curule office after 367 B.C.

Notitia Dignitatum: A list of Roman military units compiled circa 406–423 A.D.

novus homo ("new man"): A Roman elected to the consulship whose ancestors had not held a curule magistrate.

numen (pl. *numina*): Sacred power innate to any object or symbol.

oppidum (pl. *oppida*): An Iron Age Celtic settlement, such as Entremont or Magdelensburg.

optimates: Roman politicians favoring supremacy of the Senate in the late republic.

ordo (pl. *ordines*; "order"): A legally defined rank. Roman society was initially divided into the two orders of patricians and plebians.

Ostrogoths: The Goths settled in Pannonia under imperial treaty who migrated to Italy under King Theoderic (r. 489–526 A.D.). These Goths were descended from those who had submitted to the Huns after 375 A.D.

Parthians: Iranian-speaking nomads who settled in Khursan (northern Iran) in the 3rd century B.C. and, under the Arsacid kings, ruled a rival eastern empire to Rome.

patrician: The original Roman order (*ordo*) alone permitted to hold office in the early republic. The plebians, who formed an order of voters, gained rights and redress of grievances that climaxed in 367 B.C., when they also gained the right to be elected consul.

pax Romana ("Roman peace"): Described the conditions of the Principate, specifically the collective reigns of the Five Good Emperors.

peregrines (Latin *peregrinus*; pl. *peregrini*): Free foreigners residing in the provinces.

Periplous ("Sailing Around"): A manual for navigation.

pilum (pl. *pila*): The legionary thrusting and throwing spear.

plebian: See **patrician**.

popularis (pl. *populares*): A politician favoring reform in the name of the Roman people.

populus Romanus ("Roman people"): The Roman citizens as a whole in public actions.

praetor: A curule magistrate with *imperium* below the rank of consul; their number was increased to six by the late republic.

Praetorian Guards: The garrison of Rome commanded by the equestrian Praetorian Prefect.

prefect (Latin *prefectus*; pl. *prefectus*): A Roman officer of equestrian rank who commanded an auxiliary unit or administered a province.

prefecturate: One of four great regional divisions of the Roman Empire (Gaul, Italy, Illyricum, and the East) in the 4th and 5th centuries A.D. Each prefecturate comprised several dioceses.

princeps Senatus ("prince of the Senate"): The leading senator whose superior *auctoritas* was recognized by his peers. The term *princeps* ("prince") was an informal way of designating the Roman emperor.

Principate (27 B.C.–284 A.D.): The imperial government created by Augustus, in which the emperor ruled in accordance with the symbols and powers of the republic.

proconsul: An ex-magistrate with the *imperium* of a consul who was, thus, granted an extension of command within a province. The *imperium* of a proconsul ranked below that of a consul.

proletarius (pl. *proletarii*): A property-less Roman citizen not eligible for legionary service.

propraetor: An ex-magistrate with the *imperium* of a praetor who was, thus, granted an extension of command within a province. The *imperium* of a propraetor ranked below that of a praetor.

prorogatio ("prorogation"): The formal vote by the Centuriate Assembly to extend or augment the *imperium* of an ex-magistrate in a province.

prosopography ("the study of faces"): The analysis of family and matrimonial links that dictated politics at Rome.

provincia (pl. *provinciae*; "province"): Originally a theater of operation where a magistrate exercised his *imperium* or *pro-imperium*. By the mid-2nd century B.C., overseas provinces had evolved into administrative districts defined in Roman law.

Res Gestae divi Augusti ("*Deeds of the Deified Augustus*"): A monumental inscription in Latin and Greek erected throughout the Roman Empire that narrated the accomplishments of the emperor Augustus.

res publica: The Latin designation for republic or commonwealth.

Roxolani: Sarmatian nomads dwelling in modern Wallachia and Moldavia, just north of the lower Danube, between the 1st and 3rd centuries A.D.

runes: Germanic magical letters inspired from northern Italic alphabets at least since the 2nd century B.C.

sacramentum: The oath of soldiers to their commander (*imperator*).

Sassanid dynasty: These shahs of the neo-Persian Empire (227–651 A.D.) overthrew Arsacid Parthia and challenged Rome in the Near East.

Saxons: West Germanic peoples dwelling along the shores of northwestern Germany who raided Britain and northern Gaul from the mid-3rd century A.D. Saxons, along with Angles and Jutes, settled in Britain between 450 and 550 A.D.

scutum (pl. *scuta*): The rectangular, semi-cylindrical shield of the legionary.

Scythians: The Iranian-speaking steppe nomads of southern Russia between the 7th and 2nd centuries B.C.

Senate: The advisory council of the Roman state, composed of ex-curule magistrates whose collective influence (*auctoritas*) dominated politics, diplomacy, and finances of the republic. Under the Principate, the Senate became an administrative body and supreme judiciary.

Senatorial class: By the mid-2nd century B.C., this class was defined as those aristocratic families whose members undertook a political career. Augustus redefined the senatorial order as the premier legal and social order of the Roman Empire.

Social War (90–88 B.C.): The revolt of Italian allies (*socii*) in central and southern Italy when Rome denied them citizenship.

socius (pl. *socii*; "ally"): Any Roman ally, but in the republic, the term was applied foremost to the Italian allies owing military service *ex formula togatorum*.

SPQR (*Senatus Populusque Romanus*; "Senate and People of Rome"): The abbreviation applied to official acts of the Roman Republic.

Strata Diocletiana: The Roman military highway and forts along the Syrian desert; initiated by the emperor Diocletian (r. 284–305 A.D.).

Sueves: A coalition of the West Germanic tribes, the Marcomanni and Quadi.

Tax farming: The practice of letting out contracts to private companies organized by equestrians to collect provincial taxes under the Roman Republic.

Tetrarchy ("rule of four"): The collective rule of four emperors, two Augusti and two Caesars, devised by Diocletian (r. 284–305 A.D.).

thing: The sovereign assembly of free German males.

transhumance: A pattern of seasonal movements by desert nomads and their herds among the oases and pre-desert zones.

tria nomina ("three names"): The Roman nomenclature of males with a *praenomen* (personal name), *nomen* (clan name), and *cognomen* (family name).

Tribal Assembly: See **assemblies**.

Tribune of the plebians (Latin *tribunus plebis*): One of 10 sacrosanct representatives of the Roman plebians who had the power to veto ("I forbid") any action by a magistrate that threatened a plebian. Tribunes, elected by the *concilium plebis* and with the right to initiate legislation, were the main agents for *popularis* reform in the late republic.

Tribune of the soldiers (Latin *tribunus militum*): One of six junior officers (of senatorial or equestrian rank) attached to a legion.

Tribunician power (*tribunica potestas*): The power of the tribune voted to Augustus in 27 B.C. and later emperors without the limitations of office. This power was the legal basis for the constitutional position of the Roman emperor.

tributum (pl. *tributa*): Direct provincial taxation (head and land taxes).

triumph (Latin *triumphus*): The parade displaying booty and captives that glorified a successful Roman magistrate who had slain more than 5,000 foreign foes in battle. A lesser *ovatio* ("ovation") was voted for lesser victories.

triumvirate ("rule of three"): The First Triumvirate was an informal agreement by Pompey, Julius Caesar, and Crassus to cooperate and, thus, dominate the republic in 58–49 B.C. The Second Triumvirate (42–31 B.C.) was a legal alliance of Octavian, Marc Antony, and Lepidus to punish the assassins of Julius Caesar, then reorder the Roman world.

tumultus ("tumult"): A Gallic migration that required a state of emergency by the Roman Republic.

Vandals: An East Germanic peoples in central Europe who migrated across Gaul and Spain to North Africa in 406–429 A.D.. The Vandal kingdom in Africa, recognized in 439–442 A.D., was overthrown by Justinian's general Belisarius in 533 A.D.

velites: Recruited from the *proletarii*; served as the light infantry of the republican legion; organized by maniples between the 4th and 2nd centuries B.C.

vexillatio (pl. *vexillationes*; "vexillation") A legionary detachment of 2,000 men withdrawn to serve in offensive expeditions.

viritim ("man by man"): Allotments of individual farmsteads to Roman citizens from public land (*ager publicus*).

virtus ("virtue"): Manliness and bravery—qualities personified by the god Virtus. Christians defined virtue in a moral sense.

Visigoths: Descended from Goths who entered the Roman Empire in 375–377 A.D. and migrated under Alaric (r. 395–410 A.D.) to Italy. In 417–418 A.D., the Visigoths founded a territorial kingdom in southern Gaul under imperial treaty.

White Huns (or Ephthalites): Turkic-speaking nomads who attacked the northeastern frontiers of the Sassanid Empire in the late 4th and early 5th centuries A.D.

Zoroastrianism: The monotheist creed of Iran based on the teachings of Zorathustra.

Biographical Notes

Aemilian (born c. 208; r. 253 A.D.). Marcus Aemilius Aemilianus, governor of Moesia, was declared emperor by his legions. He defeated and slew the emperor Trebonnianus Gallus, but three months later, Aemilian was defeated and slain by Valerian, who was declared emperor by the Rhine legions.

Alaric (r. 395–410 A.D.). King of the Visigoths, had served under Theodosius I. Alaric, denied high command by the imperial government, led the Visigoths into Greece in 395–397, then to Italy in 400–402. Stilicho checked Alaric until 408. In 410, Alaric sacked Rome in a bid to pressure the emperor Honorius for a command, but Alaric died soon after.

Aetius (d. 454 A.D.). Flavius Aetius, *magister militum* (425–454), was from a military family in Moesia. By his influence with the kings Ruga and, later, Attila, Aetius secured Huns as federates and dominated policy at the court of Western emperor Valentinian III. In 454, Aetius was executed on grounds of treason.

Agrippina, "the Elder" (14 B.C.–33 A.D.). Daughter of Agrippa and Julia, married Germanicus circa 5 A.D., and bore three sons and three daughters.

Amalasuntha (r. 526–535). Queen of the Ostrogoths, daughter of Theoderic, and regent for her son Athalaric, who died in 534. Amalasuntha was compelled to marry and elevate to the throne her cousin Theodahad, who arranged the queen's murder. Justinian seized on the murder of Amalasuntha to invade Italy.

Ammianus Marcellinus (c. 330–395). Soldier and historian, born of a military family from the Roman colony of Berytus (modern Beirut). Ammianus, a pagan who served under Christian emperors, is hailed as the last historian of the imperial reign. Only the last portions of his history, covering the reigns from Trajan to Valens, survive.

Antiochus III (born 242 B.C, r. 223–187 B.C.). King of the Seleucid Empire, emulated the career of Alexander the Great. He blundered into a war with Rome (192–188 B.C.). His defeat at Magnesia (190 B.C) reduced the Seleucid state to a power of the second rank.

Antony, Mark (83–30 B.C.). Marcus Antonius, of a noble family, distinguished himself as a cavalry commander under Julius Caesar. Mark

Antony was tribune of the plebians in 49 B.C. and consul in 44 B.C. He joined the Second Triumvirate in 43 B.C. and won the victory over the Liberators at Philippi (42 B.C.). Mark Antony, charged with reordering the Roman East, lost support at Rome by his marriage to the Ptolemaic Queen Cleopatra VII. In 31 B.C., he was decisively defeated by Octavian at Actium. Antony fled to Egypt and committed suicide in 30 B.C.

Appuleius Saturninus, Lucius (c. 145–100 B.C.). *Popularis* tribune of the plebians in 103 B.C., entered into political alliance with Gaius Marius. His radical politics and use of violence during the consular elections of 100 B.C. alienated Marius. Saturninus was arrested and murdered during the rioting.

Arcadius (r. 395–408 A.D.). Elder son of Theodosius I and Aelia Flaccilla, born in 377 A.D. He was proclaimed Augustus in 383 and, in 395, succeeded to the eastern half of the Roman Empire. He proved a weak-willed emperor, dominated by his ministers, who averted the crisis posed by Alaric and the Visigoths.

Ardashir (r. 227–241 A.D.). The first Sassanid shah of Persia, who overthrew the Parthian king Artabanus V and waged war against the emperor Severus Alexander in 229–232.

Arminius (c. 18 B.C.–20 A.D.). Prince of the Cheruscii who led the revolt that destroyed the three legions under Publius Quinctillius Varus in the Teutoburger Forest in 9 A.D. Arminius, resented as a tyrant, was overthrown and murdered by his tribesmen circa 20 A.D.

Arrian (c. 90–150 A.D.). Flavius Arrianus, born of a wealthy Greek provincial family of Nicomedia. He entered imperial service under Trajan (r. 98–117). As governor of Cappadocia in 134–135, he defeated an Alan invasion. He wrote the best surviving account of the campaigns of Alexander the Great.

Athaulf (r. 411–415 A.D.). King of the Visigoths, succeeded his brother-in-law Alaric. He arranged with the emperor Honorius a treaty whereby the Visigoths departed Italy and, as imperial allies, restored order in Gaul and Spain. He established the Visigothic kingdom at Toulouse in southern Gaul.

Attila (born c. 410; r. 434–452 A.D.). He and his brother Bleda succeeded their uncle Ruga (r. 420–434) as joint kings of the Huns. In about 445, Bleda was murdered by Attila. In 442–443 and 447, Attila launched devastating raids into the Balkans, earning the sobriquet "Scourge of God."

In 451, he invaded Gaul and suffered a strategic defeat at Châlons from a Roman-Gothic army under Aetius. In 452, he invaded northern Italy but withdrew as a result of the intercession of Pope Leo I. Attila died from overindulgence at his wedding celebrations. The Hun Empire collapsed within two years after his death.

Augustus (born 63 B.C.; r. 27 B.C.–14 A.D.). By the settlements of 27 and 23 B.C., Augustus (previously Octavian) established the constitutional basis of the Principate. Augustus, a genius in organization, founded the fundamental institutions of the Roman Empire, sponsored Latin letters and Roman arts, and gave 45 years of peace to the Mediterranean world. He was succeeded by his stepson Tiberius (r. 14–37). See also **Octavian**.

Aurelian (born c. 207; r. 270–275 A.D.). Lucius Domitius Aurelianus, born of a military family in Dalmatia, distinguished himself as a cavalry commander under Gallienus and Claudius II. In 270, the Danube army saluted Aurelian as emperor, and he secured Rome after a brief civil war. Aurelian restored the political unity of the Roman Empire, defeating Zenobia of Palmyra in 272 and the Gallo-Roman emperor Tetricus in 274.

Aurelius, Marcus (born 121; r. 161–180 A.D.). Marcus Aurelius Antoninus, perhaps the noblest of Roman emperors, succeeded his adoptive father, Antoninus Pius. In 161–169, he shared power with his adoptive brother Lucius Verus. Marcus Aurelius waged tough frontier wars against the Parthians (161–166) and Germans (167–180), but his hard-won victories over the Germans were thrown away by his unbalanced son Commodus.

Avidius Cassius, Gaius (d. 175 A.D.). Son of a Greco-Roman equestrian, Avidius Cassius was adlected into the Senate, holding a consulship in the early 160s. He commanded the Parthian expedition of Lucius Verus in 161–166. In 175, he led a revolt of the army of Syria on false reports of the death of Marcus Aurelius, but the revolt collapsed and Avidius Cassius committed suicide.

Belisarius (c. 505–565 A.D.). Born of an humble Illlyrian family, Belisarius rose to commander of the Eastern army in 530–532. His victories marked him as the emperor Justinian's most brilliant general. Belisarius overthrew the Vandal kingdom in 533 and commanded the forces against the Ostrogoths in Italy in 535–540 and 546–549. With the death of Theodora, his patroness at court, Belisarius fell into disfavor in 549 and was forced to retire.

Boudicca (died 60 A.D.). Queen of the Iceni, she led the revolt of Britons in 60 A.D. The insurgents were defeated by Gaius Suetoninus Paullinus, and Boudicca committed suicide.

Caecilius Metellus Numidicus, Quintus (consul 109 B.C.). An optimate senator who commanded the Roman army against Jugurtha in 109–107 B.C. Metellus was undermined and replaced by his own protégé, Gaius Marius. Thereafter, Caecilius Metellus headed the opposition to Marius.

Caligula (born 12 A.D.; r. 37–41 A.D.). The son of Germanicus and Agrippina the Elder, Gaius Julius Caesar was nicknamed Caligula ("little boots") by soldiers of the Rhine legions. He succeeded his uncle Tiberius as a popular ruler of Julian descent. But Caligula's arbitrary and savage rule, aggravated by madness, led to his assassination by officers of the Praetorian Guard.

Caracalla (born 188; r. 211–217 A.D.). Marcus Aurelius Antoninus, the elder son of Septimius Severus and Julia Domna, was nicknamed Caracalla after his favorite Gallic cloak. He ruled as co-emperor with Septimius Severus from 198. In 211, he succeeded jointly with his brother Geta. In 212, Caracalla murdered Geta, then issued the *Constitutio Antoniniana*, granting citizenship to all free residents of the Roman Empire. He was murdered by his Praetorian prefect Macrinus during the Parthian expedition (214–217).

Caratacus (r. 40–51 A.D.). King of the Catuvellauni; succeeded his father, Cunebolinus. After the Romans captured his capital, Camulodunum, in 43, Caratacus organized resistance among the tribes in Wales in 44–51. In 51, he fled to Queen Cartimandua of the Brigantes, who surrendered Caratacus.

Carausius (r. 287–293 A.D.). Marcus Aurelius Carausius, a naval officer under Maximianus, repelled Saxon pirates raiding Britain, then declared himself emperor. He ruled a Romano-British Empire until his murder by his finance minister, Allectus (r. 293–296).

Cartimandua (r. c. 40–69 A.D.). Queen of the Brigantes, she proved a loyal ally of Rome, surrendering the exiled Caratacus. In 69, she was expelled by her husband, Venutius.

Carus (r. 282–283 A.D.). Marcus Aurelius Carus, the Praetorian prefect of Probus, was declared emperor by the Eastern legions. He elevated his sons, Carinus (r. 283–285) and Numerian (r. 283–284), as co-emperors. He invaded Mesopotamia, defeating the Persian army, but he was killed by lightning near Ctesiphon.

Cicero. See **Tullius Cicero, Marcus**.

Claudius Caecus, Appius (consul 307 and 296 B.C.). Distinguished himself as censor in 312 B.C. when he reformed the census and Senate. He ordered the construction of the Appian Way (*Via Appia*), the first great highway project. An eloquent orator, Appius Claudius persuaded the Senate to reject the overtures of King Pyrrhus of Epirus in 279 B.C.

Claudius (born 10 B.C.; r. 41–54 A.D.). Tiberius Claudius Drusus was the second son of Drusus and Antonia Minor. His stutter and grotesque appearance due to infantile paralysis led the family to assume he was weak-minded, and he received no political training. In 41 A.D., after the assassination of Caligula, the Praetorian Guard declared Claudius emperor. He proved an able administrator and, in 43 A.D., led the invasion of Britain. He is believed to have been murdered by his fourth wife and niece, Agrippina the Younger, in the interests of her son Nero.

Claudius II Gothicus (born c. 215, r. 268–270 A.D.). An Illyrian provincial, Claudius rose through the ranks to become a senior officer of Gallienus. He participated in the murder of Gallienus and ascended the throne as the first "soldier emperor." In 269, he defeated a major Gothic force at Naissus in upper Moesia and was hailed "Gothicus." He died of plague early in 270.

Clovis (r. 482–511 A.D.). King of the Franks, Clovis made the Merovingian kingdom the most important state in Western Europe. In about 496, he converted to Catholic Christianity and won the cooperation of the Gallo-Roman elites.

Constantine I, the Great (born c. 272; r. 306–337 A.D.). Flavius Valerius Constantinus, son of Constantius I and St. Helena, initiated the transformation of the Roman Empire into a Christian world. He served as an officer under Diocletian and Galerius. In 306, he joined his father, Constantius, Augustus of the West, in a British expedition. Upon his father's death, Constantine was declared emperor by the Western army. Based at Treveri (Trier), Constantine waged civil wars, reuniting the Roman world in 323. At the Battle of the Milvian Bridge (312), Constantine defeated Maxentius and credited his victory to the Christian God. In 325, he summoned the First Ecumenical Council at Nicaea and, in 330, dedicated Constantinople, "New Rome," as a Christian capital.

Constantius I Chlorus (r. 305–306). Flavius Valerius Constantius, from an Illyrian military family, served under Probus and Diocletian. In 293, Maximianus adopted Constantius as his heir and Caesar. In 305, Constantius I succeeded as Augustus of the West. He died in 306 after conducting an expedition against the Picts.

Constantius II (born 317; r. 337–361). Flavius Julius Constantius, son of Constantine I and Fausta, was proclaimed Caesar in 324 and succeeded jointly as Augustus with his brothers Constantine II and Constans in 337. Constantius ruled in the East, waging a war against the Persians. He crushed the rebellion by Magnentius and the Western army in 350–353. In 361, Constantius died of illness while en route to face his cousin Julian, who had been declared emperor by the Western army.

Cornelius Scipio Asiaticus, Lucius (consul 190 B.C.). The younger brother of Scipio Africanus, Lucius decisively defeated King Antiochus III at the Battle of Magnesia in 190 B.C.

Cornelius Scipio, Publius (consul 218 B.C.; died 211 B.C.). In 218 B.C., Publius sent his main forces into Spain under his brother Gnaeus, while he opposed Hannibal. In December 218 B.C., Scipio and his consular colleague, Tiberius Sempronius Longus, were defeated by Hannibal at the Battle of Trebia. In 217 B.C., Publius, with *pro-imperium*, joined his brother Gnaeus in Spain. He was defeated and slain by the Carthaginians on the upper Baetis River in 211 B.C.

Cornelius Scipio Africanus, Publius (236–183 B.C.). The son of Publius Cornelius Scipio (consul 218 B.C.) and one of the greatest Roman commanders. In 210 B.C., he arrived in Spain with proconsular *imperium*. Scipio captured New Carthage (209 B.C.), won over the Celtiberian tribes, reformed Roman tactics and weapons, and expelled the Carthaginians from Spain by 206 B.C. He was elected consul of 205 B.C., and by invading Africa (204–201 B.C.), he compelled Hannibal to withdraw from Italy. Scipio defeated Hannibal at Zama (202 B.C.) and ended the Second Punic War.

Cornelius Scipio Aemilianus Africanus, Publius (185–129 B.C.). The second son of Lucius Aemilius Paullus (consul 168 B.C.), adopted by the son of Scipio Africanus so that he became Publius Cornelius Scipio

Aemilianus. In 147 B.C., he was elected consul. In 146 B.C., he captured and razed Carthage. In 134, he was again elected consul and captured Numantia in 133 B.C., ending the third Celtiberian war.

Cornelius Sulla, Lucius (138–77 B.C.). Sulla, descended from a patrician family, led a dissolute youth. As Marius's quaestor, Sulla negotiated the surrender of Jugurtha in 105 B.C. Sulla distinguished himself in the Social War and was elected consul, with the command against Mithridates VI of Pontus in 88 B.C. When the *populares* transferred the command to Marius, Sulla marched his legions on Rome, thereby initiating the first civil war. In 87–84 B.C., Sulla defeated Mithridates VI, restored Roman rule in the East, then invaded Italy. In 84–82 B.C., he crushed the *populares*, and as dictator (82–78 B.C.), he rewrote the Roman constitution in favor of the Senate and the optimates.

Cornelius, Tacitus (56–120 A.D.). From a northern Italian or southern Gallic provincial family, Tacitus entered a senatorial career under Vespasian. In 77, he married Julia, daughter of Gnaeus Julius Agricola. In 97, he was consul, and in 112–113, proconsul of Asia. He is the greatest historian of imperial Rome. He wrote *Annals* and *Histories*, covering the periods 14–68 and 69–96 A.D., respectively. His *Germania* and *Agricola* are fundamental sources for the northern barbarians.

Crassus. See **Licinius Crassus, Marcus**.

Cunobelinus (r. 10–40 A.D.). Shakespeare's Cymbeline. King of the Catuvellauni, he made his tribe paramount in southeastern Britain. Rome saw his actions as violations of an agreement made by his predecessor, Cassivellaunus, with Julius Caesar in 54 B.C.

Decebalus (r. 85–106 A.D.). King of Dacia, he raided the provinces of Pannonia and Moesia and defeated Roman expeditions sent against him in 85–88. In 92 A.D., Domitian concluded a favorable treaty with Decebalus. Trajan defeated Decebalus in two wars (101–102 and 105–106), and the king committed suicide in 106 A.D.

Dio Cassius Cocceianus (c. 150–235 A.D.). A native of Nicaea, Dio Cassius was descended from a noble Greek family and entered the Senate under Commodus. He was twice consul, in 194 and 229. He wrote a Roman history in 80 books; the earlier books do not survive. His account of the late republic and Augustus is a fundamental source.

Diocletian (born c. 248; r. 284–305 A.D.). Gaius Aurelius Valerius Diocletianus, from an humble Dalmatian family, was hailed emperor by the Eastern legions in a civil war in 284–285. Diocletian reformed imperial administration, established the emperor as an autocrat, and upheld the worship of the pagan gods. He created collegial rule, the so-called Tetrarchy, whereby imperial power was shared by two senior emperors, Augusti, and two junior emperors, Caesars. His reforms put the Roman Empire on a sound fiscal footing, but his efforts to secure the succession by collective rule failed.

Domitian (born 51; r. 81–96 A.D.). Titus Flavius Domitianus was the younger son of Vespasian and succeeded his popular brother Titus as emperor. Domitian warred against the Chatti in 82–85, but he faced criticism for setbacks in Dacia and his treaty with Decebalus in 92. Domitian, suspicious by nature, terrorized the Senate after 93 and was murdered in a palace plot.

Domitius Corbulo, Gnaeus (c. 4–66 A.D.). Consul in 39, Corbulo was linked to the imperial family and distinguished himself as legate of Lower Germany in 47. He commanded the Roman forces in Armenia in 54–64. Corbulo was too successful; Nero forced the general to commit suicide in 66.

Drusus, the Elder (39–9 B.C.). Drusus Claudius Nero was the second son of Tiberius Claudius Nero (praetor 42 B.C.) and Livia Drusilla. Drusus, a popular prince, was married to Antonia Minor, daughter of Mark Antony and Octavia. Their children were favored by Augustus. In 16–9 B.C., Drusus campaigned in Rhaetia and Germany. He died in Germany from injuries sustained from the fall of his horse.

Gaiseric (r. 427–477 A.D.). King of the Vandals, Gaiseric invaded North Africa in 429 and, in 439–442, secured a Vandal kingdom based in Carthage and the cities of the province of Africa. In 455, he sacked Rome when the court of Ravenna failed to fulfill matrimonial and treaty obligations.

Galerius (born c. 250; r. 305–311 A.D.). Gaius Galerius Valerius Maximinus, a Balkan officer, was created Caesar of the East in 293 and married Diocletian's daughter Galeria Valeria. In 305, Galerius succeeded Diocletian as Augustus of the East, but his political arrangements denied the succession to both Constantine and Maxentius (each the son of an emperor) so that civil war erupted after 306. Galerius was credited with the initiative for the Great Persecution of Christians in 303–313 A.D.

Gallienus (born 218; r. 253–268 A.D.). Publius Licinius Egnatius Gallienus, son of Emperor Valerian I, ruled as co-emperor with his father, taking charge of the western and Danube frontiers. The death of his two sons and the capture of his father by the Persians ended any hopes for founding a dynasty. After 260, Gallienus faced rival emperors in Gaul and the East, as well as repeated Gothic invasions and rebellions in the Balkans. He was the last emperor of the traditional senatorial elite.

Germanicus (15 B.C.–19 A.D.). Gaius Julius Caesar Germanicus was the elder son of Drusus the Elder and Antonia Minor. In 4 A.D., Augustus had Tiberius adopt Germanicus as his heir. In 5 A.D., Germanicus married Agrippina the Elder, the favored granddaughter of Augustus. In 14–16 A.D., Germanicus campaigned against the Germans, recovering two Varian eagles. He clashed with his uncle Tiberius over policy. The dashing prince died of fever while in Syria, but his son, Caligula, succeeded Tiberius.

Gordian III (born 225; r. 238–244 A.D.). Marcus Antoninus Gordianus was the grandson of Gordian I (a senatorial emperor who had opposed Maximinus I in 238). His father-in-law and Praetorian prefect, Timisitheus, directed policy. In 242–244, Gordian took the field against the Persian Shah Shapur I. The young emperor was slain in a mutiny staged by his prefect Philip the Arab (who had succeeded Timisitheus in 243).

Gratian (born 359; r. 367–383 A.D.). Flavius Gratianus, son of Valentinian I, was elevated as co-Augustus in 367 and succeeded his father as Western emperor in 375. A Nicene Christian, he had stormy relations with his uncle Valens, the Eastern emperor. In 379, he elevated Theodosius to emperor to restore the situation in the East after the defeat at Adrianople. In 383, Gratian was overthrown and murdered in a revolt by the Western army led by Magnus Maximus (r. 383–388).

Hadrian (born 76; r. 117–138 A.D.). Publius Aelius Hadrianus, left fatherless as a child, was reared as the ward of his second cousin, the future emperor Trajan and his wife, Plotina. He succeeded his adoptive father and relinquished Trajan's eastern conquests. By inclination an architect and philhellene, Hadrian was unpopular with the Senate, but he proved a brilliant emperor.

Hamilcar Barca (died 229 B.C.). From a distinguished military family, Hamilcar commanded Carthaginian forces in Sicily late in the First Punic War (247–241 B.C). In 241–238 B.C., he crushed the revolt of the mercenaries in Africa. In 237–229 B.C., he founded the Carthaginian colonial empire in Spain. His three sons—Hannibal, Hasdrubal, and Mago—all swore vengeance against Rome.

Hannibal (247–183 B.C.). The son of Hamilcar Barca, Hannibal succeeded as Carthaginian commander in Spain in 221 B.C. One of the greatest commanders, Hannibal invaded Italy and fought the Romans to a strategic draw during the Second Punic War (218–201 B.C.). In 202 B.C., he was defeated by Scipio Africanus at Zama. As *sufete* (chief magistrate) of Carthage, Hannibal sponsored popular reforms in 196 B.C. that resulted in his exile. He committed suicide lest he fall into Roman hands.

Heraclius (r. 610–641 A.D.). Son and namesake of the *exarch* (governor-general) of Carthage, Heraclius seized the Byzantine throne during a civil war. He defeated the armies of Shah Chosroes II and recovered the Eastern provinces. But he witnessed the loss of Syria and Egypt to the Islamic armies in 636–641. Heraclius's reign marked the shift from the late Roman to the Byzantine Empire.

Herodotus (c. 490–425 B.C.). A prominent citizen of Halicarnassus, a Greek city on the shores of Asia Minor, Herodotus is hailed as "the father of history." His *Histories*, dealing with the Persian wars, provides a wealth of information on the "barbarians" known to the Greeks.

Honorius (born 384; r. 395–421 A.D.). Flavius Honorius, second son of Theodosius I and Aelia Flaccillia, was created Augustus in 393 and succeeded as Western emperor in 395. Real power was in the hands of Stilicho down to 408. Honorius, at his capital at Ravenna from 402 on, witnessed the loss of northwestern and Spanish provinces.

Jovian (born 337; r. 363–364 A.D.). Flavianus Jovianus, a Nicene Christian commanding the imperial guard, was elected as emperor after the death of Julian. Jovian surrendered provinces in Mesopotamia to Shah Shapur II in exchange for the safe return of the Roman army. In February 364, Jovian was found dead in his tent during the march to Constantinople.

Jugurtha (r. 118–105 B.C.), King of Numidia, Jugurtha was a grandson of Masinissa. In warring against his cousins Adherbal and Hiempsal for mastery of Numidia, Jugurtha blundered into a war with Rome (112–105

B.C.). The *popularis* politicians and Gaius Marius exploited outrage over Jugurtha's atrocities. In 107–105 B.C., Marius drove Jugurtha out of Numidia, and the exiled king was surrendered by Bocchus, king of Mauretania. After gracing Marius's triumph in 104 B.C., Jugurtha was executed.

Julia (39 B.C.–14 A.D.). The daughter of Augustus and his second wife, Scribonia. She was married successively to Marcus Claudius Marcellus (25–23 B.C.), Agrippa (21–12 B.C.), and Tiberius in 11 B.C. By Agrippa, she had five children. In 2 B.C., Julia was banished by Augustus for scandalous affairs to the island of Pandataria, where she died in exile.

Julian II, the Apostate (born 332; r. 360–363 A.D.). Flavius Claudius Julianus, nephew of the emperor Constantine, had been reared for a religious career. Julian converted secretly to paganism. In 355, he was created Caesar by Constantius II to restore the situation in Gaul. In 357–359, Julian expelled barbarian invaders, but in 360, the Western army declared Julian emperor. Julian, sole emperor with the sudden death of Constantius II, restored the worship of the old gods. In 363, Julian was killed on his Persian expedition, and the efforts to restore paganism ended.

Julius Agricola, Gnaeus (c. 40–93 A.D.). From a senatorial family of Forum Iulii (Fréjus) in southern Gaul, Agricola was consul in 77, then legate of Britain (78–85). He completed the conquest of Britain, save for Caledonia. Agricola, recalled by Domitian, retired to private life. His biography was penned by his son-in-law Tacitus.

Julius Caesar, Gaius (101–44 B.C.). Julius Caesar, a brilliant commander and politician, created the Roman imperial monarchy. He joined the First Triumvirate as a junior member. As consul in 59 B.C., he passed *popularis* laws. As proconsul (58–49 B.C.), he conquered Gaul. Caesar's primacy threatened Pompey and the optimates devoted to republican rule, who chose war to humble Caesar. Caesar won the civil wars (49–45 B.C.) and, as dictator, reformed Rome. His monarchical aspirations led to his assassination by the Liberators on March 15, 44 B.C.

Julius Civilis, Gaius (no known dates). Commander of the Batavian auxiliaries; raised a rebellion in the Rhineland against Rome in 69–70 A.D. He proclaimed an *Imperium Galliarum* and summoned German allies from east of the Rhine. The revolt collapsed in 70, and Julius Civilis obtained terms for his tribe.

Justinian I, the Great (born 482; r. 527–565 A.D.). Flavius Petrus Sabbatius Justinianus was the nephew and adopted son of Justin I (r. 518–527), the Eastern Roman emperor. Justinian aimed to restore the Roman Empire of Constantine and waged wars of reconquest in Africa (533–548), Italy (535–554), and Spain (550–551). Justinian overtaxed the resources of the empire, which suffered attacks from new barbarian foes after 565.

Licinius Crassus, Marcus (115–53 B.C.). A lieutenant of Sulla, Crassus amassed wealth during the proscriptions in 82–78 B.C. As propraetor, he crushed the slave rebels under Spartacus (72–71 B.C). Consul in 70 B.C., Crassus quarreled with Pompey. In 60 B.C., he entered the First Triumvirate, obtaining a second consulship in 55 B.C. As proconsul of Syria (55–53 B.C.), he invaded Parthia, but he was defeated and slain at Carrhae in 53 B.C.

Licinius Lucullus, Lucius (c. 118–55 B.C.). Quaestor in 88 B.C., Lucullus served under Sulla in the first Mithridatic war and civil war (83–78 B.C.). Lucullus, consul in 73 B.C., deserved the credit for defeating Mithridates VI in the third war. As proconsul (72–68 B.C.), Lucullus reformed the administration of Asia and advanced Roman frontiers into Armenia. Recalled in 68 B.C., Lucullus thereafter opposed Pompey, who assumed the command against Mithridates. Lucullus, after 59 B.C., retired into a hedonist private life.

Licinius I (born c. 265; r. 308–324 A.D.). Valerius Licinianus Licinius, a Dacian officer of Galerius, was elevated as Augustus of the West in 308. Licinius succeeded Galerius to the Balkan provinces in 311 and, thus, allied with Constantine against Maximinus II in 313. Licinius, defeated and deposed by Constantine in 323, was executed on grounds of treason.

Livia Drusilla (58 B.C.–29 A.D.). Brilliant wife of Augustus; divorced her first husband, Tiberius Claudius Nero, in 39 B.C. to marry the future emperor. Her two sons, Tiberius and Drusus, were reared in the household of their stepfather, Augustus. From 11 B.C. on, Livia managed the imperial family and aided in the adoption of Tiberius as Augustus's heir.

Livius Drusus, Marcus, "the Younger" (died 91 B.C.). Drusus, as tribune of the plebians (91 B.C.), proposed fundamental reforms, including the enfranchisement of Latin and Italian allies. Drusus failed to pass the bill on allied enfranchisement, and his assassination precipitated the Social War (90–88 B.C.).

Livy (59 B.C.–17 A.D.). Titius Livius, born at Patavium (modern Padua), enjoyed the friendship and patronage of Augustus and the future emperor Claudius. A brilliant stylist, Livy penned a history of Rome (in 142 books) from Romulus to Augustus. The extant 35 books are a fundamental source of Roman history.

Lucullus. See **Licinius Lucullus, Lucius**.

Magnentius (born c. 303; r. 350–353 A.D.). Flavius Magnus Magnentius, born of a German family settled in Gaul, commanded the cavalry under Constans. In 350, the Western army revolted, declaring Magnentius emperor and slaying Constans. In the ensuing civil war, Constantius II defeated Magnentius, who committed suicide. The fighting weakened defenses on the Rhine, enabling the Franks and Alemanni to overrun Gaul in 355–357.

Marcian (born c. 390; r. 450–457 A.D.). Flavius Valerius Marcianus, an officer of Illyrian origin, was adlected into the Senate at Constantinople. In 450, the empress Aelia Pulcheria married Marcian, and he was hailed as Eastern Roman emperor. Marcian refused to pay tribute to Attila, reformed the Eastern army, and summoned the Fourth Ecumenical Council (451).

Marius, Gaius (157–87 B.C.). Marius, a *novus homo* ("new man"), exploited *popularis* outrage against the Senate to gain seven consulships (107, 104–100, and 87 B.C.). In 107–105 B.C., he won the Jugurthine War; in 104–101, he defeated the Cimbri and Teutones. In 88 B.C., he intrigued with Publius Sulpicius Rufus to secure the command against King Mithridates VI, but he provoked his rival Sulla to march on Rome. In 87 B.C., Marius, an embittered man, reoccupied Rome after Sulla departed to the East and conducted brutal reprisals. Marius died shortly after entering his seventh consulship.

Maroboduus (r. c. 20 B.C.–19 A.D.). King of the Marcomanni, he led his tribesmen from the upper Main to Bohemia, where he established an effective Germanic kingdom. In 6 A.D., Augustus planned to attack Maroboduus, but the revolts of the Batones and of Arminius distracted Rome and saved Maroboduus. In 19 A.D., Maroboduus, expelled by his subjects, was received by Tiberius.

Masinissa (born c. 240; r. 205–148 B.C.). Masinissa, a Numidian prince commanding cavalry in Carthage's employ in Spain, won the admiration of Scipio Africanus. In 204 B.C., he joined Scipio, and his cavalry were decisive at the Battle of Zama. As a client and friend of Scipio Africanus, Masinissa united the Numidian tribes. He waged border wars against Carthage and, thus, exploited his ties among Roman senators to bring on the Third Punic War (149–146 B.C.).

Maximianus (born c. 250, r. 285–305 A.D.). Marcus Aurelius Valerius Maximianus, a Pannonian comrade of Diocletian, was promoted as Augustus in the West. Maximianus abdicated in 305, but he reentered politics, first as co-emperor with his son Maxentius, then with his son-in-law Constantine. Maximianus committed suicide at Massilia in 310 after he failed to raise a revolt against Constantine.

Maximinus I Thrax (born 173; r. 235–238 A.D.). Gaius Julius Verus Maximinus was a Thracian peasant who rose through the ranks and entered the equestrian order. In 235, he was proclaimed emperor after the murder of Severus Alexander. His reign marked the inception of 50 years of civil wars. Maximinus, the first soldier-emperor of low social origin, was detested by the landed classes despite his success in waging frontier wars. In 238, a revolt first in Africa, then at Rome, precipitated his downfall.

Maximinus II Daia (r. 309–313 A.D.). Galerius Valerius Maximinus Daia, nephew of Galerius, was named Caesar of the East in 305. In 309, he proclaimed himself Augustus and warred against Galerius and, later, Licinius. In 313, Maximinus II, defeated by Licinius, died a refugee at Tarsus.

Mithridates VI Eupator (r. 121–63 B.C.). King of Pontus in northeastern Asia Minor; forged a powerful state based on the lands surrounding the Black Sea. In 90 B.C., Mithridates declared war on Rome. In 89 B.C., he overran Bithynia and Asia, while the cities of Greece revolted. The proconsul Sulla drove Pontic armies out of Greece and ended the first Mithridatic war (90–85 B.C.) by treaty. Mithridates amassed resources to renew the contest. The third Mithridatic war (74–63 B.C.) ended in the defeat of the Pontic kingdom and the suicide of Mithridates, an exile in the Crimea.

Nero (born 37; r. 54–68 A.D.). The last Julio-Claudian emperor, Nero, born as Lucius Domitius Ahenobarbus, was the son of Gnaeus Domitius Ahenobarbus (consul 32) and Agrippina the Younger (the great-granddaughter of Augustus). In 49, his mother married Claudius and secured Nero's adoption as Claudius's heir. Nero took the name Nero Claudius Caesar. In 54, Nero succeeded as emperor, but because he craved popularity as an artist, he entrusted the affairs of state to his ministers down to 62. Nero, by his outrageous conduct, alienated the ruling classes and frontier legions and precipitated his own downfall and suicide in 68.

Octavia (died 11 B.C.). Elder sister of Augustus; first married to Gaius Claudius Marcellus (consul 50 B.C.). In 40 B.C., after Marcellus's death, she married Mark Antony, by whom she had two daughters, Antonia Maior and Antonia Minor. She supervised the imperial household until her death.

Octavian (63 B.C.–14 A.D.). Born Gaius Octavius, he was the grand-nephew and adopted son of the dictator Gaius Julius Caesar. Called by convention Octavian, his legal name was Gaius Julius Caesar Octavianus. In 43 B.C., Octavian allied with Mark Antony and Marcus Aemilius Lepidus in the Second Triumvirate to defeat the Liberators. Octavian secured Italy, while his popular colleague Antony ordered the Roman East in 41–32 B.C. In 31 B.C., Octavian defeated Antony and his consort, Cleopatra VII, queen of Ptolemaic Egypt, at Actium. The suicides of Antony and Cleopatra left Octavian master of the Roman world. In 27 B.C., Octavian relinquished his extraordinary powers as triumvir. The Senate voted Octavian tribunician power, proconsular *imperium*, and the name Augustus. Henceforth, Octavian ruled as the emperor Augustus. See also **Augustus**.

Odenathus (r. 262–267 A.D.). Septimius Odenathus, merchant prince of the caravan city Palmyra, was also a Roman senator and general (*dux*). He imposed his authority over the Roman Eastern frontier after the capture of Valerian I in 260. In 262, he captured Ctesiphon and imposed a treaty on Shah Shapur I.

Odoacer (r. 476–491 A.D.). King and commander of the barbarian federates in Italy, Odoacer deposed the last Western emperor, Romulus Augustus, in 476. Odoacer ruled as king of Italy and *magister militum*. In 489–491, he was defeated and executed by Theoderic, king of the Ostrogoths.

Otho (born 32, r. 69 A.D.). Marcus Salvius Otho, a dissolute senator, was a friend of Nero. Otho supported Galba as emperor in 68, but when Galba failed to name Otho as his heir, Otho arranged the murder of the emperor on January 15, 69. Otho then faced the invasion of Italy by the Rhine legions. His forces suffered a setback at Bedriacum; on April 17, 69, Otho committed suicide to spare the empire civil war.

Petillius Cerealis, Quintus (consul 70 and 74 A.D.). A kinsman of the emperor Vespasian, Petillius Cerealis served as legate of Legion IX Hispana in Britain (58–60). In 70, he crushed the insurgents under Gaius Julius Civilis, then served as governor in Britain (71–73).

Philip I, "the Arab" (r. 244–249 A.D.). Marcus Julius Philippus, an equestrian of Arabian origin, succeeded Timisitheus as Praetorian prefect of Gordian III in 243. Philip instigated the murder of Gordian and succeeded as emperor. In 249, he was defeated and slain by Trajan Decius, who had been hailed as emperor by the Danube legions.

Polybius (c. 200–118 B.C.). A historian and statesman of the Achaean League, Polybius was a native of Megalopolis in the Peloponnesus. In 168 B.C., he was deported to Rome. As an honored prisoner, Polybius attached himself to the circle of Scipio Aemilianus and wrote an insightful history explaining the rise of Roman power and offering a wealth of information on Roman political, religious, and social institutions.

Pompey the Great (106–48 B.C.). Gnaeus Pompeius Magnus, son of Pompeius Strabo, raised three legions and joined Sulla in 83 B.C. Pompey gained rapid advancement, by extraordinary military commands and the threat of violence. He defeated the Marians in Sicily, Africa, and Spain in 82–72 B.C. In 70 B.C., he was elected consul. In 67 B.C., he was granted *imperium infinitum* to defeat the Cilician pirates, then concluded the third Mithridatic war and reorganized the Roman East (66–62 B.C.). He joined Julius Caesar and Crassus in the First Triumvirate, gaining consulships in 56 and 52 B.C. The rise of Caesar and death of Crassus drove Pompey into the optimate camp at the outbreak of the civil wars. In 48 B.C., Julius Caesar defeated Pompey at Pharsalus. Pompey fled to Egypt and was murdered on orders of King Ptolemy XIV.

Porcius Cato, Marcus, "the Elder" (234–149 B.C.). A pragmatic conservative of peasant origin, Cato attained the consulship in 195 B.C. Although a new man (*novus homo*), Cato upheld Roman tradition in his writings and actions. He served as governor in Nearer Spain (195–194 B.C.) and volunteered to serve as a military tribune in the war against Antiochus III in 191 B.C. In 184 B.C., he was elected censor and henceforth presided over the Senate as the senior statesman (*princeps Senatus*). On Cato's recommendation, the Third Punic War was declared against Carthage. A prolific writer of more than 150 tracts, Cato was praised by Cicero for his oratory and historical prose.

Postumus (r. 260–269 A.D.). Marcus Cassianius Licinius Postumus, commander of the Rhine legions, rebelled against Valerian and Gallienus. Postumus founded a Gallo-Roman Empire (260–274).

Quinctilius Varus, Publius (consul 13 B.C.). Married to Claudia Marcella, grand-niece of Augustus, Varus administered well the provinces of Africa and Syria. As legate of Germany in 9 A.D., Varus and three legions were lured into the Teutoburg Forest and slaughtered by Arminius and the German insurgents.

Sallust (86–35 B.C.). Gaius Sallustius Crispus, a Caesarian, penned partisan accounts of the Jugurthine War and the Catalinarian conspiracy. His general history of Rome survives in fragments. Of equestrian birth, Sallust owed his advancement to Julius Caesar. He was elected praetor in 47 B.C., but his public service was marred by charges of corruption.

Scipio Aemilianus. See **Cornelius Scipio Aemilianus Africanus, Publius**.

Scipio Africanus. See **Cornelius Scipio Africanus, Publius**.

Sempronius Gracchus, Gaius (died 121 B.C.). The second son of Tiberius Sempronius Gracchus and Cornelia, Gaius, elected tribune of the plebians in 124–122 B.C., revived the legislation of his brother Tiberius. Gaius offered a comprehensive reform of the Roman state. His proposal to enfranchise Latin and Italian allies forfeited him many voters, and he failed to be elected to a third tribunate. In 121 B.C., as a private citizen, he demonstrated in protest of the repeal of his legislation and was killed in a riot.

Sempronius Gracchus, Tiberius (died 154 B.C.). He owed his career to Scipio Africanus, whose daughter, Cornelia, Gracchus married. Gracchus, praetor in 180 B.C., pacified Nearer Spain by offering generous settlements to the Celtiberians in 179 B.C. As consul (177 B.C.), he ruthlessly pacified Sardinia, and he was elected censor in 169 B.C.

Sempronius Gracchus, Tiberius (died 133 B.C.). The son of his namesake and Cornelia (daughter of Scipio Africanus). He was a cousin and brother-in-law of Scipio Aemilianus. As tribune of the plebians in 133 B.C., Tiberius Gracchus proposed a moderate land bill to reclaim public land, which was to be distributed as long-term leases to poor citizens so that they could be eligible for the draft. Many senators objected to Gracchus's methods, and his decision to stand for an unprecedented second tribunate provoked rioting in which Tiberius and his supporters were slain.

Septimius Severus (born 148; r. 193–211 A.D.). Lucius Septimius Severus, a native of Lepcis Magna in Africa, was legate of Upper Pannonia in 193. In 193–195, he defeated his rivals in the second civil war of imperial Rome and founded the Severan dynasty. Septimius Severus took harsh reprisals against opponents in the Senate, but he secured the frontiers and forged links with the provincial elites, especially those in the East and Africa.

Sertorius, Quintus (c. 125–73 B.C.). An officer of Gaius Marius, Sertorius fled Italy in 82 B.C. and organized resistance in Spain. Sertorius forged a coalition of Celtiberian tribes and provincial Romans that checked optimate forces. In 76–73 B.C., Pompey waged a war of attrition, in which Sertorius was deserted by his allies and murdered by his own officers.

Severus Alexander (born 208; r. 222–235 A.D.). Marcus Aurelius Severus Alexander was the last Severan emperor. Severus Alexander ruled judiciously under the guidance of his mother, Julia Mamaea. He respected the Senate, but his inconclusive wars against the Persians and Germans led to his assassination by mutinous soldiers of the Rhine army.

Severus II (r. 306–307 A.D.). Flavius Valerius Severus, an Illyrian officer, was created Caesar of the West by Galerius in 305. In 306, after the death of Constantius I, Galerius elevated Severus II to Augustus of the West. In 307, Severus invaded Italy, but he fell into the hands of Maxentius, who executed Severus.

Shapur I (r. 241–272 A.D.). The second Sassanid shah of Persia, Shapur I waged three successful campaigns against the Roman Empire (242–244, 253–255, and 258–260). In 260, he captured the emperor Valerian and sacked Antioch, third city of the Roman Empire, either in 253 or 260.

Shapur II (r. 309–379 A.D.). Sassanid shah of Persia, he pursued aggressive policies against Armenia and Rome. In 255–261, he waged a desultory frontier war over the Roman fortresses of Mesopotamia. In 363, he checked the invasion of Julian and compelled Jovian to surrender the strategic fortresses of Mesopotamia, thereby giving Persia the initiative in future wars against Rome.

Stilicho (died 408 A.D.). Flavius Stilicho, *magister militum* of the Western army (395–408), directed the policy of the Western court. In 395–397 and in 402–408, Stilicho used the threat posed by Arcadius to secure control over Honorius. Stilicho's policies led to the loss of the northwestern provinces in 406. In 408, he was arrested and executed on grounds of treason.

Suetonius Paullinus, Gaius (consul 42 and 66 A.D.). As legate of Mauretania, he pacified the Gaetulians and was the first Roman to cross the Atlas Mountains. As legate of Britain (58–60), he sacked Mona, the Druid sanctuary, and crushed the insurgents under Boudicca. He fought for Otho in 69 and survived into the reign of Vespasian.

Sulla. See **Cornelius Sulla, Lucius**.

Theoderic the Great (r. 489–526 A.D.). Theoderic, king of the Ostrogoths, invaded Italy at the behest of the Eastern emperor Zeno in 489. In 491, Theoderic treacherously murdered Odoacer and, henceforth, ruled as king of Italy. Theoderic, although an Arian, cooperated with the papacy and Roman senate so that Italy prospered under his reign.

Theodosius I, the Great (born c. 346; r. 379–395 A.D.). The son of Count Theodosius, a leading general of Valentinian I, Flavius Theodosius rose to high command under Gratian. In 379, as Augustus of the East, Theodosius restored order, granting a treaty to the rebellious Goths who henceforth served as federates. A devout Nicene Christian, Theodosius outlawed pagan sacrifices, resulting in the revolt of the Western army in 392–394. By the victory at Frigidus (394), Theodosius crushed the rebels and reunited the Roman Empire. In 395, he was succeeded by Arcadius and Honorius, his sons by his first wife.

Theodosius II (born 401; r. 408–450 A.D.). Flavius Theodosius, the son of Arcadius and Eudocia, succeeded as a minor. The emperor was directed by his ministers and his older sister, Aelia Pulcheria. Theodosius agreed to humiliating treaties dictated by Attila the Hun in 443 and 447.

Tiberius (born 42 B.C., r. 14–37 A.D.). Tiberius Claudius Nero was the son of Livia Drusilla and her first husband, Tiberius Claudius Nero (praetor 42 B.C.). Reared in the household of Augustus, Tiberius married Vipsania, daughter of Agrippa, in about 20 B.C. In 11 B.C., Tiberius, as the new heir of Augustus, divorced Vipsania and married Julia, but he retired from public life to Rhodes in 6 B.C. In 14 A.D., Tiberius succeeded as emperor on the death of Augustus. After 26 A.D., Tiberius withdrew to Capri and fell into depravity. The suspicious Tiberius, although an able administrator, feared his family and failed to prepare for the succession. He was succeeded by his great-nephew Caligula, the son of Germanicus and Agrippina.

Tigranes I, the Great (r. 99–56 B.C.). He forged the kingdom of Armenia and married Cleopatra, daughter of King Mithridates VI of Pontus. He conquered Media and Mesopotamia, Syria, and Cilicia and assumed the title "King of Kings." He erred in receiving the fugitive Mithridates VI. In 69 B.C., Lucullus defeated Tigranes at Tigranocerta. In 66 B.C., Tigranes submitted to Pompey and surrendered his conquests.

Titus (born 39; r. 79–81 A.D.). Titus Flavius Vespasianus, the elder son of the emperor Vespasian, served on his father's staff in the first Jewish war. In 70, Titus, elected as consul, captured Jerusalem and ended organized Jewish resistance.

Totila (r. 541–552 A.D.). Totila, elected king by the Ostrogoths at Pavia, resumed the offensive against the Byzantine garrisons. Totila reconquered most of Italy and compelled Justinian to send out, first, Belisarius (546–549), then Narses (549–552). Totila fell at the decisive Battle of Busta Gallorum (552) that ended the Ostrogothic kingdom.

Trajan (born 52; r. 98–117 A.D.). Marcus Ulpius Traianus was the son of the senator and namesake of a Hispano-Roman family of Italica. Trajan was adopted by Nerva (r. 96–98) and succeeded as the first Roman emperor of provincial origin. Trajan conquered Dacia (101–102, 105–106) and smashed Parthian power in 113–117. He initiated a spectacular building program at Rome. Hailed *optimus princeps*, Trajan founded the third dynasty of imperial Rome and was succeeded by his adopted son, Hadrian.

Trajan Decius (born 201; r. 249–251 A.D.). Gaius Messius Quintus Traianus Decius, a Pannonian provincial, attained senatorial rank under Severus Alexander. As legate of Upper Pannonia, he was declared emperor by the Danube legions. He defeated and slew the emperor Philip at Verona (249), but was himself slain by the Goths at Abrittus in Lower Moesia. Trajan Decius initiated the first empire-wide persecution of Christians in 250–251.

Trebonnianus Gallus (r. 251–253 A.D.). Gaius Vibius Trebonnianus Gallus, a legate of Trajan Decius, was declared emperor by the Roman army after Decius's death. Gallus faced attacks by northern barbarians and Persians. In 253, he was defeated and slain by Aemilian, governor of Moesia.

Tullius Cicero, Marcus (106–43 B.C.). Cicero, son of an equestrian, made his career as a forensic orator. In 70 B.C., he successfully prosecuted Gaius Verres, praetor of Sicily, for extortion, and he won the consulship in 63 B.C. Cicero became the spokesman for the optimates and a supporter of Pompey. Opposed to the First Triumvirate, he labored to win Pompey back to the optimate cause. After 49 B.C., Cicero retired, but he emerged from private life to oppose Mark Antony in 44–43 B.C.; hence, he was murdered on Antony's orders. Cicero's letters, orations, and philosophical works set the standard for Latin prose.

Vaballathus (r. 267–282 A.D.). Lucius Julius Septimius Vaballathus Athenodorus was the son of Odenathus of Palmyra and Zenobia. The young prince was advanced by Zenobia as Augustus of the East, but he never received recognition by Gallienus. In 272, he was defeated and captured by Aurelian.

Valens (born c. 328; r. 364–378 A.D.). Flavius Valens, born of a military family in Pannonia, served under Julian and Jovian. In 364, his brother Valentinian I created Valens emperor of the East. His Persian war was inconclusive. In 378, he was decisively defeated and slain by the Goths at Adrianople.

Valentinian I (born 321; r. 364–378 A.D.). Flavius Valentinianus, of a Pannonian military family, was a senior officer acclaimed emperor by the Eastern army after the death of Jovian. Valentinian appointed his brother Valens emperor of the East. Valentinian campaigned against the Germans on the Rhine and upper Danube and strengthened fortifications. He was succeeded by his two sons, Gratian (r. 367–383) and Valentinian II (r. 375–392).

Valentinian III (born r. 419; 425–455 A.D.). Placidius Valentinianus, son of Galla Placidia and Constantius III; as Western Roman emperor, he lost the remaining provinces in Spain and North Africa. His mother, Galla Placidia, who directed affairs of state, clashed with the powerful *magister militum* Aetius. Valentinian III, murdered by a clique of senators, left no heirs, and the Western Roman Empire disappeared within 20 years.

Valerian I (born c. 195; r. 253–260 A.D.). Publius Licinius Valerianus, a senator of noble origins, was legate of Raetia in the civil war of 253. He was proclaimed emperor by the Rhine legions and defeated his rival, Aemilian. Valerian faced barbarian assaults along the northern and eastern frontiers. He waged two Persian wars (253–256, 258–260) but was treacherously captured by Shah Shapur in 260 and died in captivity.

Varus. See **Quinctilius Varus, Publius.**

Vercingetorix (died 46 B.C.). Prince of the Gallic Averni, he headed the great Gallic revolt against Julius Caesar in 53 B.C. He was defeated and besieged in Alesia. Vercingetorix was compelled to surrender to Caesar in 52 B.C. He was executed after Caesar's triumph in 46 B.C.

Vespasian. (born 9; r. 69–79 A.D.). Titus Flavius Vespasianus, born of an Italian equestrian family, was adlected to the Senate and served as praetor in 40. He commanded Legion II Augusta in Britain in 43–47. He was consul in 51 and, in 66–69, commanded Roman forces against the Jewish rebels. On July 1, 69, he was declared emperor by the Eastern legions. Vespasian, the victor of the civil war, founded the second imperial dynasty, the Flavian. A tough, pragmatic emperor, he reformed the imperial army and frontiers, restored finances, and reorganized provincial administration.

Vispanius Agrippa, Marcus (64–12 B.C.). An equestrian and boyhood friend of Augustus, Agrippa proved the emperor's most brilliant general. He was a close friend of Octavia, the sister of Augustus. In 21 B.C., he married Julia, ensuring that his children were destined to succeed Augustus. In 12 B.C., he died after the exertions of campaigning in Illyricum.

Viriathus (died 138 B.C.). A Lusitanian shepherd, he escaped the massacre by the praetor Servius Sulpicius Galba in 150 B.C. A superb guerrilla leader, Viriathus defeated successive Roman armies sent into Farther Spain until he was assassinated on Roman orders.

Vitellius (born 15; r. 69 A.D.). Lucius Vitellius, son of the distinguished senator Aulus Vitellius, was appointed legate of Lower Germany in 68. He was declared emperor by the legions of the Rhine in 69, but Vitellius, of indolent character, was a figurehead for his ambitious junior officers. He was murdered during the final fighting in Rome on December 20, 69.

Vologaeses I (r. 51–78 A.D.). Arsacid king of Parthia, he placed his brother Tiridates on the Armenian throne and, thereby, precipitated a war over the Armenian succession. After 66, with the Armenian succession resolved, Vologaesus remained on cordial terms with Rome.

Wittigis (r. 536–540 A.D.). Wittigis, elected king by the Ostrogoths when Belisarius invaded Italy, conducted a war of attrition against the imperial army. He besieged Rome in 537–538. In 540, Wittigis and his court at Ravenna were compelled to surrender to Belisarius.

Zenobia (r. 267–272 A.D.). Septimia Zenobia was the wife of Odenathus of Palmyra and mother of Vaballathus. In 267, she succeeded to her husband's position in the Roman East. Styling herself as empress, Augusta, she advanced her son Vaballathus as emperor in 270. In 272, she was defeated by Aurelian and allowed to retire to a Campania villa.

Bibliography

Sources in Translation:

Ammianus Marcellinus. *The Later Roman Empire (A.D. 354–378)*. Translated by W. Hamilton. New York: Penguin Books, 1986. Abridged translation of a vital source for the later Roman Empire and the barbarians.

———. *Roman History*. 3 vols. Translated by D. Magie. Cambridge, MA: Harvard University Press (Loeb Classical Library Series), 1950–1953. Complete translation, including fragments of lost books.

Appian. *The Civil Wars*. Translated by John Carter. New York: Penguin Books, 1996. Modern translation of a fundamental source on the Roman Revolution.

———. *Roman History*. 4 vols. Translated by H. White. Cambridge, MA: Harvard University Press (Loeb Classical Library Series), 1912. Complete translation of an account of the republic's civil wars and the overseas wars, notably in Spain and the Greek East.

Birley, A., trans. *Lives of the Later Caesars*. New York: Penguin Books, 1976. Translation of a selection of imperial lives from Nerva to Elagabalus, filled with scandal and probably composed at the end of the 4th century A.D.

Brunt, P. A., and J. M. Moore, trans. and eds. *Res Gestae Divi Augusti: The Achievements of the Divine Augustus*. Oxford: Oxford University Press, 1967. The monumental inscription of the emperor Augustus, with an excellent concise discussion of the constitutional powers of Augustus.

Caesar, Gaius Julius. *The Civil War*. Translated by J. E. Gardiner. New York: Viking Press, 1976. Caesar's eyewitness account of 49–45 B.C.

———. *The Conquest of Gaul*. Translated by S. A. Handford. New York: Penguin Books, 1981. Caesar's account of the Gallic War, with his observations on Gauls, Britons, and Germans.

Cassius Dio. *The Roman History: The Reign of Augustus*. Translated by I. Scott-Kilvert. New York: Penguin Books, 1987. Translation of the relevant books by a senator of the Greek East; the main historical account for the reign.

———. *Roman History*. 9 vols. Translated by E. Cary. Cambridge, MA: Harvard University Press (Loeb Classical Library Series), 1914–1927. Complete translation of a major account of Roman imperial history, especially for the 2nd and early 3rd centuries.

Casson, Lionel, trans. and ed. *The Periplus Maris Erythraei*. Princeton: Princeton University Press, 1989. Translation and analysis of the Julio-Claudian account of the trade route to India.

Gordon, C. G. *The Age of Attila: Fifth-Century Byzantium and the Barbarians*. Ann Arbor: Michigan University Press, 1972. Useful collection of narrative sources.

Heather, P., and J. Matthews. *The Goths in the Fourth Century*. Liverpool: Liverpool University Press, 1992. Translations of literary sources otherwise not readily available.

Herodian. *History*. 2 vols. Translated by C. R. Whittaker. Cambridge, MA: Harvard University Press (Loeb Classical Library Series), 1969–1979. Major source for 180–238 A.D. written by a Greek provincial; this edition has excellent notes and introduction.

Herodotus. *The Histories*. Translated by A. de Selincourt. New York: Penguin Books, 1972. Delightful account of barbarian peoples encountered by the Greeks; indispensable for Greek attitudes inherited by the Romans.

Lewis, Naphtali, and Meyer Reinhold. *Roman Civilization Sourcebook*. 2 vols. 3rd ed. New York: Columbia University Press, 1990. Collection of translated sources, including important inscriptions and legal texts otherwise unavailable.

Livy. *Rome and the Mediterranean*. Translated by H. Bettenson. New York: Penguin Books, 1976. Abridged translation of overseas expansion by Rome in 200–168 B.C.

———. *The War with Hannibal*. Translated by A. de Selincourt. New York: Penguin Books, 1965. Inspired patriotic account of the Second Punic War.

Pliny the Younger. *The Letters of Pliny the Younger*. Translated by B. Radice. New York: Penguin Books.1970. Invaluable source on Roman imperial social attitudes and provincial administration.

Plutarch. *Fall of the Roman Republic*. Translated by R. Warner. New York: Penguin Books, 1972. Six lives: Marius, Sulla, Crassus, Pompey, Caesar, and Cicero.

———. *Makers of Rome*. Translated by I. Scott-Kilvert. New York: Penguin Books, 1965: Nine lives, notably Cato the Elder, the Gracchi, Sertorius, Brutus, and Mark Antony.

Polybius. *The Rise of the Roman Empire*. Translated by I. Scott-Kilvert. New York: Penguin Books, 1979. Major source for the Roman Republic, written by an insightful Greek historian attached to the circle of Scipio Aemilianus.

Procopius. *The Secret History*. Translated by G. A. Williamson. New York: Penguin Books, 1966. Lurid account of the reign of Justinian, written by an out-of-favor courtier.

———. *Works*. 7 vols. Translated by H. B. Dewing. Cambridge, MA: Harvard University Press, 1914–1940. Complete translations of *Persian Wars*, *Vandal War*, *Gothic War*, *Buildings*, and *Secret History*

Sallust. *Jugurthine War and Conspiracy of Catiline*. Translated by S. A. Handford. New York: Penguin Books, 1963. Partisan account by a Caesarian supporter of two scandalous events of the late republic.

Scriptores Historiae Augustae ("*Writers of the Augustan History*"). 3 vols. Translated by D. Magie. Cambridge, MA: Harvard University Press (Loeb Classical Library Series), 1921–1932. Complete translation of scandalous imperial lives (117–285 A.D.).

Suetonius. *The Twelve Caesars*. Translated by B. Radice. New York: Penguin Books, 1980. Entertaining and scandalous lives of Julius Caesar and the emperors from Augustus to Domitian.

Tacitus, Cornelius. *The Agricola and the Germania*. Translated by H. Mattingly. New York: Viking Press, 1971. Indispensable sources for Celtic Britain and the early Germans.

———. *The Annals of Imperial Rome*. Translated by M. Grant. New York: Penguin Books, 1996. The magnificently written Roman history under the Julio-Claudian emperors from a senatorial perspective.

———. *The Histories*. Translated by K. Wellesley. New York: Penguin Books, 1975. Excellent translation of Tacitus's account of 68–70 A.D. with a useful bibliography.

Thompson, E. A. *A Roman Reformer and Inventor*. Oxford: Oxford University Press, 1952. Translation and study of anonymous *De Rebus Bellicis*, outlining a plan for military reforms and fanciful inventions in the late Roman Empire.

Vegetius. *Epitome of Military Science*. Translated by N. P. Milner. Liverpool: Liverpool University Press, 1993. Late-4th-century author who urged a return to the legion.

Velleius Paterculus. *Compendium of Roman History*. Translated by F. W. Shipley. Cambridge, MA. Loeb Classical Library, Harvard University Press, 1924. Bound with a translation of *Res Gestae divi Augusti*. Velleius is the main source for the Varian disaster and the wars of Augustus and Tiberius.

Atlases:

Cornell, T., and J. Matthews. *Atlas of the Roman World*. New York: Facts on File, Inc., 1982. Extremely useful maps for Roman history with an emphasis on the provinces.

Haywood, J., and B. Cunliffe. *Atlas of the Celtic World*. London: Thames and Hudson, 2001. Superb maps and illustrations.

General Histories:

Brunt, P. A. *Social Conflicts in the Roman Republic*. New York: W. W. Norton and Company, 1971. Recommended introduction for republican history.

Cambridge Ancient History. 2nd rev. ed., Vols. VII to XIV. Cambridge: Cambridge University Press, 1982–2001. Scholarly reference work for advanced study, with extensive bibliographies, maps, and plates. These volumes cover from the Hellenistic period to the early Byzantine Age, 323 B.C.–600 A.D.

Cameron, Averil. *The Mediterranean World in Late Antiquity, A.D. 395–600*. London/New York: Routledge, 1993. Masterful survey of the transition from the late Roman world to the early medieval period.

Cary, Max. *A History of Rome down to the Reign of Constantine*. Revised by H. H. Scullard. 3rd ed. New York: St. Martin's Press, 1975. The standard reference work.

Jones, A. H. M. *The Decline of the Ancient World*. London/New York: Longman House, 1966. Strong on institutions and sources, with an excellent glossary of terms.

Marsh, F. B. *A History of the Roman World from 146 to 30 B.C.* Revised by H. H. Scullard, 3rd ed. London: Methuen and Co. Ltd., 1963. Classic narrative account of the period.

Millar, Fergus. *The Roman Empire and Its Neighbors*. 2nd ed. New York: Holmes and Meyer Publishers, Inc., 1981. Excellent discussion of Roman imperial institutions and policies, as well as chapters by leading experts on the provinces and barbarians.

Parker, H. M. D. *A History of the Roman World, A.D. 138 to 337*. 2nd ed., rev. London: Methuen and Co., Ltd., 1958. Classic study, with excellent political and narrative account.

Salmon, E. T. *A History of the Roman World from 30 B.C. to A.D. 138*. 6th ed. London/New York: Routledge, 2002. Reissue of a classic narrative account.

Scullard. H. H. *From the Gracchi to Nero*. 5th ed. London/New York: Routledge, 1990. Classic narrative account of the transition from republic to Roman Empire.

———. *A History of the Roman World, 753 to 146 B.C.* 5th ed. London/New York: Routledge, 2002. Reissue of a classic narrative account of the rise of Roman power.

Southern, Pat. *The Roman Empire from Severus to Constantine*. London/New York: Routledge, 2001. Updating of the classic study of the period by Parker.

Wells, Colin M. *The Roman Empire*. 2nd ed. Cambridge, MA: Harvard University Press, 1995. Best concise survey and excellent introduction.

Monographs:

Alcock, Leslie. *Arthur's Britain*. New York: Penguin Books, 1971. Analysis of sources for the transition from Roman Britain to Anglo-Saxon England.

Alföldy, G. *Noricum*. Translated by A. Birley. London/Boston: Routledge and Kegan Paul, 1974. History of Celtic and Roman Austria.

———. *The Social History of Rome*. Translated by D. Braund and F. Pollock. London: Croom Helm Routledge, 1986. Recommended on society and the ties of patron and client.

Astin, A. E. *Scipio Aemilianus*. Oxford: The Clarendon Press, 1967. Focuses on his role in the politics of later Rome.

Badian, E. *Foreign Clientelae: 264–70 B.C.* Oxford: Oxford University Press, 1958. Seminal study on Roman diplomacy and social relations.

———. *Lucius Cornelius Sulla: The Deadly Reformer*. Sydney: University of Australia Press (Todd Memorial Lectures), 1970. Brilliant analysis of the Sullan reforms.

———. *Publicans and Sinners: Private Enterprise in the Service of the Roman Republic*. Ithaca: Cornell University Press, 1972. Study on the rise of the equestrian order and overseas expansion under the republic.

———. *Roman Imperialism in the Late Republic*. Ithaca: Cornell University Press, 1968. Provocative analysis of Rome's expansion, linked to the drive for security.

Bennett, Julian. *Trajan, Optimius Princeps*. 2nd ed. Bloomington: University of Indiana Press, 2001. Excellent use of inscriptions and archaeology to recreate the reign.

Birley, Anthony. *Hadrian: The Restless Emperor*. London/New York: Routledge, 1997. Discursive biography of the emperor; best on senatorial politics.

———. *Marcus Aurelius: A Biography*. New Haven: Yale University Press, 1987. Thoughtful modern biography, with an excellent discussion of the frontier wars.

———. *The People of Roman Britain*. Berkeley: University of California Press, 1980. Recommended study of provincials and barbarians based on archaeology and inscriptions.

———. *Septimius Severus: The African Emperor*. New Haven: Yale University Press, 1972. Modern biography with fine chapters on dynastic policies and frontier wars.

Bowersock, G. W. *Julian the Apostate*. Cambridge, MA: Harvard University Press, 1978. Recommended modern biography for the personality and policy of the emperor.

———. *Roman Arabia*. Cambridge, MA: Harvard University Press, 1983. Well-written survey; recommended.

Broughton, T. R. S. *The Romanization of Africa Proconsularis*. Baltimore: Johns Hopkins University Press, 1933. Classic study.

Brunt, P. A. *Italian Manpower, 225 B.C.–A.D. 14*. Oxford: Oxford University Press, 1971. Definitive demographic study; essential for colonization and military potential.

Burns, Thomas S. *Barbarians within the Gates of Rome: A Study of Roman Military Policy and the Barbarians, ca. 375–425 A.D.* Bloomington: Indiana University Press, 1994. Recommended for imperial failure at Adrianople and the aftermath.

———. *A History of the Ostrogoths*. Bloomington: Indiana University Press, 1984. Excellent on the Ostrogothic kingdom in Italy.

———. *Rome and the Barbarians, 100 B.C.–A.D. 400*. Baltimore: Johns Hopkins University Press, 2003. Superb survey of the subject; excellent on the 3rd through 5th centuries A.D.

Bury, J. B. *History of the Later Roman Empire*. 2 vols. New York: Dover Press, 1958. Reissue of the classic narrative of 395–565 A.D. by the leading Victorian historian of late Rome.

———. *The Invasion of Europe by the Barbarians*. New York: W. W. Norton Co., Inc., 1967. Reissue of the lively narrative penned by the leading Victorian historian of late Rome.

Campbell, H. B. *The Emperor and the Army, 31 B.C.–A.D. 235*. Oxford: Clarendon Press, 1984. Recommended for conditions of service and army life.

Carney, T. F. *A Biography of C. Marius*. Chicago: Argonaut Publishers, 1970. Reprint of a classic biography; strong on the generalship of Marius.

Cary, M., and E. H. Warmington. *The Ancient Explorers*. Rev. ed. Baltimore: Penguin Books, 1963. Best introduction to trade and exploration by the Greeks and Romans.

Casey, P. J. *Carausius and Allectus: The British Usurpers*. New Haven: Yale University Press, 1994. Main study of the Romano-British Empire (287–296 A.D.).

Cheesman, G. L. *The Auxilia of the Roman Army*. Oxford: Oxford University Press, 1914; reprinted, Chicago: Ares Press, 1975. Fundamental work.

Cherry, David. *Frontier and Society in Roman North Africa*. Oxford: Clarendon Press, 1966. Reassessment of the Roman impact by a leading archaeologist.

Chilver, G. E. F. *Cisalpine Gaul: Social and Economic History from 59 B.C. to the Death of Trajan*. Oxford: Oxford University Press, 1941. A study of the transformation of Celtic society into a Roman municipal-based society.

Connolly, Peter. *Greece and Rome at War*. London: Macdonald Phoebus, 1981. Accurate illustrations of Greek, Roman, and barbarian armies based on literary and archaeological sources; superb photos and maps.

Cunliffe, Barry. *The Celtic World*. New York: McGraw-Hill Book Company, 1979. Lavishly illustrated oversized volume with superb photos.

———. *The Extraordinary Voyage of Pytheas the Greek*. New York: Penguin Viking, 2003. Text and analysis of the voyage to northern Europe by the Massiliot merchant in 325 B.C.

———. *Iron Age Communities in Britain: An Account of England, Scotland, and Wales from the Seventh Century B.C. until the Roman Conquest*. 2nd ed. London: Routledge and Paul Kegan, 1978. Fundamental study.

Curchin, L. A. *Roman Spain: Conquest and Assimilation*. London/New York: Routledge, 1991. Concise, recommended introduction.

Dill, Samuel. *Roman Society in Gaul in the Merovingian Age*. London: Macmillan, 1926. Classic study based on the literary sources to recreate the society of early medieval Gaul.

———. *Roman Society in the Last Century of the Western Empire*. 2nd ed., rev. London: Macmillan, 1921. Remarkably thoughtful study of the transformation of late Roman society with an emphasis on Italy and Gaul.

Drinkwater, John F. *The Gallic Empire: Separation and Continuity in the North-western Provinces of the Roman Empire, A.D. 260–274*. Stuttgart: Franz Steiner Verlag, 1987. Definitive study.

———. *Roman Gaul: The Three Provinces, 58 B.C.–A.D. 260*. Ithaca: Cornell University Press, 1983. Excellent survey and recommended introduction.

Duncan-Jones, R. *Structure and Scale in the Roman Economy*. Cambridge: Cambridge University Press, 1990. Statistical studies on the limits of the Roman economy.

Dyson, Stephen L. *The Creation of the Roman Frontier*. Princeton: Princeton University Press, 1985. Excellent account of Rome's conquest and assimilation of barbarian peoples in the republican period.

Ebel, C. *Transalpine Gaul: The Emergence of a Roman Province*. Leiden: Brill, 1976. Fundamental study for Romans in southern Gaul.

Elton, Hugh. *Warfare in the Roman Empire, A.D. 350–425*. Oxford: Clarendon Press, 1996. Revisionist argument against structural weakness in the late Roman army.

Ferrill, Arther. *The Fall of the Roman Empire: The Military Explanation*. London: Thames and Hudson, 1986. Critical study of cultural continuity in Late Antiquity, arguing for the older view of an abrupt military fall.

Frere, Sheppard S. *Britannia: A History of Roman Britain*. London/New York: Routledge and Kegan Paul, 1987. Definitive study.

Garnsey, Peter. *Famine and Food Supply in the Greco-Roman World: Responses to Risk and Crisis*. Cambridge: Cambridge University Press,

1988. Invaluable study on subsistence, trade, and limits of the ancient economy.

———, and Richard Saller. *The Roman Empire: Economy, Society and Culture*. Berkeley: University of California Press, 1987. Recommended introduction for social and economic conditions and structure of the imperial government.

Geary, P. J. *Before France and Germany: The Creation and Transformation of the Merovingian World*. Oxford: Oxford University Press, 1988. Best introduction to the transition from the late Roman world to early medieval Gaul.

Gelzer, Matthias. *Caesar, Politician and Statesman*. Translated by Peter Needham. Cambridge, MA: Harvard University Press, 1968. Definitive biography of his political career.

Goffart, Walter. *Barbarians and Romans, A.D. 418–584: The Techniques of Accommodation*. Princeton: Princeton University Press, 1980. Major restudy of the sources on how federate barbarian tribes were settled in the Roman Empire.

Goldsworthy, A. K. *The Roman Army at War, 100 B.C.–A.D. 200*. Oxford: Clarendon, Press, 1996. Excellent introduction to Roman warfare, as well as that of the barbarian opponents.

Greene, Kevin. *The Archaeology of the Roman Economy*. Berkeley: University of California Press, 1986. Well-argued reassessment stressing the achievements of the Roman economy; highly recommended.

Griffen, M. T. *Nero: The End of a Dynasty*. New Haven: Yale University Press, 1984. Recommended modern biography of the most notorious of emperors.

Gruen, Erich S. *The Hellenistic World and the Coming of Rome*. 2 vols. Berkeley: University of California Press, 1984. Recommended discussion of Roman diplomacy; emphasis on Rome's relations with the Greek world.

———. *The Last Generation of the Roman Republic*. Berkeley: University of California Press, 1974. Reassessment of 77–49 B.C. by a leading scholar of prosopography.

Hanson, W. S. *Agricola and the Conquest of the North*. Totowa, NJ: Barnes and Noble Books, 1987. Career of the most famous Roman governor of Britain.

———, and G. S. Maxwell. *Rome's North West Frontier: The Antonine Wall*. Edinburgh: Edinburgh University Press, 1983. Definitive study of the wall.

Harl, K. W. *Civic Coins and Civic Politics in the Roman East, A.D. 180–275*. Berkeley: University of California Press, 1987. Political and social history of the Eastern provinces during the wars of the 3rd century.

———. *Coinage in the Roman Economy, 300 B.C.–A.D. 700*. Baltimore: Johns Hopkins University Press, 1996. Monetary and fiscal history of the Roman world, with discussion of long-distance trade and prices and wages.

Harris, William V. *War and Imperialism in Republican Rome, 327–70 B.C.* Oxford: Clarendon Press, 1985. Fundamental study with excellent discussions of Roman values and aims, as well as the economic motives for expansion.

Heather, Peter. *Goths and Romans, 332–489*. Oxford: Clarendon Press, 1991. Important reassessment of Gothic society prior to 378 A.D.

Henderson, Bernard W. *Civil War and Rebellion in the Roman Empire, A.D. 69–70*. London: Macmillan, 1908. Still the definitive military study.

Holmes, T. Rice. *Caesar's Conquest of Gaul*. New York: Macmillan, 1899. Still the best analysis of the military operations.

———. *The Roman Republic and the Founder of the Empire*. Oxford: Clarendon Press, 1923. Unfinished work, but with an excellent analysis on Lucullus and Pompey in the third Mithridatic war.

Hopkins, Keith. *Conquerors and Slaves*. Cambridge: Cambridge University Press, 1982. Brilliant analysis of Roman society and economy with a superb discussion on slavery.

———. *Death and Renewal*. Cambridge: Cambridge University Press, 1983. Seminal essays on social rank and legal status in the Roman Empire.

Huzar, E. G. *Mark Antony: A Biography*. Minneapolis: University of Minnesota Press, 1978. A modern study.

Isaac, Benjamin. *The Limits of Empire: The Roman Army in the East*. Oxford: Oxford University Press, 1992. Revisionist study of frontier policy by a leading Israeli scholar.

Johnson, Stephen. *The Roman Forts of the Saxon Shore*. London: Elek, 1979. Archaeological study arguing for the arrival of German federates in Britain during the 4th century.

Jones, B. W. *The Emperor Domitian*. London/New York: Routledge, 1992. Strong on Domitian's frontier policies.

Jones, A. H. M. *Constantine and the Conversion of Europe*. Oxford: Oxford University Press, 1948; reprinted, Toronto: Medieval Academy of America Reprints for Teaching. Classic study with emphasis on religious policy.

———. *The Later Roman Empire, 284–602: A Social, Economic and Administrative Survey*. 2 vols. Norman: University of Oklahoma Press, 1964. Scholarly analysis of institutional history and sources.

Kaegi, Walter E., Jr. *Byzantium and the Decline of Rome*. Princeton: Princeton University Press, 1966. Thoughtful study of the reaction of the imperial court at Constantinople to the political collapse of the Western Roman Empire.

———. *Byzantium and the Early Islamic Conquests*. Cambridge: Cambridge University Press, 1992. Recommended for the wars of Heraclius and the Arabic impact.

Keaveney, Arthur. *Lucullus: A Life*. London/New York: Routledge, 1992. Only modern narrative account, but weak on his military career in the East.

———. *Sulla: The Last Republican*. London: Croom Helm, 1982. Narrative biography best read in tandem with Badian's monograph.

Kennedy, David, and D. Riley. *Rome's Desert Frontier from the Air*. Austin: University of Texas, 1990. Study of aerial photographs of the 1930s, archaeology, and literary sources for the frontiers of Roman Syria and Arabia.

Keppie, Lawrence. *The Making of the Roman Army from Republic to Empire*. London: Batsford Ltd., 1984. Recommended introduction.

Lengyel, A., and G. T. B. Radan. *The Archaeology of Roman Pannonia*. Lexington: University of Kentucky with Akademiai Kiado, Budapest, 1980. Important select studies of pre-Roman and Roman Pannonia (Hungary).

Lenski, N. *Failure of Empire: Valens and the Roman State of the Fourth Century A.D.* Berkeley: University of California Press, 2002. Well-written study of a critical reign.

Lepper, F. A. *Trajan's Parthian War*. London: Clarendon Press, 1948. Definitive study of topography and sources.

———, and Sheppard S. Frere. *Trajan's Column*. London: Alan Sutton, 1988. Catalogue of each panel, with an excellent discussion of Dacia and Trajan's wars.

Levick, Barbara. *Claudius*. New Haven: Yale University Press, 1990. An institutional study of the reign.

———. *Roman Colonies in Southern Asia Minor*. Oxford: Oxford University Press, 1967. Model study of the social and cultural impact of Roman colonies.

———. *Vespasian*. London/New York: Routledge, 1999. Strong on the institutional reforms of the Flavian dynasty.

Liddell Hart, B. H. *Scipio Africanus, Greater than Napoleon*. Novato, CA: Presidio Press, 1992. Reprint of a 1926 study of one of Rome's greatest commanders by a renowned British strategist.

Liebeschuetz, J. H. W. G. *Barbarians and Bishops: Army, Church, and State in the Age of Arcadius and Chrysostom*. Oxford: Clarendon Press, 1990. Excellent discussion of the Eastern court's military policies and relations with barbarians.

Luttwak, E. N. *Grand Strategy of the Roman Empire from the First Century A.D. to the Third*. Baltimore: Johns Hopkins University Press, 1979. Controversial analysis of imperial frontier policy with a wealth of details and maps and a complete bibliography.

MacKendrick, Paul. *The Dacian Stones Speak*. Chapel Hill: University of North Carolina Press, 1975. Introduction to Dacian civilization based on archaeology and inscriptions.

———. *The North African Stones Speak*. Chapel Hill: University of North Carolina Press, 1980. Survey of archaeological studies by region and city.

MacMullen, Ramsay. *Constantine*. New York: The Dial Press, 1969; reprint, London/New York: Routledge, 1987. Recommended introduction to the career and society of Constantine.

———. *Corruption and the Decline of Rome*. New Haven: Yale University Press, 1988. Controversial study on corruption as undermining imperial government.

———. *Enemies of the Roman Order: Treason, Unrest, and Alienation in the Empire*. Cambridge, MA: Harvard University Press, 1966. Insightful analysis with excellent chapters on brigands and provincial resistance to Romanization.

———. *Roman Government's Response to Crisis, A.D. 235–337*. New Haven: Yale University Press, 1975. Elegantly written analysis of the changes wrought by the 3rd-century crisis.

———. *Soldier and Civilian in the Later Roman Empire*. Cambridge, MA: Harvard University Press, 1967. Well-written and seminal study on social transformation of the Roman army and society by the leading social historian of Rome.

Maenchen-Helfen, O. J. *The World of the Huns: Studies in Their History and Culture*. Berkeley: University of California Press, 1973. Learned discussion of various aspects of Hun society and history based on archaeological evidence.

Magie, David. *Roman Rule in Asia Minor to the End of the Third Century after Christ*. 2 vols. Princeton: Princeton University Press, 1950. Fundamental study on Eastern frontiers.

Mattern, S. P. *Rome and the Enemy: Imperial Strategy in the Principate*. Berkeley: University of California Press, 1999. Written as a response to Luttwak, explaining the limits of imperial policy; thoughtful on Roman knowledge about barbarian foes.

Matthews, John. *The Empire of Ammianus*. Baltimore: Johns Hopkins University Press, 1989. A series of historical studies based on the account of Ammianus Marcellinus; fine discussion of frontier policy and wars.

Millar, Fergus. *The Roman Near East, 31 B.C.–A.D. 337*. Cambridge, MA: Harvard University Press, 1993. Discursive study of the Eastern frontier; weak on archaeology.

Mitchell, Stephen. *Anatolia: Land, Men, and Gods in Asia Minor*. 2 vols. Oxford: Oxford University Press, 1993. Major study on Anatolia and the Eastern frontier, especially on the Galatians and the Roman impact on eastern Anatolia.

———, and M. Waelkens. *Pisidian Antioch: The Site and Its Monuments*. London: Gerald Duckworth and Co., Ltd., 1998. Definitive study on the Roman colony.

Mócsy, A. *Pannonia and Upper Moesia: A History of the Middle Danube*. London/Boston: Routledge and Kegan Paul, 1974. Standard account by a leading Hungarian archaeologist.

Moorhead, John. *Justinian*. London/New York: Longman, 1984. Best modern biography.

———. *Theoderic in Italy*. Oxford: Clarendon Press, 1992. Emphasis on the achievements of Theoderic in reconciling the Roman elite classes.

Nicolet, Claude. *The World of the Citizen in Republican Rome*. Translated by P. S. Falla. Berkeley: University of California Press, 1980. Re-creation of the life of citizens in the republic by a leading French social historian.

O'Flynn, J. M. *Generalissimos of the Western Roman Empire*. Alberta: University of Alberta Press, 1983. Fine study of the evolution of high commands in the 4th and 5th centuries.

Parker, H. M. D. *The Roman Legions*. Rev. ed. New York: Barnes and Noble Inc., 1971. Study of the individual legions from the late republic to the Antonine age.

Pedley, John, ed. *New Light on Ancient Carthage*. Ann Arbor: Michigan University Press, 1980. Important studies of North Africa based on recent excavations.

Piggott, Stuart. *Ancient Europe from the Beginnings of Agriculture to Classical Antiquity: A Survey*. Edinburgh: Edinburgh University Press, 1965. Fundamental study for Celtic Europe.

———. *The Druids*. London: Thames and Hudson, 1985. Standard study.

———. *The Earliest Wheeled Transportation from the Atlantic Coast to the Caspian Sea*. Ithaca: Cornell University Press, 1983. Fundamental study for trade and society in prehistoric Europe.

———. *Wagon, Chariot, and Carriage: Symbol and Status in the History of Transport*. London: Thames and Hudson, 1992. Important for Celtic religious and social life.

Platnauer, Maurice. *The Life and Reign of the Emperor Lucius Septimius Severus*. Oxford: Oxford University Press, 1918. Important for analysis of sources.

Richardson, J. S. *Hispaniae: Spain and the Development of Roman Imperialism, 218–82 B.C.* Cambridge: Cambridge University Press, 1986. Study of the evolution of institutions under the republic.

Rossi, L. *Trajan's Column and the Dacian Wars*. Translated by J. M. C. Toynbee. Ithaca: Cornell University Press, 1971. Excellent discussion of the imperial army (especially *auxilia*) based on the column.

Roth, Jonathan. *The Logistics of the Roman Army at War (264 B.C.–A.D. 235)*. Leiden: Brill, 1999. Definitive study with excellent analysis of Roman strategy and frontier policy.

Schutz, Herbert. *The Prehistory of Germanic Europe*. New Haven: Yale University Press, 1983. Wide-ranging analysis of archaeology of Celtic and early Germanic Europe; recommended study.

———. *The Romans in Central Europe*. New Haven: Yale University Press, 1985. Focuses on the Roman impact on Celtic and nascent Germanic cultures.

Scullard, H. H. *Roman Britain: Outpost of the Empire*. London: Thames and Hudson, 1979. Recommended introduction with excellent illustrations.

———. *Scipio Africanus: Soldier and Politician*. Ithaca: Cornell University Press, 1970. Scholarly biography with emphasis on the Second Punic War and politics.

Seager, Robin. *Pompey: A Political Biography*. Berkeley: University of California Press, 1979. Best modern scholarly study, with emphasis on Pompey's political career.

———. *Tiberius*. Berkeley: University of California Press, 1972. Fine modern biography with excellent discussion of frontier wars and dynastic policy.

Sherwin-White, A. N. *Roman Foreign Policy in the East, 168 B.C. to A.D. 1*. Norman: University of Oklahoma Press, 1985. Best modern account of the Mithridatic wars and insightful analysis of the limits of Roman power.

Sinor, Denis. *The Cambridge History of Early Inner Asia*. Cambridge: Cambridge University Press, 1990. Excellent discussion of nomadic life; with chapters on Scythians, Sarmatians, Hsiung-nu, Huns, and Avars.

Smith, R. E. *Service in the Post-Marian Army*. Manchester: University of Manchester Press, 1958. Standard study of the impact of the Marian reforms.

Southern, P., and K. R. Dixon. *The Late Roman Army*. New Haven: Yale University Press, 1996. Thoughtful essays on selected topics, rather than a comprehensive study.

Spann, Philip O. *Quintus Sertorius and the Legacy of Sulla*. Fayetteville: University of Arkansas Press, 1987. Modern biography, with good analysis of Roman Spain in the 1st century B.C.

Stockton, David. *The Gracchi*. Oxford: Clarendon Press, 1979. The best modern study of two fraternal *popularis* reformers.

Stoneman, R. *Palmyra and Its Empire: Zenobia's Revolt against Rome*. Ann Arbor: Michigan University Press, 1984. Recommended study for the Palmyrene hegemony in 262–273 A.D.

Syme, Ronald. *The Roman Revolution*. Oxford: Oxford University Press, 1939. Seminal and masterful work on Roman politics from Pompey to Augustus.

Talbert, Richard J. A. *The Senate of Imperial Rome*. Princeton: University of Princeton Press, 1984. Definitive study, with important analysis of motives and careers of imperial senators and growth of the imperial administration.

Taylor, Lily Ross. *Party Politics in the Age of Caesar*. Berkeley: University of California Press, 1995 (Reissue edition). Brilliant and well-written study; best introduction to the constitution of the Roman Republic.

———. *Roman Voting Assemblies from the Hannibalic War to the Dictatorship of Caesar*. Ann Arbor: University of Michigan Press, 1966. The definitive scholarly study.

Thompson, E. A. *The Early Germans*. Oxford: Oxford University Press, 1965. Delightfully written study based on classical literary sources.

———. *A History of Attila and the Huns*. Oxford: Oxford University Press, 1948; rev. ed. issued as *The Huns*. Oxford: Blackwell Ltd., 1996. Well-written and definitive narrative of Attila's reign.

———. *Romans and Barbarians: The Decline of the Western Empire*. Madison: University of Wisconsin Press, 1982. Delightfully written essays on Visigoths, Sueves, Ostrogoths, and Vandals.

Wallace-Hadrill, J. M. *The Barbarian West: The Early Middle Ages, A.D. 400–1000*. New York: Harper and Row, 1962. Concise survey of the Germanic peoples.

Ward, A. M. *Marcus Crassus and the Roman Republic*. Columbia: University of Missouri Press, 1977. Recommended modern biography.

Warmington, B. H. *Carthage*. Baltimore: Pelican Books, 1960. Still the best introduction.

———. *The North African Provinces from Diocletian to the Vandal Conquest*. Cambridge: Cambridge University Press, 1954. Classic narrative.

Watson, A. *Aurelian and the Third Century*. London/New York: Routledge, 1999. Fine biography with an excellent discussion of institutions and conditions during the 3rd century.

Webster, Graham. *Boudicca*. 2nd ed. London/New York: Routledge, 2001. Third of a series on the Roman conquest, focusing on the queen of the Iceni.

———. *The Roman Imperial Army*. 3rd ed. Totowa, NJ: Barnes and Noble Books, 1985. Classic study with fine maps, line drawings, and plates.

———. *The Roman Invasion of Britain*. London/New York: Routledge, 1999. First volume of a study combining archaeology and literary sources for the Roman conquest of Britain; a wealth of details on the Roman army and Celtic life.

———. *Rome against Caratacus: The Roman Campaigns in Britain, A.D. 48–58*. New York: Barnes and Noble, 1982. Second volume on the Roman conquest with details on archaeology in Wales and northern Britain.

Wellesley, Kenneth. *The Long Year, A.D. 69*. Boulder, CO: Westview Press, 1976. Well-written narrative; recommended as an introduction.

Wells, Colin M. *The Germany Policy of Augustus*. Oxford: Oxford University Press, 1972. Definitive study of archaeology and literary sources, with insightful analysis of Augustan imperialism.

Wells, Peter S. *The Battle That Stopped Rome: The Emperor Augustus, Arminius and the Slaughter of the Legions in the Teutonburg Forest*. New York: W. W. Norton Co., Inc., 2002. Popular book based on current archaeological evidence for the Varian disaster.

———. *Beyond Celts, Germans, and Scythians: Archaeology and Identity in Iron Age Europe*. London: Gerald Duckworth and Co., 2000. Summation of archaeological evidence written from an anthropologist's perspective.

———. *Farms, Villages, and Cities: Commerce and the Urban Origins of Prehistoric Europe*. Ithaca: Cornell University Press, 1984. Reassessment of archaeology by a leading anthropologist of early Europe.

Wheeler, Mortimer, Sir. *Rome beyond the Imperial Frontiers*. London: G. Bell and Sons, Ltd., 1954. Recommended introduction to Rome's trade with the barbarian worlds.

Whitby, M. *The Emperor Maurice and Historian: Theophylact Simocatta on Persian and Balkan Warfare*. Oxford: Oxford University Press, 1988. Excellent on the invasions of Avars and Slavs and ethnic transformation of the Balkans.

Whittaker, C. R. *Frontiers of the Roman Empire: A Social and Economic Study*. Baltimore: Johns Hopkins University Press, 1994. Masterful use of archaeology to reconstruct frontier and barbarian societies in the Roman imperial age.

Wilkes, J. J. *Dalmatia*. Cambridge, MA: Harvard University Press, 1969. Fundamental study of the Balkans and the Roman conquest.

Williams, Stephen. *Diocletian and the Roman Recovery*. New York: Methuen Inc., 1985. The only modern account on the reign, but dated and superficial in analysis.

———, and G. Friell. *Theodosius: The Empire at Bay*. New Haven: Yale University Press, 1994. The only modern narrative account, but weak in analysis and institutions.

Wilson, A. J. N. *Emigration from Italy in the Republican Age of Rome*. Manchester: Manchester University Press, 1966. Standard study of overseas settlements by Rome.

Wolfram, Herwig. *History of the Goths*. Translated by T. J. Dunlap. Berkeley, 1979; revision of German edition. Comprehensive history with excellent bibliography.

Yarshater, E., ed. *Cambridge History of Iran: The Seleucid, Parthian and Sassanid Period*. Vol. 3, parts 1–2. Cambridge: Cambridge University Press, 1983. Recommended survey of steppe barbarians from Scythians to Mongols.

Zanker, Paul. *The Power of Images in the Age of Augustus*. Translated by H. A. Shapiro. Ann Arbor: University of Michigan Press, 1988. Comprehensive study of arts, coins, and letters as part of the imperial ideology created by Augustus.

Notes

Notes

Notes

Notes